A Year at the Fights

A Year at the Fights

By Thomas Hauser

The University of Arkansas Press
Fayetteville
2003

Designer: John Coghlan

⊚ The paper used in this publication meets the minimum requirements
of the American National Standard for Permanence of Paper for Printed
Library Materials Z39.48-1984.

Library of Congress Cataloging-in-Publication Data

Hauser, Thomas.
  A year at the fights / by Thomas Hauser.
     p. cm.
  ISBN 1-55728-733-3 (pbk. : alk. paper)
  1. Boxing. I. Title.

  GV1133 .H345 2003
  796.83—dc21

2002012288

For Cathy and Jessica, their own book.

But they have to share it with Jim and Geri

Contents

Author's Note

A Year at the Fights contains the articles about professional boxing that I authored in 2001 and early 2002. The articles I wrote about the sweet science prior to that date have been published in *Muhammad Ali & Company* and *A Beautiful Sickness*. Special thanks are due to Secondsout.com, Houseofboxing.com, and *Boxing Digest* under whose aegis the articles in this book first appeared.

Round 1
Fights and Fighters

In the United States, Henry Cooper is viewed as part of the Muhammad Ali legend. But in England, it's the other way around.

Sir Henry Cooper

It's a moment frozen in time, fixed in the collective consciousness of a nation. A memory that has been conjured up, told, and retold so many times that for many in England it has become the equivalent of religious lore.

In one corner, a brash young American named Cassius Marcellus Clay Jr. The twenty-one-year-old Clay had won a gold medal at the 1960 Olympics in Rome and was undefeated in eighteen professional fights with fourteen knockouts. He was loud, cocky, and beginning to irritate people as much as he charmed them.

And in the other corner, Henry Cooper, the patron saint of modern British heavyweights. The twenty-nine-year-old Cooper had been born in Bellingham, Kent, and been fighting professionally since 1954. He'd won the British and Commonwealth heavyweight titles in 1959 and would hold them for a record ten years.

The date was June 18, 1963. Clay entered the ring wearing a crown embedded with imitation precious stones and a red robe emblazoned with the words "Cassius the Greatest." Prior to the bout, he'd predicted that he would knock Cooper out in round five, and fifty-five thousand fans had jammed into Wembley Stadium to see if "Our Henry" could make the American eat his words.

For three rounds, two minutes, and fifty-five seconds, everything went as Clay had planned. From round one on, he was in control. By round three, Cooper was bleeding badly, and it appeared as though the bout would end whenever Cassius wanted it to. But instead of taking care of business, Clay seemed intent on prolonging the Englishman's agony and making good on his prediction of a fifth-round knockout.

Then THE PUNCH landed. "'Henry's Hammer," the British called it.

"It came from a long way back," one ringside observer later wrote, "with Cooper lunging forward as hard as he could. It caught Clay on the side of the jaw, and Cassius went over backwards through the ropes. He rolled back into the ring and got dazedly to his feet, gazing off into the distance, starry-eyed. He wobbled forward, gloves low, and started to fall, but his handlers caught him. Wembley Stadium was in an uproar."

But the round was over. And for British fans, a tale of woe followed. Earlier in the fight, Clay's trainer, Angelo Dundee, had noticed a split on one of Clay's gloves on the seam near the thumb. Now, with his fighter in desperate straits, Dundee, in his own words, "helped the split a little, pulled it to the side, and made the referee aware that there was a torn glove. I don't know how much time that got us," Dundee later reminisced. "Maybe a minute, but it was enough. If we hadn't gotten the extra time, I don't know what would have happened."

But Clay did have the extra time. And in round five, a barrage of punches ripped open the skin around Cooper's eyes, causing a torrential flow of blood. The fight was over, as Clay had predicted, on a fifth-round knockout.

Henry Cooper is now sixty-six years old. He retired from boxing in 1970 with a record of 40 wins, 14 losses, and 1 draw. He's still a hero in England, the most beloved fighter in the history of British boxing. Last year, he served as national spokesman for a campaign encouraging people age sixty-five and older to get flu shots. Cooper's message—"Get your jab in now!"—was in print ads and on television for weeks on end. Health-care personnel later reported that many citizens coming into clinics said simply, "I want a Henry Cooper."

Cooper is also chairman of the Executive Committee of the Variety Club in London. In that capacity, last year he supervised thirty golf tournaments that raised more than one million pounds for charity. He does extensive fundraising to support a school for mentally handicapped children. And in perhaps the ultimate tribute, he has been knighted by Queen Elizabeth.

Cooper still cuts a striking figure, with rugged features and an aura of honesty and decency about him. He and his wife, Albina, have been married for forty years. One of their sons operates a charter boat. The other is a chef in an Italian restaurant. They have two grandchildren—

Henry James, age six, and Lilly Maria, who's two-years-old. With his boxing days far behind him, Cooper plays golf with an eleven handicap. "I
shoot my 85s," he says. "Take eleven off, and I'm all right."

As for boxing, Cooper has a lot to say about the sweet science today.
"It's killing itself," he says with dismay. "If it keeps going the way it is,
there will be no professional boxing in England in ten years. It's not boxing now. It's fighting. You're supposed to learn your basic defensive moves
as a kid. But trainers today don't know their trade, and fighters aren't being
properly schooled as amateurs or professionals. They're not learning
defensive skills anymore. All their trainers tell them to do is go forward."

"There are too many one-sided fights," Cooper continues. "You have
all this hype for thirty minutes. Searchlights, posing in front of the searchlights, lasers, dancing, bands. Then the fight lasts a minute-and-a-half. In
the old days, there were one-round fights, but people didn't know which
ones they'd be in advance."

Cooper supported the decision of the British Home Office to allow
Mike Tyson to fight Julius Francis in England. "Tyson's done three years
in prison," he said at the time. "How long does he have to keep paying
for it? We know he's a bit of a nutcase, but they're talking about Julius
Francis losing money if Tyson isn't allowed in."

And despite the debacles surrounding Iron Mike's fights in the
United Kingdom against Francis and Lou Savarese, Cooper's opinion on
the matter is unchanged. "What's the worst crime?" he posits. "It's not
rape; it's murder. Don King has killed two men that we know of. Don
King served time in prison [for manslaughter]. Yet we allow Don King
to come here and promote fights. Why should Tyson be any different?
Besides," Cooper notes, "if Tyson wants to fight Lennox Lewis in London,
you know they'll let him in."

And who does Cooper think would win a bout between Lewis and
Tyson? "Tyson was a great fighter for the first few years of his career," he
answers. "He's still dangerous. The last thing a puncher loses is his punch.
But Tyson has lost it mentally and physically since then. There's no move-
ment; he's getting hit. I think Lennox will stop him. You have to measure
fighters by the standards of their era," Cooper continues. "Jack Johnson,
Jack Dempsey, Joe Louis, Rocky Marciano, Muhammad Ali, and Larry
Holmes all had great talent and a great fighting brain. In my view, they

were the greatest heavyweights ever. Lennox Lewis is in the next group. He's a good fighter and he dodges no one."

Meanwhile, Cooper's own place in British boxing history is secure despite his "Achilles heel"—the tendency to cut.

"If you gave Henry a rough towel, you needed a basin to catch the blood," says Hugh McIlvanney, England's foremost sports journalist. "When he fought the serious Americans, you wouldn't have bet him. But he was a good boxer. For a man of his weight, he was a wonderful puncher. He fought to the limit of his powers and never let anyone down. He was a marvelous presence for the game."

And McIlvanney's American counterpart, Jerry Izenberg, adds, "If Henry Cooper had a different facial bone structure, he would have been heavyweight champion of the world. He could punch; he could box; he came to fight; he always gave people trouble. But at the end of almost every fight, he was red with his own blood because those jagged edges betrayed him."

Cooper himself prefers not to dwell on the cuts. He has a different memory to look back on—round four on the night of June 18, 1963. "The greatest heavyweight ever," he says. "And I had him on his bum. It's still vivid in my mind. I remember everything."

"I was confident going into the fight," Cooper continues. "Clay, which was his name then, had looked good against big guys, but small quick fighters like Doug Jones had given him trouble. And he was a novice inside fighter. He hadn't learned how to defend himself in close. I only weighed thirteen-and-a-half stone [190 pounds], but I was messing him up inside. Then I knocked him down. And when I looked in his eyes, I knew he was gone. The eyes register everything. There's no way he would have come around in one minute. But Angelo saw that the stitching on the glove had ripped a bit. That's what you pay top trainers for."

Hugh McIlvanney says simply, "If Ali had gone out with only one-minute's rest, it might have been over." That conforms to the view of BBC boxing commentator Harry Carpenter, who viewed Clay between rounds and later reported, "His eyeballs were still rolling in their sockets."

"But there's nothing I can do about it now," says Cooper. "And you know the rest. I was a bleeder. I'd come to expect cuts. They were part of every fight for me. It's a shame, really. If I'd had flatter rounder features, who knows. But the worst cut I ever had was against Cassius Clay. I could feel the warm blood dripping on my chest. Of course, I think about the torn glove and the extra time it brought. There's no bitterness; I'm content with the way my life has worked out. Still, I have to say, you expect to be disadvantaged like that when you're abroad. I had a fight in Germany when I knocked my opponent down in the second round and they rang the bell a minute early. Then, when I knocked him out in the next round, I was disqualified. If Clay had been fighting a German in Germany, they would have let the fourth round go another ten seconds in the pandemonium after the knockdown and he would have been knocked out. I never asked for that. All I wanted was a level playing field. And to have it happen the way it happened in England was a bit hard."

There was a second fight between the two men in 1966, but it was little more than a postscript to the first. Cassius Clay had become Muhammad Ali. He was heavyweight champion of the world by then and well-respected as a boxer with an aura of menace about him.

"Ali was a quick learner," Cooper remembers. "By the second time we fought, he'd learned how to defend himself inside. Whenever I got near him, he'd clamp down on me like I was in a vice, hold on until the referee made us break, and step back out of harm's way."

Cooper fought valiantly, as he had three years earlier. But this time, there was no left hook. Otherwise, things were pretty much the same. Ali stopped him on cuts in round six.

And as for what might have been had Cooper won the first fight—

"Probably I would have fought Sonny Liston next," Cooper acknowledges. "I always thought the press built Liston up more than he deserved until Ali exposed him. If you were a mover and a good boxer and could punch a little, you could beat Liston, so I would have been confident going in. As for Ali, even if I'd won, someday he still would have become heavyweight champion. Joe Louis lost before he won the title. Jack Dempsey lost before he won the title. Ali was such a brilliant boxer, he was destined to become heavyweight champion of the world."

Cooper, of course, would have his own destiny. "You think you've got all the honors you're going to get," he says with pride. "And then this letter arrived in the mail. I saw the return address, Ten Downing Street, which is the office of the Prime Minister. I opened it up, and the letter said, 'You are under consideration for knighthood. Will you accept?' I showed the missus. She couldn't believe it. We were sworn to secrecy for seven weeks. Then we went for the big event. You're allowed to bring three guests, so I took my wife, my youngest son, and my grandson, which was what my older son wanted. It was at Buckingham Palace, and no one does ceremony like the British. They tell you the etiquette before you go. You kneel before the Queen, and she touches you with a sword on your shoulder. There's a bit of small talk. The Queen said to me, 'You had a long career, didn't you, Mr. Cooper?' I told her, 'I did, ma'am; seventeen years.' Then she shook hands with me. And according to the etiquette, when the Queen shakes hands with you, you know it's over. You don't keep talking to her."

So there it is. Lennox Lewis might be the "King." Naseem Hamed might be the "Prince." But Henry Cooper is a knight. That much is clear when an admirer approaches and asks Cooper if she can have his autograph. He signs with a flourish:

Best Wishes,
Sir Henry Cooper

One of the nice things about being a writer is getting to know the people you write about. Meeting Naseem Hamed in January 2001 was no exception.

In Search of Naseem Hamed

The public image of Naseem Hamed is of someone who's loud, arrogant, flamboyant, and obnoxious. That's the part of his persona known as the "Prince." But Hamed is a complex person, and most people who meet him are surprised at how nice he is. Or phrased differently, many people who root hard against the "Prince" find themselves rooting for Naseem.

Hamed began fighting professionally at age eighteen. At present, his record stands at thirty-five wins and no losses with thirty knockouts. At the relatively young age of twenty-six, he's financially secure and the pre-eminent featherweight in the world.

Also, despite Hamed's manic public image, he has handled his success well. He's a positive person. He knows who he is. And rather than fall victim to the roller-coaster ride of fame, he is in many ways thoughtful and well-grounded.

Hamed's character has been shaped by myriad influences: foremost among them his family, his religion, and his natural talent. He was born and raised in Sheffield, which offers an environment very different from London. Sheffield is an industrial town with high unemployment. And while Hamed might be on stage away from home, in Sheffield he keeps largely to his family and himself. The core of that family is his parents, who were born in Yemen; four brothers; four sisters; a wife; and two sons, who will celebrate their first and third birthdays later this year.

As for who he is, Hamed offers the following:

> • I have a lot of respect for my parents, and I'm so grateful to them for my upbringing. My biggest hero is my father, the way the man is, what he believes, the way he raised nine children in a foreign country with none of us ever getting in trouble. My father taught me values and manners and how to speak with people. And my mother taught me how to treat women, to be right and honest with women and not treat

them as secondary people. One of my biggest satisfactions is being able to look after my family with the success I've had in boxing. And I want to bring my children up the same way my parents brought me up.

• The most important thing in my life is to worship Allah. I believe that everything is created by Allah, and everything is created by Allah for a reason. I want people to know that I'm a Muslim, and I want to be a vehicle for Islam. I thank Allah for everything I have and everything that I'm going to get. The gifts Allah has given me go far beyond boxing.

• I believe that Islam is God's final religion. I believe that Allah loves to be worshipped in a certain way and accepts only one religion, and that religion is Islam. That's a harsh statement to make, but I will also say that no one can tell another person that he or she is going to Hell because no one except Allah is all-knowing and no one except Allah is entitled to judge. Only Allah knows what will happen to virtuous non-believers.

• I'll never forget my pilgrimage to Mecca. It was fantastic to see so many people. People of all colors and people from all countries, millions of people as far as my eyes could see and as wide as my eyes could see. And not one person looked at anybody in a wrong way. Everyone was there for one purpose: to worship Allah. It gave me strength and purified my soul.

• I created the "Prince." If all I did was sit at a press conference and say things like, "I've trained hard; I'll do my best," no one would care. But when I'm loud and cocky, it makes people switch on their televisions and that means I'm doing my job. It's the same thing with my ring entrances. When I started fighting on television, SkySport came up with a few ideas and I added to them and people liked it. It's one of the reasons people come to see me fight. It sells tickets. There's a show; there's music; and then there's a proper fight. And there are times when I like being the Prince. It lets me say things that are fun to say; but without a fight to promote, I'd tell myself not to go that far.

• I don't have anything against my opponents. I don't want to hurt them, and I don't want them to hurt me. All I want to do is win. But if I ever lose—or worse, get knocked out—I'll hold out my hand and say to the man who did it, "Congratulations, you were the better fighter tonight."

• People ask, why don't I move up in weight and fight Mayweather and Corrales and Freitas. I started as a flyweight. Now I'm a natural featherweight. With my height and frame and the way I punch, I'm perfect at 126 pounds. Why should I move up? I'm a perfectionist. I like to do things in the best way, and I fight best at this weight. There's no reason I should disadvantage myself and go into the ring at less than my best to please other people. Hey, sometimes I think of myself as a heavyweight. I'd have been a great heavyweight. But at the end of the day, I've come to realize that I'm a five-foot-three-and-a-half-inch guy, and I have what I have, and I have to be grateful for it.

• I was on pilgrimage when I heard about Paul Ingle. I hoped and prayed for him in Mecca, and I still do. He's in every one of my prayers. As soon as I got back to Sheffield, I went to the hospital. Paul's eyes were closed. They told him, "Naz is here." Finally, he opened his eyes and I told him, "Paul, I want you to know, if there comes a time when I fight Mbulelo Botile, I'll dedicate the fight to you and I'll beat him for you; not to hurt him, but to win for you." Paul couldn't speak, but he put his thumb up. And that was a very moving moment for me, to know that Paul understood.

• What makes me sad? Ignorance makes me sad. Sinful people make me sad. People who are asleep and don't realize why we're here make me sad. My father smokes and it's hard to get him to stop. That makes me sad. People smoke; they take drugs; they drink alcohol. And it's like going to someone and saying, "Here's a cup of poison. It won't kill you, but it will start you on your way." They wouldn't drink the poison, but if it's camouflaged, they will.

All of that brings us then to April 7: Naseem Hamed versus Marco Antonio Barrera.

Confidence is important for any athlete, and it's particularly important for a fighter. Hamed is supremely confident. In Islam, he has found something larger than himself to flow into. It's true that there are times when he looks like a less-than-complete boxer, particularly when he's under pressure. But Barrera is a one-dimensional fighter, and Hamed should be able to beat him with speed.

Also, with the possible exception of Mike Tyson, Hamed is pound-for-pound the hardest active puncher in boxing and among the hardest punchers ever in the featherweight division. When a fighter hits as hard as he does, it often renders other considerations irrelevant.

In the days leading up to April 7, Naseem Hamed will be in "Prince mode." But once the bell rings, it won't be an act.

One of the challenges in writing is to find a different angle to a story that hundreds of other writers are covering. Watching Naseem Hamed rehearse his ring entrance prior to fighting Marco Antonio Barrera was part of that process.

Illusion, Reality, and Naseem Hamed

Las Vegas is the capital of illusion. Whatever fantasy you have, the men and women who run the casinos will help you pursue it. On April 7 in Las Vegas, illusion and reality collided for Naseem Hamed, and his carefully constructed world came tumbling down.

Hamed made his United States ring debut in 1997 with a fourth-round knockout of Kevin Kelley at Madison Square Garden. At the time, HBO was committed to developing the Prince into a media sensation. There were giant ads featuring a sneering Hamed on bus shelters throughout Manhattan, a fifty-foot-wide billboard in Times Square, national advertisements, luncheons, bus trips, even a forty-foot banner in Los Angeles; all designed to raise Hamed's profile in the United States from ground zero to the sky at a cost of one million dollars. On fight night, 150 seats were removed from the Garden's normal seating plan so the Prince could dance down a two-hundred-foot runway amidst flashing strobe lights and confetti before somersaulting over the top rope into the ring.

But after the Kelley bout, HBO became an enabler for Hamed. In the succeeding years, he fought two shot fighters (Wilfredo Vazquez and Vuyani Bungu), three guys who couldn't punch (Wayne McCullough, Paul Ingle, and Cesar Soto), and one guy who couldn't take a punch (Augie Sanchez). Finally, Hamed came to understand that he needed a true inquisitor to prove his claims of ring greatness. Enter WBO super-bantamweight champion Marco Antonio Barrera.

Barrera had 52 wins coupled with 3 losses and 38 knockouts. In his four defining fights, he had scored a victory over Kennedy McKinney in the first *Boxing After Dark* show ever, lost a disputed decision to Erik

Morales, and suffered two defeats at the hands of Junior Jones. In his most recent bout, he looked impressive in stopping Jesus Salud. Barrera would be Hamed's toughest opponent ever.

Hamed-Barrera was the Prince's pay-per-view debut in the United States and his first fight in Las Vegas. The promotion was a tribute to his showmanship and the skill of both pugilists. The formula it followed was simple. Put the two best fighters in any weight division in the ring together, and you're likely to have a good fight. The bout was marketed as the heavyweight championship of featherweights.

The task of readying Hamed for battle fell in significant measure on the shoulders of Emanuel Steward. Ever since Naseem left Brendan Ingle, he has in effect had two trainers. Before each fight, Steward comes in for several days at the start of training to plan strategy. Then Oscar Suarez takes over the day-to-day chores, and Emanuel resurfaces from time to time before assuming command a week or so before the fight. On fight night, they're co-trainers, although Steward has the lead role in the corner.

Steward had been with Hamed for four fights before Barrera, and he spoke glowingly of his charge. "Naz has an uncanny ability to sense things in the ring," the trainer said. "He's very smart and adaptable during a fight. He has the ability to trap his opponents in a slugfest. And when he does, he has unbelievable punching power. His punching power is phenomenal early and late. And Naz attacks from unorthodox angles, which means his punches are even more devastating because often the opponent doesn't see them coming. And he's tough inside. He's a rare gifted kid who always finds a way to win."

Steward loves big fights. But for this one, he'd been spread pretty thin. He had wanted Hamed to train in Las Vegas so he could continue his own work with Lennox Lewis and also spend time on a movie with Wesley Snipes. But Hamed had opted for a gated community in Rancho Mirage, where a conference center was converted to a makeshift gym. For six weeks, the fighter had lived in this compound, leaving only on Fridays for a two-hour round trip to a mosque in the town of Hemet. Stewart flew in by charter plane twice a week until April 1, when Hamed broke camp and flew to Las Vegas.

"When I started working with Naz, I was amazed at the way things had been done before," Steward said shortly before the fight. "Prior to our association, Naz had never done roadwork. He'd never been to a real training camp. He was still preparing for fights surrounded by kids at an amateur center in Sheffield. He'd never even had his hands properly wrapped before sparring. In fact, when Naz sparred, he and his sparring partners never punched to the head because they were afraid of hurting their hands. I know that's hard to believe, but it's true. It's only in the past two years, that Naz has become a true professional fighter."

But if Hamed was getting better, so was Barrera. And Steward knew it. "Everyone is saying that this will be an easy fight for Naz," the trainer cautioned. "But I just don't see it. Barrera has become a complete fighter. He began his professional career in Mexico when he was fifteen. That means he completed his amateur training as a pro and became a champion before he was seasoned. He's like a lot of these Mexican kids, who lose some fights early because they haven't fully learned their trade. But Barrera's defense has gotten a lot better since he lost to Junior Jones. That fight is long in the past. Back then, Barrera was a kid fighting for money. Now he's a complete fighter. Now he rolls away from punches that used to catch him solid. And the Morales fight showed me that he's the kind of fighter who rises to the occasion. I thought Morales was going to beat the hell out of him. But in the end, believe me, Barrera won that fight. And he looked very good against Jesus Salud. Regardless of Salud's age, it was an impressive performance. So Barrera is good. And what I'm most worried about is, Naz throws lunging punches and, when he misses, he's off-balance when he finishes up. That's why he gets knocked down so much. It's not that he's hurt as much as he's off-balance. I've never really seen Naz hurt, on or off his feet. But Barrera can take advantage of Naz being off-balance. And if Naz doesn't shorten his punches and keep his left hand close to his chin, Barrera could nail him."

Lest anyone think that Steward was just blowing smoke and hyping the fight, it had to be remembered that he'd predicted a relatively easy win for Lennox Lewis over David Tua and had gone so far as to say before that fight, "David Tua is stepping out of his league. If he thinks he's prepared to fight Lennox, he's mistaken."

Adding to Steward's concern before the Barrera bout was the fear that Hamed was underestimating his opponent. Naseem was working with two Mexican sparring partners. "He's getting used to smashing

Mexicans," one entourage member noted. But Hamed was coming off a 230-day layoff, the longest of his career. "Naz should have had tougher sparring, more sparring and better sparring partners," Emanuel acknowledged to one follower several days before the fight.

As the bout approached, both fighters were confident. "I've seen his weakness. I'll win; I'm sure," Barrera offered. "We're both in the same boat," Hamed countered. "For both of us, it's the fight of our lives. There will be a collision; I promise you that. Someone is going to get knocked out, and it won't be me."

On the afternoon of the fight, Hamed sat in his suite on the twenty-ninth floor of the MGM Grand Hotel and watched the videotape of a documentary entitled *a/k/a Cassius Clay*. Occasionally, he sipped water that had been brought to him from an underground spring that runs through Mecca. The water is believed to be blessed. Hamed had ingested a bit of it every day since his training began.

At 2:30 P.M., Hamed left his hotel suite. Ten minutes later, accompanied by several family members and friends, he arrived at the Grand Arena and journeyed to its upper reaches to the point where his ring entrance would begin. There, standing on a platform, he examined six signs that would be spotlighted for his entrance. Three of the signs bore the name of the prophet Muhammad. The other three bore the inscription "Allah."

"How do I get up to this platform before the fight?" Hamed queried.

"An elevator lift will bring you up," the man responsible for the technical direction of the Prince's ring entrance answered. "You'll be back lit; there will be smoke. Once the fog dissipates, you walk down two steps to this white-tape 'X' right here. Fountains will rise behind you and confetti will rain down."

"I don't want to get any confetti on my body."

"No problem. It will be way behind you."

"How do I get from here down to the ring?"

"You have two options. Option number one is a fly-rig. Once you're strapped in, it will lift you off the platform. As it goes up, flame projectors will shoot out, and then you'll fly down."

Hamed crossed the platform to examined the fly-rig. Somewhat skeptically, he pulled at the two supporting cables.

"Are these little things all that hold it up?"

"They're steel cables," he was told. "Each one is capable of supporting 980 pounds."

"Before I ride down in that thing, I want to see someone else do it first."

"We can show you the pyrotechnics and fountains, too."

"I want to see the dangerous part first."

Someone from the technical crew sat down on the fly-rig, and a harness was strapped around his waist.

"Good luck," Hamed offered.

The fly-rig lifted up off the platform, and Hamed watched intently as it descended one hundred feet to the floor below. Then he turned to the director.

"What's Plan B if I refuse to do this?"

"You walk down."

"That's a lot safer, isn't it."

The remark was a statement, not a question. Hours before the biggest fight of his life, Naseem Hamed was deliberating whether or not to take the risk of flying on a thin steel contraption to a boxing ring. One had to wonder why he'd be willing to put that extra pressure, perhaps even fear, on himself moments before the fight. The answer was twofold. First, he was aware of his obligations as a showman. The Prince is expected to be bigger than life. And second, in the past, Naseem Hamed had fed off the frenzy of the crowd.

Once again, Hamed stared down at the ring below. "Maybe they should just put a rope up here," he suggested, "and I can swing down like Tarzan." Then, wordlessly, he walked down the arena stairs, climbed into the ring, and looked back up at the platform. "All right," he called out, standing in ring center. "Show me what it will look like."

The director narrated the effects as the demonstration unfolded.

"First, there will be smoke and lights; then the effects. Effect number one will be an airburst with the platform empty. As you come into view on the elevator lift, ten flamethrowers will shoot up. That's effect number two. Number three will be a six-second fountain."

At this point, the demonstration stalled. There was no fountain.

"We've got a dead battery," someone shouted.

The dead battery was not lost on Hamed, who was being asked to trust these people and their technology on a one-hundred-foot drop to the ring.

A new battery was inserted, and the six-second fountain blazed. That, in turn, was followed by effect number four: twenty sparklers flaming downward, creating the illusion of a waterfall.

"Have you added up how long the whole thing will take?" Hamed asked.

"The fly-rig will take a maximum of forty seconds from lift-off to the floor."

"Not just the flight, the whole thing. I'll want to get to the ring."

"That depends on how long you spent on the platform before you take off."

"Can the whole thing be done in under three minutes?"

"Absolutely."

Hamed was businesslike and polite at the same time. "I want to ride down on that thing myself," he told the director. "I need to know exactly how high and how fast it will go."

Hamed walked back up the stairs to the platform, where his father was waiting. His father expressed concern over the safety of the fly-rig. Naseem has total respect for his father. If his father said, "Don't do it," most likely, he wouldn't. But Mr. Hamed left the decision to his son.

At 3:35 P.M., Hamed was harnessed into the fly-rig. "Let's do it," he said with bravado. The flight from the platform to arena floor lasted thirty seconds. At 3:40 P.M., Hamed left the arena. He had been there for over an hour.

Outside, a light rain was falling. "It means something when it rains on the day of a fight," Hamed told his father. "A desert rain. Allah is bestowing His blessing upon us."

■ ■ ■

Virtually everyone in the media agreed that Hamed-Barrera shaped up as a good fight. And virtually everyone in the media was picking the Prince. The match-up was seen as the equivalent of a test for a gifted student who had studied hard and was expected to pass. Hamed was a solid three-to-one favorite.

As the moment of reckoning approached, the MGM Grand Arena was awash with British and Mexican flags. Both groups of followers were fervent. The Brits were loud and the Mexicans were louder. The atmosphere had the chaotic passionate feel of a World Cup football contest.

Meanwhile, a problem was unfolding. As of 6:45 P.M., Hamed still hadn't arrived at his dressing room; the fight was scheduled to start at eight o'clock; and the fighters' gloves had yet to be chosen.

The glove controversy had been brewing since the previous day's weigh-in. The fighters' contracts called for both boxers to wear Reyes gloves. The Nevada State Athletic Commission had agreed to requests that Hamed be allowed to wear green gloves and Barrera yellow. Then, at the weigh-in, Barrera had chosen a pair of yellow gloves for himself. But Hamed had first choice of gloves under the contract and, changing his color preference, he decided suddenly that the pair chosen by Barrera was the one he wanted. Thereafter, everything degenerated into uncertainty and the unorthodox colors were discarded.

At 6:48 P.M., finally, Hamed arrived in his dressing room. Two minutes later, Marc Ratner (executive director of the Nevada State Athletic Commission) entered with six pairs of red Reyes gloves. Naseem began trying on the gloves. In the background, rap music incorporating the word "motherfucker" blared. Hamed looked up angrily. "Turn that off," he ordered. The room fell silent. "Who put that on?" he demanded. There was no answer.

One by one, Hamed tried on the gloves, with Ratner placing the discards in a large black plastic bag. None of the gloves satisfied the fighter.

"I'm sorry to be taking so long," Hamed told Ratner.

"That's all right," Ratner responded. "These are your guns. Take your time, and make sure you have the right ones."

At seven o'clock, three more pairs of gloves were brought into the dressing room. Finally, after Hamed had examined every glove and pumped a series of punches into Oscar Suarez's outstretched hands, a pair marked "Naz #1" was chosen. Then Ratner journeyed to Barrera's dressing room, where Emanuel Steward was watching Barrera's hands being taped. Ratner set the remaining eight pairs of gloves on a table. A Barrera second walked over and, without looking twice, pointed to a pair at random.

Referee Joe Cortez entered Barrera's dressing room and gave the fighter final instructions. Then he went to Hamed's dressing room, but was refused entry because the fighter was deep in prayer. Finally, at 7:25 P.M., Cortez was allowed in. Hamed's hands were still not taped, nor had he taken off his street clothes. With Cortez waiting, Naseem went into a back room and changed into his ring garb. He was moving deliberately at his own pace, completely in control of the situation, meeting his own strategic and emotional needs; or so it seemed.

At 7:30, Hamed reappeared in leopard-skin boxing trunks, ring shoes, and a plain gray T-shirt. Cortez gave him final instructions. Emanuel Steward and a second from Barrera's camp returned from the Mexican's dressing room, and Hamed's hands were taped. Over the next hour, he would glove up, warm-up, remove his right glove to retape his thumb, and warm-up again. Meanwhile, Barrera waited stoically.

"Everything is already written," Hamed said to no one in particular. "Allah knows now who will win."

As for the fight itself, it can be said simply that Barrera fought a brilliant tactical fight, counterpunching for much of the evening and getting off first when he wanted to. Meanwhile, Hamed spent most of the night looking for one big punch and never found it. The Prince might be a great puncher, but Barrera exposed him as a less-than-great boxer. Neither Hamed's ring skills or his confidence had ever been so sorely tested and, on this particular occasion, he came up short.

Also, as the fight wore on, Hamed's corner seemed to slide into chaos with his two trainers giving him diametrically opposed instructions. Indeed, after round nine, Suarez told him, "I know you're going to take him out now, but not with one single shot. Concentrate more on his body. Work the body." Meanwhile, sensing the urgency of the moment, Steward implored, "You've got three rounds to go. Every punch has to have knockout on it. All you got to do is land one shot. You may miss three or four, but if you land the fifth, you can still knock him out."

The judges' decision was unanimous for Barrera: 115-112, 115-112, and 116-111. Those who gave Hamed four rounds were being kind to him. Steward himself said afterward that his fighter won three rounds maximum.

In the dressing room, Hamed's father did his best to console him. "This is a sport," he told his son. "There's a winner and a loser. You won them all before tonight, and now you've lost one. There's no shame in this."

As for Hamed himself, he took his first loss like a champion. His performance in the ring might have validated his critics, but his serenity and grace afterward disarmed them. "I make no excuses," he told the media. "Barrera boxed well. He won the fight clearly. Credit is due to him. He was better than me tonight. I can accept this defeat because it comes from Allah. It's part of Allah's plan for me, and I accept what was written." And then, somewhat pensively, Hamed added, "If I can find out the reason for this, I will."

In truth, it was a hard loss to swallow. Hamed had expected to win big against Barrera, cement his place in boxing history with a victory over Erik Morales later this year, and retire from the sweet science in the near future as a ring immortal. The chapter of his life after boxing had seemed to be beckoning. Now the dream of retiring undefeated is gone forever.

Most likely, there will be a rematch. It's in the fighters' respective contracts, and Hamed says he wants one. Maybe he'll win it. People made the mistake of overestimating Naseem Hamed as a fighter before this bout. They shouldn't make the mistake of underestimating him as a fighter after it.

Marilyn Cole Lownes and I were at ringside together to co-author what was supposed to be a celebration of boxing on the night that Beethavean Scottland was killed.

Anatomy of a Tragedy

It began as a festive occasion. On the night of June 26, 2001, Duva Boxing was promoting the first professional fights ever held on the deck of the *U.S.S. Intrepid*. The nine-hundred-foot aircraft carrier went to sea in August 1943. It saw extensive action during World War II, and was involved in numerous other military missions such as the blockade of Cuba during the 1962 missile crisis and naval operations off the coast of Vietnam. The *Intrepid* also served as a prime NASA recovery vehicle for the Mercury and Gemini space capsules. It was decommissioned in 1974 and opened to the public as a museum in 1982.

The ring was set up on the flight deck surrounded by folding chairs with aluminum bleachers on two sides. Arriving fans were greeted by round-card girls styled as World War II pinups. Wherever one turned, there were panoramic views: to the east, the towering skyscrapers of midtown Manhattan; to the north, the George Washington Bridge; south, New York Harbor and the World Trade Center; west, the Hudson River and New Jersey Palisades. But a boxing ring is a boxing ring wherever it is.

There was a patriotic picnic-like atmosphere. Red, white, and blue ring ropes cordoned off the red, white, and blue ring canvas. Everything sparkled. The sky was a perfect, almost surreal, backdrop for the fighters: aquamarine at first; after that, dark with just enough haze to resemble a black velvet curtain.

Then tragedy struck.

Beethavean Scottland entered the ring against George "Khalid" Jones for the first of the evening's two co-featured bouts. Scottland, regardless of what he tipped the scales at, was a super middleweight. Jones had weighed in for all but two of his last twelve fights at more than 180 pounds.

Scottland took a beating. On three occasions in three different rounds, he came back from the brink. And rather than just try to survive, he kept trying to win. Indeed, after referee Arthur Mercante Jr. seemed on the verge of stopping the fight in round seven, Scottland won rounds eight and nine. Then, in round ten, his condition went beyond taking a beating. His eyes wandered. Clearly, he was no longer functioning properly. And Mercante let the fight continue to its brutal knockout end.

Scottland lapsed into a coma seconds after the bout and was taken in critical condition to Bellevue Hospital, where he underwent emergency brain surgery. Six days later, he died. His courage carried him too far.

The day after the following article appeared online, my telephone rang at 5:55 A.M. It was Bernard Hopkins. Prior to doing his roadwork, he'd checked the Internet for stories about himself, read this one, and was calling to thank me. The thought crossed my mind that he could have called after his roadwork. But the truth is, I always enjoy talking with Bernard, and he's easy to write about. All that's necessary is to listen and take notes.

Bernard Hopkins—Y4145

Felix Trinidad is the box-office star of the ongoing middleweight championship series. But the most compelling personality to emerge from the tournament is Bernard Hopkins.

Hopkins minces no words when it comes to boxing. "In the ring," he says, "all fights are grudge matches. I'm a dangerous guy. I destroy careers. I ruin other people's dreams. There's a time to be humble and a time for war. Boxing is war. Boxing is serious. It ain't no joke; it ain't no show. You have to think violent. Don't cry and complain to the referee, 'Bernard is hurting me.' We're not in church; we're fighting. If you want to not get a bruise, then go play golf."

Hopkins grew up on the mean streets of Philadelphia. He was one of eight children, four boys and four girls, born to Bernard Hopkins Sr. and his wife Shirley. "I always had leadership qualities," he reminisces. "Fifth grade, sixth grade, if someone was messing with another kid, he'd come to me for protection. It wasn't free. Maybe it was just a peanut butter sandwich with bananas, which was my favorite sandwich, but I always charged something. Later on, I was the guy that girls came to for protection if their boyfriend was beating up on them. But the truth is, I was ignorant; I was a thug. You have two kinds of people, lambs and wolves; and I was a wolf."

Hopkins' story is best told by the perpetrator himself, so let him continue.

"Most of the people I preyed on were tough, but I was tougher. I never stole anything from a woman, and I didn't use a weapon. Mostly, I took things by intimidation. I'd see someone with a chain I liked and it was, 'Nice chain. Can I see it? . . . I said I want to see the chain . . . Let me see the chain . . . Give me the fucking chain now.' They weren't going to fight me. I had the reputation. Sometimes, I'd just look at a guy and he'd take his chain off without my even asking. My reputation preceded me . . . 'Like those shoes, man . . . Give me the shoes . . . Give me those shoes now!' I was tired of wearing hand-me-down clothes and looking like I'd been dressed by Jehovah's Witnesses. I thought respect was having chains and nice clothes and money to spend. I'd go out gambling and, whether I lost or won, I'd be the one who went home with the money. I'd lose, beat someone up, and take it all back again. None of the situations were big money. It was all petty stuff, but it gave me an adrenaline rush. One time, I was wearing nine gold chains."

"At home, I'd hide what I stole," Hopkins continues. "If my mother or father caught me with a chain, I'd lie and say I borrowed it from a friend. After a while, they knew. You could have taken the police administration desk and put it on our front porch. My mother used to say to me, 'You know, someday, you're going to jail.' And she was right. I don't know how many times I was suspended from school. I didn't respect life; I put myself in a lot of positions to be six feet under. My teachers used to tell me that I wouldn't live to be eighteen, and I believed them. When I was fourteen years old, I got stabbed with an ice pick over a craps game. My lung was punctured inches from my heart. I spent thirty days in the hospital. A year later, I got stabbed again, this time in the back. The guy who did it; I know I did something wrong to him. But I did so much wrong to so many people that I don't know what it was. I have teeth marks all over my hands from the street fights I was in. Why was I spared? I don't know."

At age seventeen, Hopkins was sentenced to prison for multiple offenses. One sentence was five to twelve years. The second, which ran consecutively, was three to six. In other words, at age seventeen, Bernard Hopkins was facing up to eighteen years in prison. He had just finished eleventh grade.

"I don't blame the judge," Hopkins says reflectively. "I'd been in court thirty times in two years. What else was he supposed to do? The truth is,

I had to go to the penitentiary to be saved from the graveyard. I'm not happy about the things I did back then, but the way I turned my life around speaks for itself."

For fifty-six months, from 1984 through 1989, Hopkins was one of three thousand inmates in Graterford State Penitentiary in Pennsylvania. "In prison, the sharks are waiting for any fear you might show from the moment you walk in," he remembers. "You get off a big blue bus, shackled from your ankles to your waist to your wrists. You can't even spread your legs, so you sort of shuffle forward. The inmates who are already there are checking you out in the receiving room like you're a fresh young chicken. Y4145 was the number they gave me. That was my name in prison. I'll never forget that number."

"I saw a lot of things in prison that aren't clean or nice to talk about," Hopkins continues. "I was seventeen years old. I didn't consider myself dangerous, but I was surrounded by killers, rapists, child molesters, skin-heads, Mafia types, so I was in a dangerous situation. I saw a guy stabbed to death with a makeshift ice pick in an argument over a pack of cigarettes. You see rapes. You don't go in the shower with no clothes on. You take a shower wearing your shorts because, no matter how tough you are, it's not enough if you're up against four or five people. That HBO show *Oz* is like cartoons compared to what I saw in prison."

Not long after Hopkins was imprisoned, his brother Michael was shot in the back and killed in a street fight over a girl. "I was on the phone," he remembers. "The way it works in prison is, you make your calls collect and you're allowed ten minutes before it's the next person's turn. So I'm talking with my mother, and I can hear in her voice that something is wrong. I said to her, 'Mom, I know something is wrong. What is it?' So she passed the phone to my sister Bernadette who passed it to my sister Marcy, and finally my mother got back on the phone and said, 'Michael got shot last night. He died.' And the guy behind me is saying, 'Come on, man! Your ten minutes is up. It's my turn.'"

Twice a week, every week for fifty-six months, Shirley Hopkins journeyed to Graterford State Penitentiary to visit her son. "Twice a week is all you're allowed," Hopkins explains. "I don't think she missed more than three or four visits ever in a year. My girlfriend left me. My friends wouldn't accept collect calls. But my mother was always there, in the rain, in the snow, going through the indignity of having her body touched when they searched her everywhere from her pocketbook to her bra."

Whose fault was it?

"I'm not blaming anyone but Bernard Hopkins for putting myself and my family in that situation," Hopkins continues. "Maybe society put the traps there for me to fall into. But if you fall into them, it's your own fault. There's not a day that goes by that I don't remember those fifty-six months in prison. It was all I could do to maintain my sanity. I did the best I could to mind my own business. I put a front on; I tried to look tough. But I hated it. I wanted to get out as soon as possible. In fifty-six months, I never had a write-up. And I told myself, I promised myself every day, 'If I ever get out of here, I'm not coming back again.' But I also had to get ready for when I got out. I was seventeen years old, couldn't spell, could barely read. If I said a word, I didn't know if I was using it right. I said to myself, 'I've got to fix this.' So I started studying in prison and got my graduation equivalency diploma. And I started thinking more about what I'd done. When you commit a crime, you're not thinking about any-one but yourself. Then, after a while, you start to think about all the people that you let down, like your mother. But you haven't really started thinking right until you realize that the person you put in fear when you robbed them is a person too, that they're someone else's son or brother or father. And I also learned in prison that you don't have to be bad to be tough."

Boxing also played a role in Hopkins's rehabilitation. Graterford was one of six prisons that participated in a joint boxing program. While in prison, he won four national middleweight penitentiary boxing champi-onships. "Boxing was my best therapy," he remembers. "It saved my sanity. I'd boxed when I was young; started when I was seven years old and had some amateur fights. In prison, they said I was punch-drunk. They said I was crazy. I used to run the prison yard like a gerbil on a wheel, around and around, around and around, saying over and over to myself, 'Someday, I'm gonna get out of here. Someday, I'm gonna be a champion.'"

Hopkins was released from prison in 1989 with nine years of parole facing him. He had to be good to stay free. He was twenty-two-years-old at the time and, in his own words, "I haven't spit on the ground since then." It wasn't easy being on the outside. "A lot of the guys I'd known when I was younger were dead," he remembers. But some were dealers, had the big cars, fancy jewelry, and all that. I was a convicted felon with a GED, working at an unskilled job and fighting four-round preliminary fights. I wasn't allowed to vote because I'd been in prison, but you better believe I was allowed to pay taxes. And some of the prison habits died hard. Like people would say to me, 'Bernard, you're not in the penitentiary anymore. Why are you covering your plate with your left hand when you eat?'"

Hopkins lost a four-round decision in his first pro fight when he was overmatched against a more experienced foe. Then he hooked up with trainer Bouie Fisher. In forty-one fights since then, only Roy Jones has beaten him, and Bernard has held the IBF middleweight crown since 1994. But the road has been far from smooth. Or as Hopkins says philosophically, "We reap what we sow. When I started to get good in the ring, Butch Lewis, who was my promoter, took advantage of me. He did to me what I did to other people when I was taking chains, only he did it by deception instead of intimidation."

Outside the ring, Hopkins is genuinely devoted to his family, particularly the three women in his life: his mother, his wife, and his daughter.

Shirley Hopkins is now fifty-five and battling cancer. Bernard has been with her every step of the way, driving her to and from each of the chemotherapy sessions that ended this past April.

Regarding his wife, Hopkins says forcefully, "I'm thirty-six; Jeanette is thirty-one. We've been together for twelve years, been married for eight; and she's as strong as I am. When we started living together, she had a job with Community Legal Services in Philadelphia making $25,000 a year while I was struggling as a fighter. We slept on the floor. There were no shortcuts to get to where we are today. And you can write this; I want you to write this: I love my wife, and I'm one hundred percent faithful to my wife. I don't hang out at clubs. I don't have groupies. Sometimes, someone will start coming on to me, and I'll tell her, 'I'm married.' Then maybe she'll ask, 'Are you happily married?' But I love my wife enough not to hurt her like that, and I hope she feels the same way about me."

"And I have one child," Hopkins continues. "Absolutely only one child: our daughter, Latress Gerney Hopkins. Most of my friends had babies early on and, after a while, my wife and I were getting strange looks. We were trying; we were doing all the right things; but I was firing blanks. I guess it wasn't time for me to be a father."

Latress was born on June 28, 1999.

"I'd never been in an operating room and seen a baby delivered," Hopkins reminisces. "But I was there that day. It was a C-section. I was looking through a curtain; my wife was sedated. Then I saw this bloody head come out, and the nurse asked me, 'Do you want to hold her, Mr. Hopkins?' She gave me the baby all wrapped up. I held my daughter thirty seconds after she was born. And I made a promise to myself right then. I told myself, 'This baby is going to have a father.' People ask me sometimes if I think I'm a role model. Yes, I'm a role model. When I talk with young people, being a champion gives me more leverage. Automatically, it gets me respect so I have more influence with them. And the most important thing I can show other people is how a man should feel about his wife and children and his responsibilities to them."

"I've done wrong," Hopkins acknowledges, "and it shouldn't be forgotten. But good things can happen if you decide to truly turn your life around. Sometimes I think about how maybe my life would have been different if I'd had someone like Bernard Hopkins to talk to me when I was young. You know, I missed out on so much when I was young. I never went to a high school prom. I was in jail when my class graduated from high school. Someday, I'd like to take my wife back to the high school I went to and chaperone at the senior prom."

■ ■ ■

Bernard Hopkins used to take other people's gold chains. Now he's into taking other guys' belts. But he's doing it the honest way, in the ring. The middleweight championship series that he's participating in was consummated for numbers that he deserves but had never seen before. First there was a $200,000 signing bonus plus $50,000 in training expenses and a purse of $1,000,000 to fight Keith Holmes. That bout took place on April 14, and Bernard was dominant, although he was booed for what some in the crowd perceived as a lackluster performance. But as Hopkins said after a similar experience last year against Syd Vanderpool, "The boos don't bother me. I'm from Philadelphia. I've heard people boo Santa Claus."

Next up, of course, is Hopkins versus Felix Trinidad on September 15 at Madison Square Garden. For that one, Bernard will receive another $50,000 in training expenses and a purse of $2,750,000. Once Bouie Fisher and miscellaneous items such as the cost of sparring partners are paid, all of the rest will go to Bernard. Lou DiBella, who guided Hopkins to the tournament, will be compensated directly by Don King out of other revenue sources. DiBella and Hopkins have a handshake agreement, not a written contract. That's also the case with Bernard and Bouie Fisher.

Trinidad-Hopkins has the potential to measure up to Hagler-Hearns. "This fight is my future," Hopkins said recently. "It's the last fight before they open the vault for me and let me pick out anything I want. After I beat Trinidad, just give me everything he has. The big money, the covers on magazines, pound-for-pound. Everything Trinidad has, I want it."

But he has to beat Trinidad first.

"I'm the champion," Hopkins told the media when the championship series was first announced. "Holmes and Joppy are only belt-holders."

That might have been true. But like Hopkins, Felix Trinidad is a legitimate champion. Like Hopkins, he has a strong sense of pride and enjoys testing his opponent's will. He too believes in himself and is a true warrior. Indeed, Hopkins himself recently acknowledged, "Trinidad's greatest asset is his heart and willingness to get up and his determination not to lose."

If there's a lingering question about Trinidad, it's that he hasn't beaten a great fighter in his prime. Pernell Whitaker was over-the-hill; David Reid and Fernando Vargas seem to have been overrated; and the scoring of the judges in Trinidad versus De La Hoya was questionable. But if De La Hoya gave Trinidad a boxing lesson, it's a lesson that he learned well. Not only is Felix better at 160 pounds than he was at 147; he's better pound-for-pound at 160 than he was at 147. It wasn't just that he beat William Joppy; it's the way he beat him that was so impressive. With every fight, Trinidad looks more and more like the real thing and the greatest in a line of champions from Puerto Rico that includes Jose Torres, Wilfred Benitez, and Wilfredo Gomez. He's also the first Puerto Rican with a legitimate claim to boxing's pound-for-pound title.

Handicapping Trinidad-Hopkins on September 15, one has to

acknowledge that Trinidad is now a full-blown middleweight. Indeed, he walks around between fights at a weight ten to fifteen pounds heavier than Hopkins.

Speed? Felix went up to 160 pounds with no apparent loss here. There's a school of thought that he might simply be too fast for Hopkins.

Power? Trinidad appears to have brought his power with him. And unlike Felix, Hopkins doesn't have one-punch knockout power.

So how does Bernard Hopkins beat Felix Trinidad? Oscar De La Hoya showed what a skilled boxer with enough power to keep Felix honest can do against him. To beat Trinidad, Hopkins will have to give him angles, not stay in front of him, punch, grab, maul, pick his spots, tie him up, take things step by small step, and otherwise disrupt Trinidad's offensive flow. In other words, to win, Hopkins will have to win ugly. Or as he says, "There's a difference between being a rough tough fighter who's using all his skills and a fighter that's being dirty. I plan to fight Trinidad rough and tough. There's punishment that's going to be laid out on me, and I'm going to lay out punishment on him." But then, almost in the same breath, Hopkins adds, "You know, you can say I'll fight this way or I'll fight that way. But once that leather starts getting thrown, no one knows what will happen."

And last, there's the age factor. "What is age?" Hopkins asks rhetorically. "You judge a guy by his performance, not his age. I'm thirty-six; Arturo Gatti is twenty-eight. From a fighting point of view, who's older?"

But the fact remains that Hopkins is thirty-six and Trinidad is twenty-eight. So yes, Bernard is in the best shape that a thirty-six-year-old can be in. And yes, he's fueled by a powerful rage backed by a will of iron. But has his opportunity for super-stardom come too late?

There are occasions when an aging fighter has a great and inspired night. Bernard Hopkins hopes that September 15 will be one of them. "I know the odds," he says in closing. "I hear what people are saying. But I was born black in America on January 15, 1965. I was an underdog the day I was born."

Note: The Hopkins-Trinidad bout was later rescheduled for September 29 due to the September 11 attack on the World Trade Center.

I didn't agree with everything that Bernard Hopkins said and did lead-
ing up to Hopkins-Trinidad. But I thought his point of view was worth
sharing with the public.

Bernard Hopkins and
the Puerto Rican Flag

Felix Trinidad versus Bernard Hopkins is shaping up as the blockbuster fight of the year. One reason is that it's a great matchup between
two extraordinary warriors. The other reason is "the flag."

Don King and HBO are pushing Puerto Rican pride as a marketing
tool for the fight. No one should be surprised if Puerto Rican and
American flags are prominently displayed in advertisements for the bout.
But Hopkins has seized on the flag as a means of readying himself for war
and perhaps getting inside Felix's head. On two occasions this month, the
second time in front of six thousand screaming partisans in San Juan,
Bernard threw a Puerto Rican flag to the ground. Those acts stirred passions that are expected to send pay-per-view sales through the roof when
the two men meet in the ring. But some of the passions are ugly, and the
downside is obvious.

Madison Square Garden is concerned about security on fight night.
To deal with the issue, MSG management will deploy additional security personnel. In a departure from past practice, uniformed New York
City police officers may well be in the building. The use of metal detec-
tors is being considered. There have been discussions regarding whether
the national anthems of the United States and Puerto Rico should be
sung at the start of the evening rather than just prior to the main event.
Beer sales will be cut off at 9:00 P.M. The ring walks for both fighters will
be carefully choreographed for security purposes. Access to the ring and
ringside area will be curtailed.

"We know tensions are high," says MSG vice president Eric Gelfand.
"And because we're aware of the situation, we'll be in a position to pro-

tect everyone. Bowe-Golota [the July 1996 riot] just happened; there was no advance warning. But here, we know what's going on, and we're devising procedures now that will be in place on fight night."

In a way, it's ironic. Hopkins has long said that he respects the way the Hispanic community supports its fighters and wishes the black community was as fervent in its support. He also believes that, insofar as the flag incidents are concerned, he was set up by Don King and that all of the flag waving had been orchestrated to intimidate and inflame him.

Recently, Bernard and I talked about the flag incidents. The following is an explanation of what happened from his point of view:

All the talk, all the shouting, but people don't understand what happened. My contract says equal billing. I'm supposed to get the same respect as Trinidad. But what we had wasn't a Hopkins-Trinidad tour. It was a pro-Trinidad tour without giving me any props. All the big powers, all the big money is lined up behind Trinidad. I'm fighting Don King. I'm fighting HBO. I'm fighting Madison Square Garden.

The disrespect started when I got to HBO for a photo shoot to advertise the fight. I did shots for seven or eight hours. I was the test rat for Trinidad. I was on that little thing that goes around and around. Then Trinidad comes in, and he's out in an hour. I was pissed. But as much as I talk, I didn't say anything. Then I had to listen to [HBO Sports president] Ross Greenburg saying to me, "Bernard, if you beat Trinidad, your picture will be right there where his is." All I said was, "That's nice, Mr. Greenburg." But what I was thinking was, "I know your kind. You'll be jumping on my bandwagon after I win, because I'll be hot."

The next day [at the press conference in New York], they're handing out flags. I didn't hand out the flags. Trinidad got in my face with a flag, so I threw it down. Then we go down to Puerto Rico. Don King gets up in San Juan and starts talking about "we Puerto Ricans." There's ten thousand people shouting and waving flags. And Trinidad tried to test my heart. He's making a big thing of it. Getting in my face, saying things like, "When you threw my flag down," and all that stuff. I've seen that before; that's penitentiary stuff. And then Don starts waving a flag in my face. So either I do it again or I back down. And if I back down, I'll be running every day until the fight. So I did what I did. I knocked the flag out of Don's hand. It wasn't even Trinidad's hand. It was Don's hand. No one ever knows for sure what will happen in a boxing ring, so I demanded my respect right there. I took control of the mental war. The physical fight won't be until September 15, but the mental war is on now.

If they want me to be the bad guy, I'll be it. No one will intimidate me. They took me to Quito, Equador, in 1994 to fight Segundo Mercado, nine thousand feet above sea level, two days before the fight. Do you think I'm going to worry about who's waving flags at Madison Square Garden?

And another thing; it's not Bernard Hopkins who's making this Puerto Rico against America. It's not a race thing to me. It's not a hate thing to me. To me, this is a thing between me and Trinidad. It's Trinidad and his fans and HBO and Don King who are making it country against country. I got nothing against Puerto Rico. I'm not the one who's bombing that island, Vieques. I didn't start the flag-waving in this contest. Trinidad's fans booed the national anthem at Madison Square Garden before Trinidad fought William Joppy. I heard Kevin Wynne [vice president, MSG Sports Properties] saying that maybe the Garden should get a Latino singer to sing the national anthem on September 15 so Trinidad's fans won't boo the anthem that night. So don't talk to me about disrespect.

I've raised the stakes and I've raised them high. But I'm doing things my way. I'm nobody's whipping boy, and anybody who thinks I am has another thought coming. I've got no regrets about what I did. But now it's done, and I'm through talking about it. I know how to be quiet. When I shut down, you'll see how quiet I can be. From now on, I'm saving my talking for the fight.

*When Bernard Hopkins and Felix Trinidad finally met in the ring, I
watched the fight sitting next to Lou DiBella.*

Bernard Hopkins and Lou DiBella

Shortly before eleven o'clock on the night of September 29, Lou
DiBella settled into his fifth-row seat at Madison Square Garden. DiBella
was tired. Nerves and excitement had kept him from sleeping the night
before. Now, the same nerves and excitement had him on edge. The
Garden was jammed. Nineteen thousand spectators had gathered for the
fight of the year. Bernard Hopkins versus Felix Trinidad had stirred passions beyond anything in recent memory in boxing. The bout was also a
milestone in DiBella's transition from HBO to the present.

Last year, DiBella left the number-two slot at HBO Sports to form
DiBella Entertainment, Inc. While his long-term goals are many, his primary business to date has been packaging bouts for a select group of fighters. Olympians Ricardo Williams, Jermaine Taylor, Michael Bennett,
Clarence Vinson, Jose Navarro, Brian Viloria, Jerson Ravelo, and Paolo
Vidoz are in the fold. So are Naseem Hamed, Vernon Forrest, and two
young prospects, Paul Malignaggi and Brian Adams. DeBella has served
as matchmaker for the undercards on Oscar De La Hoya versus Arturo
Gatti and De La Hoya against Francisco Castillejo. And he was the driving force behind HBO's January 27 "Night of the Olympians" at Madison
Square Garden, a July 7 HBO doubleheader at Coney Island, and a second Olympian telecast by HBO on August 11.

After the August 11 show, DiBella reflected on his accomplishments
and noted, "The novelty has worn off. The kinks are being ironed out
and I'm hitting my stride. Overall, I'm content. I enjoy being my own
boss. I'm doing it my way, and it's working. People can argue about what
I call myself, but they know how I'm operating. A lot of people who were
looking to stick a wrench in my bicycle spokes are getting used to the
fact that I'm still around and will be around as long as I want to be."

DiBella is one of the good guys in boxing. He was fair with the fighters when he was at HBO, and he's doing right by them now. He has a sense of justice, and his frustration-slash-anger is apparent when discussing the inequities of life for those less fortunate than himself.

Then there's the matter of DiBella's relationship with Bernard Hopkins.

Hopkins marches to the beat of his own drummer. He has strong views on right and wrong, and acts upon them regardless of the consequences. "I have self-esteem," Bernard tells anyone who will listen. "I am what I want to be. It's hard to beat me down."

Hopkins is also the most verbally gifted champion since Muhammad Ali and, in some ways, even more verbally gifted than Ali. He's a walking quote-machine, extraordinarily articulate and expressive. The same can be said of DiBella, although Hopkins recently noted a significant difference between them with the observation, "I didn't go to Harvard; I went to prison."

DiBella and Hopkins are in business together on a handshake. There's no written contract between them. Sitting in his seat at Madison Square Garden, DiBella reflected on the moment at hand and acknowledged, "Tonight is far beyond anything I've done before. It's important to my company financially, but it's hugely important to me personally because Bernard will always be hugely important to me. I cherish the relationship I have with Bernard. The first guy to come to me after I left HBO and say 'I'm with you' was Bernard. Most people have no idea what a good person Bernard is, and this is the most important night of Bernard's life."

"I think Bernard will win this fight," DiBella continued. "He believes with everything that's in him that he's going to win, and his confidence has me confident. But Bernard said something the other day. He told me, 'Lou, I know there's nothing certain in a fight, but I have the opportunity and that satisfies me.' If they steal this fight, if Bernard wins and they take it away from him, Bernard will be the angriest man on Earth." DiBella's voice trailed off, then picked up again. "And I'll be the second angriest."

The night was the culmination of a madcap, often horrifying month for everyone involved. Hopkins had been incredibly focused and intense, walking around like a man with nitroglycerin in his veins. He looked like an empty frying pan that had been put on a stove over a high flame. It might seem harmless, but don't touch it.

There was a flag controversy. To Hopkins, his impending fight was a fistfight between two men, not an ethnic war. But many saw him as "anti-Puerto Rican."

There was a referee controversy, spurred in part by Bernard's past conduct in fights and his declaration, "There's no such thing as a clean fight. Fighting is always dirty."

And there was controversy about Trinidad's personal life with the revelation that a young woman named Brenda Colon was five months pregnant with the fighter's child, to which Hopkins responded, "I don't care about Trinidad's situation. I don't care if his cat got hit by a car. I don't care if his fish died because he didn't feed them. I don't care nothing about his personal life right now."

The controversies dimmed following the horrifying events of September 11. In the aftermath of the nation's loss, Hopkins followed the fortunes of several firehouses and developed a particular affinity for the Ninth Battalion, located on Eighth Avenue and 48th Street, which had lost fifteen men in the World Trade Center bombing. His concern would carry over to fight night when, for the first time in eleven years, he entered the ring without two self-styled "executioners" leading the way. Instead, two men dressed in dark suits carrying the hats of a NYC policeman and firefighter accompanied him to the fray.

"I'm sensitive to what happened," Hopkins said three days before the fight. "But I have no control over what happens around the world. I have a personal war to take care of, and I'm not going to link the two. Don't mix the war that's going on for America with the war that's going on for Bernard Hopkins. I separate what happened at the World Trade Center from Saturday night. For me, there's no love in the air, because I'm getting ready to put physical pain on someone. It's going to be him or me that feels the pain, and I want it to be him. I'm not in a mourning stage right now."

As for the fight itself, the inclination of most observers going in was to give the physical edge to Trinidad. Hopkins took issue with that view, proclaiming, "This is the first time Trinidad has been in the ring with a man who's bigger than he is. I'm too much man for Trinidad. Styles make fights, and easy fights come with styles that are made for other fighters. This fight will be easy for me."

Hopkins also noted, "Trinidad only knows one way to fight. He hasn't had to go to a Plan B in his entire career."

Still, Trinidad was seen as younger, stronger, and faster than Hopkins, whose body had seemed increasingly fragile in recent bouts. If Bernard had a edge, it was believed to be in the area of will, where his was perceived as made of iron. "I beat up guys who have heart," he said days before the fight. "I never think about a way out. I'm always looking for a way to win."

The fight was a reality check for both men. Hopkins was ready, but Trinidad was ready, too. No one had ever broken Bernard's spirit, but no one had broken Tito's spirit either. It would be champion against champion, the best fighting the best. To many, the determining factor seemed to be, "Would the difference in physical talent between the two men outweigh the difference in will between them?"

In the end, as is always the case in boxing, actions spoke louder than words. Hopkins had always wanted the spotlight. Now he had it. And in the brightest glare possible, he imposed both his will and skill on Trinidad, fighting a brilliant magnificent disciplined fight.

For a long time, Bernard has been known for "winning ugly." Nothing in his career foreshadowed a performance as artistically beautiful as this.

Rounds one through six were a tactical fight. Both men fought cautiously and respectfully of one another, with Hopkins employing lateral movement and fighting Trinidad the way Oscar De La Hoya fought him two years ago. Meanwhile, Trinidad moved inexorably forward, and one had the impression that Tito wanted to fight while Bernard wanted to box. Then, in rounds six through nine, the exchanges grew more heated. And in round ten, Hopkins began to beat Trinidad up.

The final rounds were supposed to belong to Trinidad, but Hopkins dominated. He staggered Felix at the bell ending round ten; brutalized him in round eleven; and put him down with a chopping right hand to the jaw a minute into round twelve.

Trinidad rose at the count of nine on unsteady legs. "Given the magnitude of the fight," referee Steve Smoger said later, "I was going to make a careful assessment. It's possible I would have let him continue."

That would have made for an interesting situation, since Hopkins was already lying on his back in ring center in euphoric celebration, and one of his cornermen was entering the ring to congratulate him. Fortunately, Papa Trinidad was also entering the ring to embrace his son and stop the fight.

There are no easy roads to greatness in boxing. Great fights make fighters great. And in boxing, more than any other sport, the way in which a man wins is factored into the equation. Winning alone is not enough.

Bernard Hopkins has now earned the right to be called "great." As he said before the bout, "This is my opportunity to show my greatness. This is the fight where I settle a lot of things that people have said about me. This is the fight that sets me apart."

For a long time, what Hopkins heard was, "Yes, Bernard, you're the best, but the middleweight division isn't what it used to be."

That might have been true. But Hopkins has now thoroughly dominated Felix Trinidad, a great fighter in his own right. And more significantly, he has tied Carlos Monzon's record of fourteen consecutive middleweight title defenses. In that regard, a look at opponents is instructive.

The best fighters Monzon fought during his reign were Nino Benvenuti (twice), Emile Griffith (twice), and Jose Napoles. But Benvenuti was on the downside of his career when the two men met and won only five of his last eleven fights. Griffith won only fifteen of his last thirty fights, starting with his first loss to Monzon. And Napoles was a thirty-four-year-old welterweight who weighed in against Monzon at 153 pounds. Hopkins would have been competitive against Monzon. And Hopkins versus Marvin Hagler is a fantasy fight of the highest order.

I'm not sure a fighter can go where Hopkins has gone these past few months more than once in a lifetime. Bernard spent the weeks leading up to the fight trying to transform himself into a force of nature, imperious to blows and pain. That sort of mind-set is hard to achieve and will be harder to duplicate in the future. But for now, all of that is irrelevant. The important thing for the moment is that, on September 29, 2001, Bernard Hopkins gave us all something special to savor. It was a performance for the ages.

After beating Felix Trinidad to unify the middleweight championship, Bernard Hopkins's next fight was in the unlikely venue of Reading, Pennsylvania.

Bernard Hopkins
Craftsman at Work

Greg Sirb, chairman of the Pennsylvania State Athletic Commission, stood outside the Sovereign Center in Reading, Pennsylvania, last Saturday night and savored the moment. Bernard Hopkins was about to defend the undisputed middleweight championship of the world against Carl Daniels. If successful, it would be his fifteenth defense, breaking Carlos Monzon's record of fourteen consecutive middleweight title defenses.

Reading is an old industrial town with eighty thousand residents. Victorian houses and stone churches are much in evidence, but so are signs of urban blight. Fighting back against marginalization, the community has launched an ambitious downtown redevelopment program intended to make it an economic anchor for all of Berks County. The nine-thousand-seat Sovereign Center is the linchpin of Reading's plan. Meanwhile, Hopkins-Daniels was the biggest sports event in the history of the county, and Sirb was aware of its importance.

"We do fifty fight cards a year in Pennsylvania, the most of any state in the east," Sirb said. "But we're not a gaming state, so we get very few showcase events. It's mostly club fights. But I'm going to tell you something: they're great fights. I say it all the time: If you want to see boxing, go to the casinos. If you want to see fights, come to Pennsylvania. Everyone knows about Philadelphia fighters, but some of the best fights in the world take place in Pittsburgh, Scranton, Allentown, Erie, and Reading. We don't have high rollers; we don't have beautiful people; but we have fans. In Las Vegas, people come into the arena at the last minute for the main event. Here, they're waiting outside when the doors open. The problem is we get to see the fighters coming up, but when they reach a certain level, we can't afford them anymore. Now Bernard's fans have the opportunity to see him in the ring as champion. Not on TV, in person. This is huge for us. Anyone who wants to can buy a twenty-dollar ticket to see Bernard Hopkins fight. Think about that. It's fantastic! When's the last time anyone could pay twenty dollars and see one of the greatest fighters in the world? It's Christmas in Reading."

This was Hopkins's first fight in his home state since 1993, when he stopped Wendall Hall in three rounds. Tickets were priced from twenty to one-hundred-fifty dollars. Hopkins was fighting for his legacy, but he also saw the bout as part of his ongoing quest for respect.

Bernard remembers slights; and during his career, there have been many of them. "People didn't just give me the credit I deserve," he said recently. "I forced them to give it to me."

Hopkins hasn't forgotten the photo shoot at HBO last July, when still ads and commercials were shot to advertise Trinidad-Hopkins. "I did shots for seven or eight hours," he complained later. "I was the test rat for Trinidad. I was on that little thing that goes around and around. Then Trinidad comes in, and he's out in an hour."

Hopkins beat Trinidad. And as Larry Merchant noted, "Coming off a great victory and fighting to break a historic record, you'd expect this fight to be in a historic venue or in Bernard's hometown of Philadelphia."

It didn't happen. Promoter Don King and HBO said they sought a venue in Philadelphia, but that all of the satisfactory sites had been previously booked. Hopkins himself told reporters, "I'd be lying if I said I wasn't disappointed that it isn't in Philly. That's the city where I learned my trade, and I'm proud to be part of it. If I had a magic wand and could put the fight in Philly, I would."

To some, the fact that the bout was being held in Reading was a slap in the face to Hopkins. Cynics said the venue was a good long-term business move for Don King. The gate would be small, but HBO's license fee was driving the fight. And the fact that Bernard couldn't fill a moderately sized arena at bargain prices would be a factor when everyone sat down eventually to negotiate purses for Roy Jones Jr. versus Hopkins. Economic failure would temper Bernard's feelings of empowerment and, from King's point of view, keep his purses as close as possible to the previously-agreed-upon contractual minimum.

But on fight night, a crowd of 8,243 showed up despite the fact that not a penny was spent on local advertising. That didn't put Hopkins at the head of boxing's economic pound-for-pound ratings, but it was awfully good.

Meanwhile, as noted by Peyton Sher who has been a fixture at Don King fights for three decades, "When you have a big fight in big city, you're just part of the overall picture. But here, the whole community welcomes you and supports you. The entire community feels like this is something big."

And it was. As Saturday drew close, boxing insiders were much in evidence at the Lincoln Plaza Hotel, which served as fight headquarters. The weigh-in at the hotel was open to the public and drew a standing-room-only crowd, although women were barred. "After all," one local official explained, "the boxers have to take their pants off to make weight." The night before the bout, the hotel bar and restaurant were jammed as "fight people" mingled with local residents.

Then came the fight. And it was less a competitive bout than a performance by a brutal craftsman at work.

Carl Daniels is a good journeyman fighter, but Hopkins is a warrior of legendary proportions. Everyone understood that, to win, the challenger would have to do things he'd never done before and Bernard would have to fight badly. Neither eventuality occurred. Hopkins was exquisitely prepared as always; and Daniels was never in the fight.

"It's a street thing; it's not a Harvard thing," Hopkins has said about dominating opponents. "Once I sense that slight sliver of fear, it's over."

This one was over early. Daniels fought from round one on like a man who'd be happy to lose a non-violent twelve-round decision. All night long, it was Hopkins stalking, while the challenger threw stay-away-from-me jabs and tied up the champion whenever he moved in close. Hopkins never got frustrated. For the second fight in a row, he boxed beautifully, stayed within himself, fought foul-free, and broke his opponent down while putting round after round in the bank. This time, the left hook to the body was his money punch. In round nine, the hurt began to show. After ten rounds, Daniels told his trainer Tommy Brooks, "I have no more," and the fight was stopped. Each judge gave the champion every round. It was a dominant performance by a consummate professional against an opponent who didn't want to fight.

As for what comes next, boxing fans and HBO are hoping for a Hopkins rematch against Roy Jones Jr., who defeated Bernard nine years ago for the vacant IBF middleweight crown. But any one of three problems could KO that bout.

The first problem is weight. Jones fights regularly at 175 pounds, and Hopkins at 160. Bernard wants Roy to meet him halfway at the super-middleweight standard of 168. But Jones says that would be forcing him to enter the ring at less than his best. And he has a point. When Sugar Ray Robinson challenged Joey Maxim for the light-heavyweight crown, they didn't fight at a catch-weight. Maxim entered the ring with a fifteen-and-a-half-pound advantage. That was the difference between the two men on a night when Robinson wilted from the heat. But that's boxing.

The second problem is money. Jones says that, because he won the first Jones-Hopkins fight, he's entitled to a 60-40 purse split in his favor. Hopkins is demanding 50-50. Moreover, even if the two men can agree on percentages, the numbers to make the fight happen might not be there. Jones gets $5,000,000 a pop for fighting the likes of Glen Kelly, so he'll want close to $10,000,000 for Hopkins. And if Bernard got $2,500,000 for fighting Daniels, he'll want $6,000,000 or $7,000,000 for fighting Jones. But in the past, neither man has shown himself to be a major pay-per-view attraction. Money is the real matchmaker in boxing, and lack of funds might kill Jones-Hopkins.

And then there's problem number three. Hopkins seems to want the bout, but Jones doesn't. For all his talent, it has been years since Roy Jones Jr. sought out the best available opposition. Roy is a great fighter, but he doesn't want to be great in the way that great fighters are asked to be.

Still, it's worth speculating on what will happen if the bout takes place. The last time they fought, each judge scored the bout 116–112 for Jones. But the last two rounds belonged to Hopkins. Roy says he hurt his hand. Bernard says that, as the fight wore on, he figured Roy out.

Jones has gotten bigger since then. Hopkins has gotten better. If they do meet again in the ring, it will be a fight.

I began work on this article when Francisco Bojado was considered a "can't miss" prospect and shaped it accordingly after his first professional defeat.

Francisco Bojado
The Young Phenom Stumbles

You see them in every sport: the young athletes who dazzle their peers with performances and physical skills beyond their tender years.

At age eighteen, Wayne Gretzky led the National Hockey League in scoring and was designated the league's most valuable player. He repeated that dual achievement for eight consecutive seasons.

Magic Johnson led the Los Angeles Lakers to the NBA championship when he was three years out of high school. In the final playoff game against the Philadelphia 76ers, he started at center in place of the injured Kareem Abdul-Jabbar, played all five positions, scored forty-two points, and pulled down fifteen rebounds.

Tiger Woods won three consecutive United States Amateur titles by the age of twenty. Now, at age twenty-six, he is acclaimed by many as the greatest golfer of all time.

These young men had greatness stamped all over them. But so did many other "can't miss" athletes who ultimately failed. Until this past weekend, the latest "can't miss" phenom in boxing was Francisco "Panchito" Bojado, who was considered by many to be the most promising young prospect in boxing.

Bojado was born in Mexico on May 11, 1983. Two years later, his family moved to Commerce, California, ten miles southeast of Los Angeles. As an amateur, Bojado compiled a 168-15 record with 85 knockouts. At age seventeen, he was a member of the 2000 Mexican Olympic team. Then he turned pro under the guidance of Shelly Finkel and Joe Hernandez. Said Finkel, "Within three years, he'll be a world champion."

There's something incongruous about a fighter the age of a high-school senior in the ring with grown men. Boxing is different from other sports. It eats its young. Mike Tyson, Wilfred Benitez, and Edwin Rosario are examples of fighters who had extraordinary early careers but burned out early.

"What you have to understand," says Teddy Atlas, one of boxing's most astute observers, "is that boxing is different from other sports. In all sports, young stars learn the fundamentals and develop their bodies early. But boxing requires more. It demands that you give up a normal life, which is very hard for an adolescent to do. It's not like a sixteen-year-old playing baseball during the baseball season or basketball during the basketball season. In boxing, there are no seasons, and that's a hard commitment for anyone to sustain over time. To be there year after year, to do what you have to do, you need physical gifts, you need proper training, and most definitely, you need mental toughness and a certain kind of character. It's not about age. It has to do with maturity, mindset, and—I'll say it again—character."

Still, at age twenty, Sugar Ray Robinson sported a ring record of 31 and 0 with 25 knockouts including victories over Sammy Angott and Fritzie Zivic. At the same age, Roberto Duran was 29 and 0 and a mere ten days away from a title bout with Ken Buchanan. Ezzard Charles had 27 wins in the bank before he turned twenty-one. On his twentieth birthday, Willie Pep decisioned Vince Dell'Orto to run his record to an astounding 51 and 0.

As for Bojado, the early signs were promising. His professional career began with nine knockouts in nine fights that lasted a total of fourteen rounds. Onlookers praised his speed and power. Outside the ring, he was poised and polite. The fact that he's light-skinned and bilingual added to his potential crossover appeal. More than one supporter heralded him as "the next Oscar De La Hoya."

Then, on February 17, Bojado's journey to greatness was interrupted. In his tenth professional bout, he was dominated by journeyman Carlos Rubio and lost a unanimous ten-round decision. Now he must deal with the perception that fight number ten tarnishes the first nine.

What went wrong for Bojado? Teddy Atlas thinks he knows the answer.

"To be a prodigy," says Atlas, "no matter how physically gifted you are, you need an environment that will bring out your talent. That means you need to surround yourself with people who won't coddle you. But too often, the way it works now is that young fighters are surrounded by people who do what's comfortable. It's about concessions and friendships and pretend friendships, anything that's necessary for the hangers-on to keep their business relationships in place so they can make money. What's really going on is, these guys are protecting themselves, not developing the fighter. It's a con. No one forces the fighter to deal with reality and develop the character and skills to do what has to be done. That's what happened with Bojado. Bojado has the physical tools to beat Rubio, but he hasn't been forced to develop what he needs to be great. He might have thought he was getting it, but he wasn't. He was never hardened for battle and, as a result, he wasn't prepared to deal with a game opponent who didn't submit. I honestly believe that, if Rubio was a puncher, he would have knocked Bojado out."

One might expect a wail of protest from the Bojado camp over Atlas's comments. Thus, it's refreshing to hear Shelly Finkel say, "To a degree, Teddy is right. We have a kid who, up until the Rubio fight, had been incredible, and we all got caught up in the thing about his being a super-star. Panchito got caught up in it. The rest of us got caught up in it. And what happened was, we all relaxed a little so, when Panchito got lazy, we didn't push him as hard as we should have."

Bojado concurs. "Before the fight," he acknowledges, "my weight went up almost to 170. That meant my whole training camp was con-centrating on weight. I had to lose twenty-five pounds in four weeks; and because of that, during the fight, I got tired earlier than I expected. I also made mistakes in the fight. I thought Rubio wouldn't be able to take my punches, so I was aggressive when I should have boxed and fought smart."

"It bothers me," Bojado continues. "Nobody likes to lose, but I've lost before. I lost in the Olympics; I lost other amateur fights. The great-est fighters in boxing have had losses. So I have to look at it as a learning experience that will help me in the long run. I wish it hadn't happened; but if it had to happen, better now than when I'm going for a title. Hey, it was my fault, and I'm not blaming anyone else but me."

That's an honest approach, one that augers well for the future if Bojado means it.

Also, as Atlas notes, "Let's not forget we're talking about an eighteen-year-old kid. He still has the ability to be special. He's just not there yet."

In other words, Francisco Bojado still could evolve into a special vessel. Time will tell whether he does or not.

The build-up to the rematch between Lennox Lewis and Hasim Rahman took place in federal court, in TV studios, and at press conferences like the one I reported on below.

Rahman–Lewis II
The Countdown Begins

Don King, considered by some to be the greatest show on earth, brought his latest bit of theater to the Plaza Hotel in Manhattan on August 29. The Great One was costumed in black judicial robes. Hasim Rahman wore shorts, while Lennox Lewis opted for a more formal three-piece suit. A drum and fife core played *Yankee Doodle,* and there was a mock trial presided over by "Judge King" in a quest to determine who is the true heavyweight champion of the world. American and British flags were strewn about.

All of this, of course, is prelude to the November 17 rematch between Hasim Rahman and Lennox Lewis, which will take place at Mandalay Bay in Las Vegas and be televised as a pay-per-view attraction by TVKO. Ticket prices range from $1,200 to $100. And while the press conference might have been lacking in nationalistic fervor, a pretty good drama is building.

Rahman KO'd Lewis in round five of their April 22 bout in South Africa to capture the heavyweight crown. Considerable legal maneuvering followed and, in New York, Hasim pronounced himself satisfied with the outcome. "November is when I wanted to fight Lennox," he told the assembled media. "All Lennox did by going to court was cost me a few million dollars by not letting me fight David Izon first."

As for the fact that he'll be getting far less for fighting Lewis than the twenty million dollars that King originally promised him, Rahman noted, "The court took away some of my leverage. I could have held out and tried to stick Don for the twenty million, but the ten million I'm reported to be getting isn't bad. I'm satisfied with my purse."

Actually, rumor is that Rahman's purse will be $9,500,000. That, plus the five million dollar signing bonus already received from King, would total slightly more than the $14,150,000 that HBO offered Rahman and his former promoter, Cedric Kushner, during negotiations this past May. But others put the number at far less. And the deal negotiated by Kushner contained additional compensation for options, whereas the current contract with HBO has none.

"The whole HBO thing," Rahman says, "is I feel like they were negotiating for Lennox. I don't have a problem going with HBO. But they don't understand; Lennox isn't champion anymore and he's not going to be champion. So when I win again, I'll get more money from HBO or someone else than HBO is offering me now."

Any analysis of the Rahman-Lewis rematch has to begin with their first bout. The entire Lewis camp continues to maintain that conditioning and the South African altitude were not factors in Lennox's loss. To a man, his inner circle denies that Lewis was suffering from fatigue and claims that a big right hand Rahman landed early in round five did only minimal damage. They ascribe the loss to what Lennox calls Rahman's "lottery punch."

"I was winning comfortably," says Lewis. "But I wasn't one hundred percent focussed. That's what did me in. It was just an instant. Conditioning and altitude don't matter with one punch."

"Lennox made a tactical mistake that had nothing to do with conditioning and everything to do with state of mind," adds Adrian Ogun, Lewis's friend and business manager. "It was a mental error that came from complacency and disdain for the opponent."

And Emanuel Steward, who has trained Lewis for seven years, voices a similar view, saying, "Lennox had gotten to the point where he was just going through the motions. That's what cost him against Rahman."

Thus, the party line is that Lennox should have no trouble emerging victorious against Rahman the second time around. "I'm not playing this fight," says the challenger. "I'm taking this like a Mike Tyson or Evander Holyfield fight. I'll be cautious when I need to be. Rahman has a great right hand, but if I see it coming, I can do something with it. I've been through this before. I know what it takes to get to the top again."

Meanwhile, as expected, Rahman has a different take on things. "I don't give Lennox any credibility," the reigning champion said at the

Plaza. "If you listen to what he said before the first fight, none of it came true so why should I listen to him now? The truth is, Lennox Lewis can't beat me. I've got too much heart; I've got too much power; I'm physically stronger than he is. And Lennox ain't the bravest fighter in the world. He thinks he can fight me this time the way he fought David Tua: use his reach, run, and stay away all night. But I have a jab; that's the difference between me and Tua."

"Lennox is confused," Rahman continued. "He doesn't know what happened to him in South Africa or what kind of fight he wants to fight. I'm not looking to do to him what I did last time. I want to do everything better this time. I'm improving my conditioning, my strength, everything. And whatever he does, I'll adjust to the Lennox Lewis I see in the ring on November 17. Lennox had a brilliant career, but it's over now."

Underneath it all, one gets the impression that these two guys are starting to dislike each other. Rahman seems a bit pissed off that Lewis took him to court, beat him in court, and still isn't giving him what he considers proper respect. Meanwhile, Lewis doesn't like the fact that he had to sue to get his previously-contracted-for rematch. And he might also harbor a grudge over having been knocked woozy.

"This is getting personal for Lennox," Steward acknowledges. And Lennox himself adds to that thought when he says, "Ego plays a big part in it. It's not about money anymore. I'm fighting for personal respect and history."

But Lewis's place in history is now at risk. The great ones don't get taken out with one punch. And that has happened to him twice. Lennox maintains that "being three-time heavyweight champion of the world will seal my legacy." But it would have been better for him if he had beaten Rahman the first time around and remained a two-time champion.

The pick here is that Lewis will emerge victorious. But it won't be easy. The Lewis camp has been saying that, come November 17, Hasim Rahman will be known as "Has-Been Rahman." But if Lennox isn't careful, he could become known as "Lennox Loses."

When Lewis-Rahman II finally occurred, I wrote about it in part through the eyes of Marc Ratner, who let me follow him around in the days leading up to the fight.

Guilty Pleasures
The Rematch, Marc Ratner, and Las Vegas

For many people involved with boxing, there's a guilty pleasure in following the sport. And those feelings can be even more pronounced when a fight is tied to the pleasures of Las Vegas

Marc Ratner, executive director of the Nevada State Athletic Commission, is the point person for boxing in Las Vegas. Ratner was born in Arizona in 1944, and moved to Las Vegas with his family in 1957. After graduating from the University of Nevada at Reno with a degree in business management, he joined his father in the beauty and barber supply business. Then, in the late 1970s, he went to work for Sig Rogich, who had been a friend since eighth grade.

Rogich was a power broker in Nevada. He owned a major advertising agency, was influential within the state Republican Party and, in the mid-1980s, served as chairman of the Nevada State Athletic Commission. Ratner was already interested in sports. On weekends, he officiated local high-school and college football games. In 1985, at Rogich's urging, he turned to boxing as a per diem inspector for the NSAC. Three years later, he was named chief inspector. Then, in 1992, Chuck Minker, who was the commission's executive director, died at age forty-one. The death devastated Ratner. He and Minker were close friends who had talked on the telephone virtually every day for twenty years. Soon after, Ratner followed in Minker's footsteps to become executive director of the NSAC.

The NSAC has five commissioners who are appointed to three-year terms by the governor. Ratner and three administrative assistants—Sandy Johnson, Coleen Patchin, and Barbara Barcenas—are its only full-time employees. In addition, there are thirteen inspectors, eight referees, twenty-four ring judges, six timekeepers, and ten doctors who serve on a per diem basis. The commission's annual budget is $325,000, and it takes in roughly $2,800,000 per year in gate taxes, television taxes, and license fees. As executive director, Ratner serves "at the pleasure" of the commission. In other words, three of the five commissioners can terminate his employment at any time; but that's highly unlikely to happen.

Ratner has built a national reputation for integrity and competence. "My philosophy," he says, "is to have a level playing field when fights come to Nevada and to be as fair and efficient as possible." From time to time, it's suggested that Nevada's casinos exercise more influence with the commission than they should. Ratner himself states the obvious when he says, "The reason we have as much big-time boxing as we do in Nevada is because it brings customers into the casinos." But in the next breath, he notes, "I don't deal with the presence of the casinos as much as the commissioners might."

The heavyweight championship rematch between Lennox Lewis and Hasim Rahman was a special moment for Ratner. One year earlier, Las Vegas had hosted Lewis versus David Tua against the backdrop of a disputed presidential election. Now the backdrop was more ominous. September 11 and the anthrax scare that followed had traumatized America. The eyes of the world would be focussed on Las Vegas and its flagship event. The city that urges visitors to forget all worldly cares would be a tempting target for terrorists, particularly when one considered the nationalities of Lewis (the Brit) and Rahman (the American) with Rahman's Islamic heritage thrown into the mix.

"This is a big fight for Vegas because the town has been quiet lately," Ratner said several days before the fight.

The promotion swung into high gear with a final press conference three days before the bout. There's a different feel to a Don King event. King adds excitement; he's part of the show. Moreover, Rahman-Lewis wasn't just for the heavyweight championship. More importantly for King, the outcome of the bout would determine who controlled the heavyweight champion of the world.

King was Rahman's exclusive promoter, but had no paper on Lewis beyond the rematch. Also, Lewis was tied to HBO whereas Rahman, at King's urging, had eschewed a long-term TV contract to remain a free agent.

"A TV contract is only an insurance policy for losing," King told the assembled media. "I don't want to know what Rock gets if he loses. I want to know what Rock gets when he wins. This is what you call 'rolling the dice; winner take all.' Rock ain't no one-night stand."

Meanwhile, behind the scenes, Ratner was at work. On Wednesday morning, he met with Mandalay Bay security personnel and representatives of the Metropolitan Police Department to discuss safeguarding the fight site. Next, he sat down with representatives of both fighters and Don King Productions for an organizational meeting. That was followed by a rules meeting with officials from the world sanctioning bodies that had put their championship imprimatur on the bout.

"We have an organized format for big fights," explained Ratner. "But not everything can be anticipated. I suppose the most bizarre situation we ever had was the 'Fan-Man' incident [when a nut parachuted into the ring midway through Bowe-Holyfield II]. Nothing in the boxing manual told us how to handle that one. The Tyson-Holyfield bite incident was difficult to deal with, and of course there was the ugly aftermath on the casino floor [Nevada officials refer to it as an 'alleged shooting incident']. The toughest moment for me was when Jimmy Garcia died," Ratner continued. "In my years with the commission, there have been three fatalities. Robert Wangila and Johnny Montantes were the other two. But with Garcia, I spent a lot of time with him in the hospital. We thought he was going to make it, and he didn't."

Rahman and Lewis weighed in on Thursday. Hasim tipped the scales at 236 pounds; Lennox, 10 pounds heavier. That same day, Dr. Margaret Goodman, the neurologist who serves as medical director of the Nevada State Athletic Commission, administered the final pre-fight physicals. The fighters' blood work and other tests had been conducted earlier. This was a general check of lungs, temperature, blood pressure, pulse, eyes, ears, possible hernia symptoms, and the like. Goodman knew both fighters, having worked with them before. She examined Lewis first, engaging him in conversation as she probed.

"How are you feeling?"

"Good," Lennox answered.

"Any recent colds or the flu?"

"No."

"What will you have for breakfast on Saturday?"

"Eggs and sweet plantains, fried."

"When will your last meal be?"

"Around four o'clock."

"What will you have?"

"Pasta."

The examination was over in less than ten minutes. The most significant finding was that Lewis's nose appeared to have been broken since the last time he'd fought in Las Vegas. The cartilage on the right side had collapsed, and he couldn't draw air through his right nostril as well as before. Also, Lennox's blood pressure was higher than before previous fights; 150 over 88. And his pulse was 80, which was faster than his past pre-fight norm. He seemed nervous.

Rahman was next, and Dr. Goodman repeated the process. Hasim appeared to be more relaxed than Lennox, as though he were enjoying the ride. His blood pressure was 120 over 80 and his pulse was in the mid-sixties, both of which were normal for a relaxed well-conditioned professional athlete.

"What will you eat for your last meal before the fight?" Dr. Goodman queried.

"I don't know. Probably pizza."

The physicals seemed to confirm the pre-fight buzz; namely, that Rahman had "gotten inside Lewis's head."

Confidence is important for any athlete; and that's particularly true of fighters. The Hasim Rahman who settled into Las Vegas appeared confident and focussed, but there were doubts about Lewis.

Many of those doubts sprang from the first meeting between the two men, when Rahman knocked Lewis out in the fifth round. "Lennox was winning every round and just got hit," trainer Emanuel Steward said. "It's part of boxing."

"The punch was a great punch," Lewis added. "But I never put my left hand in position to block it. My defense wasn't like it should have been. I wouldn't say I was cocky or arrogant. I think those are the wrong words. But I may have taken him a bit lightly and didn't realize he was able to throw a punch like that. I'm going to make sure my defense is up in a better position this time. There's no way I want to get caught by that punch again."

Still, a man can't go swimming without getting wet. And a fighter can't get in a boxing ring without getting hit. Wisdom decreed that some of Rahman's punches would get through to Lewis again. And more to the point, Lennox seemed to be in denial regarding some basic facts relevant to their first fight.

"I wasn't able to get off the canvas because the referee counted too fast," Lennox said of that night. "The ref was trying to count me out as fast as possible. When I was getting up, he stopped the fight."

Steward adhered to the party line, also claiming the stoppage had been quick. "When Lennox went down," Steward said, "the referee started counting like he was in a race. I know that for a fact because I was there. I've seen guys in heavyweight championship fights hurt much worse than Lennox was and come back to win. Larry Holmes did it against Earnie Shavers and Renaldo Snipes. Evander Holyfield was hurt worse than that in the second Ruiz fight, and they let it go on. The round was almost over. If the referee had given Lennox a normal count, he would have been able to go on. This was the heavyweight champion of the world defending his title. You give the man a chance."

To many observers, Lewis's cavalier attitude toward Rahman in South Africa, his failure to train at altitude before the fight, and a suspect chin had more to do with the outcome of Lewis-Rahman I than the referee's count or a lucky punch. Indeed, Lennox had seemed to be tiring badly in round five and had been hit with a damaging right hand moments before the knockout blow. Thus, if one were looking for wisdom in Steward's remarks, it might have been in the message that Lennox had to fight a careful fight the second time around. That is, even if attitude and altitude weren't problems, there was still the matter of a suspect chin. Lewis's chin, it was posited, had kept him from the ranks of boxing greats. He might not have a glass jaw; but there's always Lenox china.

Meanwhile, Rahman had his own take on things. He saw Lewis as a limited pugilist (". . . Jab . . . counterpunch . . . jab . . . counterpunch"), lacking in versatility and without heart. As for claims of a quick count in South Africa, the champion noted, "You saw the fight. The referee counted to ten. He could have counted to twenty, and Lennox wouldn't have been able to go on. They refuse to deal with the truth," Rahman concluded. "They just can't accept that I have his number."

Rahman claimed to have Lewis's number outside the ring, too. There was growing personal enmity between the two men, accentuated by the champion's frequent allusions to rumors that Lewis is gay. An ugly TV-studio brawl in August brought the matter to the fore and, throughout fight week, Rahman continued his taunts.

"Is Lennox gay?" a reporter asked on Wednesday.

"How many children does Lennox have?" Rahman countered. Then he added, "Emanuel is trying to make his baby nice and comfortable."

Lewis sat stoically through it all. "I have to store my emotions up and save them for the fight," he said. "I'll do my damage in the ring."

Still, there were doubts. Even Emanuel Steward conceded, "Lennox has an extremely complicated make-up mentally. You can talk to Lennox and still not know what's going on in his mind. Lennox thinks too much. Sometimes, I look at Lennox and it looks like he's playing chess in the ring. But it's not a chess game; it's a fistfight."

Meanwhile, Rahman seemed pleased with where the fighters were psychologically. "I've heard them say that I'm a journeyman; I'm a bum; I'm nothing," he noted. "But now Lennox is fighting the biggest fight of his life, and it's against me. I know I humiliated him. I knocked him out. I took his title. The facts speak for themselves. I'm in his head, big; you know what I'm saying? I can punch hard, and Lennox knows that now. But the thing is, even though he's aware of it this time, there's nothing he can do to stop it. I humiliated this man. I knocked him out, and the same thing is coming this time only faster."

The day before the fight, Rahman seemed totally relaxed. He was walking the hotel, mingling with fight fans. He even went to the Orleans Hotel and Casino to watch one of his stable mates, Davarryl Williamson, knock out Andre Kopolov on ESPN2's *Friday Night Fights*. Then he ate dinner at Raffles Cafe.

On the surface, all of the psychological signs appeared to favor the champion. His body language radiated confidence, whereas Lewis's seemed to radiate doubt. When the rematch was first announced, the odds had been four to one in Lennox's favor. By fight night, those numbers had been cut in half.

Meanwhile, behind the scenes, Marc Ratner was doing his job. The Nevada State Athletic Commission runs a tight ship, and November 17 was no exception. The first bout was scheduled to begin at 3:00 P.M. Lewis-Rahman was slated for nine o'clock. Ratner arrived at the arena at 1:30. He measured the ring canvas to make sure it conformed to specifications, then climbed into the ring and walked every square foot checking for dead spots. Next, he examined the ring ropes. "We're down to a science on the big fights," he said. No detail was too small for scrutiny.

At 2:15, the commission officials who would be working the card gathered at ringside, and Ratner reviewed each person's responsibilities. The level playing field he sought could be tilted by accident or design. Either way, as far as Ratner was concerned, a tilt would be unacceptable. His final words to the group were, "This is a big night for us, a huge heavyweight championship card. Have fun and concentrate on your jobs."

The undercard fights began. As they progressed, Ratner walked the floor, making certain that everything was in order—saying hello to casino executives and sanctioning body officials, ushers, and security guards, greeting everyone with the warmth of a friend. Someone asked if he was nervous. "Not really," he answered. "I get nervous if I'm compiling the scoring of the judges between rounds and the scores don't look right to me. When that happens, I say to myself, 'I hope we have a knockout tonight.' But other than that, I'm usually okay."

As is his custom, Ratner visited the dressing room of every undercard fighter before each bout ("Welcome to Las Vegas . . . I'm glad you're here . . . Good luck . . ."). And he repeated the process afterward ("Good fight . . . Congratulations . . . Are you all right? . . .").

The Mandalay Bay Events Center began to fill up. The fight had caught on within the boxing community. The arena was sold out.

At 7:50 P.M., Ratner and referee Joe Cortez entered Lewis's dressing room. The room was silent.

Cortez gave Lewis the standard rules review and pre-fight instructions. "Are there any questions?" he asked the fighter.

"Is there a standing eight count?" Lewis queried.

Cortez said there wasn't. Then he and Ratner journeyed to Rahman's dressing room. Loud voices and pulsating music filled the air. Cortez repeated his pre-fight instructions, closing again with, "Are there any questions?"

There were none.

Ratner left. At 8:15, he returned to the fighters' dressing rooms one last time with the gloves that would be worn during the fight. Lewis had an intense almost haunted look on his face. Rahman seemed like a man preparing to go to a party, as though he intended to pick up in this fight where he'd left off in South Africa.

Forty-five minutes later, with the crowd roaring, Lewis left the sanctuary of his dressing room and made his way to the ring.

Three minutes later, Rahman followed. But now, there was a change in the champion's visage. The cockiness was gone. There was no longer any joy in his face. The absence of joy was to be expected. But more telling, the aura of confidence present all week had been replaced by a look of worry and concern.

Lewis had been storing up the meanness, anger, cruelty, even hate, that would be necessary for him to do what he had to do. Lewis was coming into the ring with an attitude.

By contrast, Rahman had been too relaxed in the days leading up to the fight. In the process of talking the talk, he seemed to have never prepared mentally to walk the walk. He'd been so busy trying to get inside Lennox's head that he had never fully readied his own.

Yes, Rahman had gotten under Lewis's skin. Now, he was about to pay the price. The party was over.

In boxing, "big" is often a state of mind. In the ring, Lewis looked far more than ten pounds bigger than Rahman.

The bell rang. In round one, Lewis sliced open the skin above the champion's left eye with a jab. Then, still jabbing, he kept him at bay, boxing and punching from the first round on. Rahman's best hope seemed to lie in surviving until the middle rounds, when the rhythms of their first fight might repeat. But it wasn't to be. Midway through round four, Lewis threw a left hook that grazed the champion's chin and moved his head back into the line of fire. A monster right hand that landed flush on the jaw followed. Rahman plummeted to the canvas, rose through an act of Herculean will, and pitched back to the canvas again. It was over at 1:29 of round four.

Amidst the tumult, Margaret Goodman crossed the ring to tend to Rahman. Bleary-eyed, lying on his back, the deposed champion's first words were, "What happened?"

"You got knocked out," Dr. Goodman told him.

"I didn't see the punch."

A minute passed. Rahman gathered his senses. Then, looking up, he saw a replay of the knockout blow on the giant screen above him.

"Wow!" he said to no one in particular. "He's the real champion."

Never before had two such dramatic knockouts with such dramatically opposite results been juxtaposed in championship bouts between two men.

After leaving the ring, Rahman went to his dressing room, retreated to the adjacent bathroom alone with his wife, dressed quickly, and left. In another room down the corridor, Lennox Lewis sat on a wooden bench with a quiet smile on his face. "I knew what I wanted to do," he said. "And I went out and did it. I was keeping everything I felt inside me, saying, 'Okay, you'll pay come fight time.'"

Meanwhile, back on the floor of the arena, Marc Ratner was addressing the Nevada State Athletic Commission personnel who had worked the fight. Everything of importance that had just transpired was critiqued. Then paychecks were distributed to the per diem employees with thanks for a job well done.

Shane Mosley is one of the best, most exciting fighters in recent mem-
ory. But he has spent much of the past few years fighting in casino ball-
rooms in front of 2,500 people. I tried to explain why.

Marketing Shane Mosley

There's a difference between a fighter being good and a fighter being marketable. To be marketable, he has to appeal, not just to boxing fans, but also to the general public. He has to find his way into the "people" and "celebrity" sections of the newspaper. He needs certain personal intangibles, and he has to be willing to work at the commercial aspects of the game. Sports agent and marketing expert Leigh Steinberg states the criteria as follows: "In one sentence, how can the public identify this figure? What distinguishes him from any other person on the face of the earth? It can be personality, physical characteristics, or something the athlete stands for. The challenge is to clearly and distinctly create a persona for this individual as opposed to any other person in the world."

Enter Shane Mosley.

Jack Mosley is his son's trainer and manager. "At the very beginning," Jack remembers, "when Shane first got interested in boxing, I told him, 'Get this straight. If you're going to box, you should do it for yourself, not for me.' But I also told him, 'If you like it, you'll be good.'"

Good is an understatement. Shane Mosley is undefeated with 34 knockouts in 37 fights. He's the only man to have decisively beaten Oscar De La Hoya. Like Michael Jordan in his prime, Mosley stays in best shape possible and does everything he can to be ready when it's time to perform in the ring. Boxing is a hard sport, but there are times when Shane makes what he does look deceptively easy. No less an authority than Eddie Futch says that Mosley is better than Sugar Ray Leonard ever was, ranks number one in the world pound-for-pound right now, and would have been competitive against Sugar Ray Robinson in his prime.

That leaves Mosley as a person.

We live in a society that often ruins its athletes as people. Too many of them are surrounded by lackeys who excuse everything they do and clean up whatever mess they leave behind. But Mosley appears to have first-rate character to go with his ring skills.

"Shane has always been a good person," says his father. "In his whole life, I never had a problem with him. In a way, he's a homebody. He likes his privacy. He can entertain himself. He doesn't have to be with other people. He spends a lot of time at his computer. He loves to play basketball and listen to jazz. He has a fish tank, one of those aquariums, and he's happy when he's taking care of that."

"I think I'm a nice guy," Shane says, adding to his father's appraisal. "I'm very competitive. I work hard for what I want and to be the best. Whatever I do, I want to do it well. Respect is important to me; to give it and to get it. And truth is important. I get angry when people say something to me or about me that isn't true. Just tell it the way it is; no better, no worse."

Put it all together: great fighter, well-spoken, good-looking, fantastic smile, terrific person. One sentence—"Shane Mosley: Simply the best."

The challenge of putting Mosley in the public eye falls in large part on the shoulders of Norm Horton. Horton is Shane's publicist. That means he's responsible for making Mosley accessible to the media and providing the media with information about him. He also keeps Mosley's schedule and serves as camp coordinator for non-boxing matters such as airline reservations, hotels, and dealing with security personnel.

Boxing isn't new to Horton. His father was a fighter, who compiled a professional record of 32-6 before retiring in 1950, the year before Norm was born. "Tommy Bell was my godfather," Horton remembers. "And guys like Ike Williams, Beau Jack, and Sandy Saddler were around our house all the time."

Horton graduated from Kentucky State University in 1974 and moved to Los Angeles. From 1977 to 1993, he solicited sports display advertising for the *Los Angeles Times*. Then he transferred to the *Pasadena Star News*, where he performed essentially the same duties.

"One night," Horton recalls, "there were fights at the Olympic Auditorium in Los Angeles, and Shane was on the card. It was the first time I'd seen him fight. I was impressed. I met both Jack and Shane that night, and after that I got to know the family pretty well. Then, a few years later, Shane was fighting well, but he wasn't going anywhere commercially, and I told Jack that he needed to do some marketing. Jack suggested I try my hand at something, so I put together a highlight film and media kit, and we sent it to some of the big guns. I was still at the newspaper, but I started doing work for Shane by taking long weekends and using up my vacation time. Then, eventually, Jack said, 'Why don't you come with us and I'll pay you a salary.'"

Horton now has two boxing clients: Shane Mosley and DiBella Entertainment. He's well-liked by the media, and doesn't confuse his own status with that of his client. "I'm only as good as the fighter allows me to be," Horton acknowledges, "and Shane has spoiled me. He's punctual; he's courteous. I can always depend on him. Plus, he likes it. The media is entertainment for Shane, and he understands its importance."

Thus, the question: The sports celebrity-making machine is more elaborate now than ever. So why isn't Shane Mosley big? Why is it that the man many people consider the best fighter in the world pound-for-pound made his last title defense in front of 2,500 people in a ballroom at Caesar's Palace in Las Vegas?

For starters, Mosley is a fighter. And as far as the general public is concerned, boxing is a niche sport. Michael Jordan, Joe Montana, Ken Griffey Jr., and their brethren have all been able to piggy-back on their sport. They've had constant network TV exposure. There's no way that Allen Iverson would cross over if he were a fighter, but, as an NBA star, he has an endorsement contract with Reebok worth tens of millions of dollars. By contrast, boxing hasn't been a meaningful presence on free television for years. If a fighter is heavyweight champion of the world, he gets a certain amount of attention ex officio. And a handful of fighters cross over. Muhammad Ali is the classic example of that, but there's only one Ali. Mike Tyson in the first half of his career and George Foreman at the end were commercial phenomena. Mike Trainer did a brilliant marketing job with Sugar Ray Leonard, and Bob Arum did one for Oscar De La Hoya. But the truth is, there are NBA players sitting on the bench who have better endorsement deals than Roy Jones Jr. Also, Ali, Foreman, Leonard, and De La Hoya all had the running start of an Olympic gold medal and heavy network television exposure.

Then there's the matter of HBO. Mosley is one of HBO's franchise fighters. He has fought on the network eleven times. HBO is the greatest marketing force in boxing today. It has spent a lot of money on Mosley, but there's a perception that it has spent more on promotional campaigns for Lennox Lewis, Oscar De La Hoya, Roy Jones Jr., and Naseem Hamed. Also, less than seven weeks before Mosley's next fight, HBO didn't know where it would take place or who the opponent would be.

HBO practices what its executives like to call "separation between church and state." That is, it doesn't give its sports personnel cameo roles on feature shows unless the show's producers request them. Still, the cable giant would be well-advised to get Mosley on *Arliss* and maybe even give him a bit part on *The Sopranos*. It should use its synergy with Seth Abraham and Madison Square Garden to push Mosley as the next great fighter to fight at Radio City Music Hall. And Norm Horton for one would like HBO to promote Shane more in the black media.

Mosley's promoter, Cedric Kushner, has also been accused of being lax. There was a time when Shane was one of the hottest young prospects in boxing. But fighting in California in the shadow of Oscar De La Hoya, he was going nowhere. Then Kushner took Mosley on, got him his first title shot, and has guided him from there. At one point, the promoter went so far as to take a significant financial hit on a fight in Las Vegas because Mosley wanted the bout there. But Kushner has invested more time and money on *Thunderbox* than he has on the man who might be the best fighter in boxing. One might argue that Cedric would be less than wise to pour promotional funds into a fighter who will be contractually free to leave him after two more bouts. And conventional wisdom dictates that Mosley will in fact leave. But conventional wisdom also dictates that, unlike Hasim Rahman, Mosley will fulfill his contractual obligations to Kushner and that Cedric will be given the same chance as every other promoter to make an offer for Shane's services.

All in all, it's a frustrating situation for Mosley. Right now, he might be just one more big fight away from super-stardom. But because he's so good, he's every top fighter's last option. By the end of 2001, Oscar De La Hoya will be pointing toward Fernando Vargas; the winner of Trinidad-Hopkins will be looking toward Roy Jones Jr.; and most likely, Mosley will be odd-man-out on the dance cards.

According to his investment advisors, Mosley is financially secure for life. He's not fabulously wealthy. That will come only if he's able to cross over into the general market. But his money is conservatively invested, and he spends it wisely.

"That's the way I raised him," says Jack Mosley. "I told all my children, 'The money doesn't make you; you make the money; so don't let it control you.' Shane started boxing when he was nine years old." Jack Mosley continues. "It took him twenty years to accumulate what he has today, and he's not going to lose it all in a year or two or ever."

If there is anyone boxing should be able to convey to super-stardom, it's Shane Mosley. His contract with HBO extends for another three-and-a-half years and calls for ten more fights: seven of them on *HBO Championship Boxing* and three on pay-per-view, with adjustments possible. The first of these fights will occur on *HBO Championship Boxing* against Adrian Stone. There has been grumbling in boxing circles with regard to Stone as an opponent. To some fans, it seems as though HBO has dug itself into a hole by repeatedly approving a certain level of opponent for Roy Jones Jr. and thus set a standard that its other franchise fighters are tempted to follow. A pay-per-view title-unification bout against either Vernon Forrest or Andrew "Six Heads" Lewis is likely before the end of the year.

Meanwhile, Mosley can take comfort in the fact that his evolution as a person is more important than his growth as a marketing commodity.

The best fighting the best often makes for a great fight.

Mosley–Forrest
A Good Fight Becomes a Great One

When Shane Mosley versus Vernon Forrest first appeared on boxing's radar screen several years ago, the assumption was that, when it happened, it would be a blockbuster fight. Things didn't turn out that way. Mosley-Forrest never became a megafight, but it was a great one.

The two men entered the ring at Madison Square Garden on January 26 as the best welterweights in boxing; undefeated champions in their prime; one of them arguably pound-for-pound the best fighter in the world. That was Mosley, who held the WBC crown. Actually, technically speaking, Forrest was no longer a "champion." The IBF stripped him of his belt for not making a mandatory defense against Michele Piccirillo of Italy. But once Forrest decided he wanted to fight Mosley, giving up the IBF title was a no-brainer. If he lost to Mosley, he'd lose the IBF title anyway. And if he won, he'd be the WBC welterweight champion and a boxing superstar.

Meanwhile, "no brains" was more appropriate nomenclature for everyone who contributed to the IBF stripping Forrest. That included Forrest's management team, which didn't ask the IBF for an extension of his mandatory defense so he could engage in a title unification bout until it was too late, and also the IBF, which will wind up with the winner of Piccirillo versus Corey Spinks as its 147-pound champion. But as Joe Dwyer (chairman of the IBF Championship Committee) noted several weeks ago, "At least you know we acted on principle, because we would have gotten a much bigger sanctioning fee for Mosley-Forrest."

Regardless, even before he was stripped of his title, Forrest was cast in the role of challenger against Mosley and a six to one underdog. That irked him.

"I'm no second fiddle for Shane," Forrest said before the fight. "There's three belts. He has one and I have one, and his is no bigger than mine. He knows I'm coming for him, and I know he's coming for me. I was better than he was last time, and I'll be better on January 26, too."

"Last time" was a reference to the one previous time that the two men met in the ring. Forrest defeated Mosley in the 139-pound division at the 1992 Olympic trials, and much of the pre-fight build-up focussed on that bout. Vernon Forrest, the story-line went, was the last man to beat Shane Mosley.

"He came out doing what he still does, trying to be aggressive," Forrest said of that bout. "But I outboxed him and took him to school. It was Boxing 101. We're both older, smarter, and more experienced now. This fight isn't about what happened ten years ago. This fight is about who's the best welterweight in the world today. Shane has gotten a lot better, but it's not like I've been sitting in a time capsule. I've gotten better, too. Both of us are punching harder now. That comes with maturity. But I'm bigger than Shane and I'm stronger than Shane. This fight will be like Hopkins-Trinidad."

Meanwhile, Mosley had his own recollections of their 1992 encounter. "It was a close fight, but it was an amateur fight," he said. "And it was ten years ago. When they raised his hand, I lost. That was it. After that, I put all that behind me. We were boys then, and we're men now."

Mosley also noted that, having lost to Forrest at the 1992 Olympic Trials, he became Forrest's sparring partner as the latter prepared for Barcelona. "We sparred about three times," Mosley remembered. "And I really lit into him in those sessions. I was steadily tattooing him with right hands and jabs. I just picked up on his style. When I sparred with him, I learned him; so he's going to be very easy for me to take care of."

"This is a fight I've wanted for a long time," Mosley continued. "This man is the reason why I fight as hard as I do every fight. I'm already the best. Now I want to redeem myself. I don't have any grudge or gripe with Vernon. I just want to go ahead and take care of business. I'm going to do a lot of damage. I don't want to just beat Vernon Forrest. I want to knock him out. I'm going to show him how much I've learned and how great a fighter I really am. Power, speed, agility. I'm going to put everything into one fight and that's for Vernon Forrest. I'm so sharp and I've trained so hard. I've prepared to the utmost. I can't see him standing in the ring with me for six rounds. What I possess now is too much for

Vernon, and he doesn't realize that yet. I don't think it's going to be too
pretty for him.'"

So that was the setting. And January 26 was a memorable night. The
Theater at Madison Square Garden was sold out. The place was alive.
Arturo Gatti and Terron Millet set the stage for the main event with a
slugfest that looked like a fantasy movie and ended with Gatti reviving
his career via a brutal fourth-round knockout.

Then it was time for Mosley-Forrest. And all of a sudden, as Forrest
had pledged, Bernard Hopkins versus Felix Trinidad seemed to be echo-
ing through the Garden. For the second time in as many MSG fight cards,
a fighter with a legitimate claim to the pound-for-pound crown went
down.

Mosley started strong in round one, throwing lead right hands and
going upstairs with a pretty good left hook. But two minutes into the
fight, Forrest began to establish his jab. Mosley won the round. Clearly
though, his hands were full.

In round two, they got fuller. Twenty seconds into the round, the two
men clashed heads. Initially, Forrest seemed more stunned by the collision, but Mosley suffered a cut on the hairline above his left eye. The cut
wasn't in a bad place, but it seemed to throw Shane off a bit. Then, with
1:20 left in the round, a huge overhand right staggered Mosley and backed
him against the ropes, where a six-punch barrage punctuated by a hook
to the body, a right uppercut, and an overhand right, all of which landed
flush, put him down. Mosley was up at the count of four but badly hurt
with 1:04 left in the round. At that point, Forrest was all over him. And
suddenly the Garden was consumed by the kind of chaos that reigns when
a seemingly invincible fighter is reeling and on the verge of defeat. Mosley
survived, but barely as Forrest administered a fierce beating and a second
knockdown just before the bell.

Thereafter, the drama never ceased. In round three, Mosley moved
away from his foe, buying time to collect himself. In four and five, his
strength returned. But each time he seemed to be getting back into the
fight, Forrest took things up a notch and fired back harder. Still, Mosley
persevered, showing enormous heart and courage. And by round seven,
miraculously, he was back in the fight. Yes, he was way behind on points.
But Vernon was tiring and holding whenever Shane got in close. Mosley

won rounds seven, eight, and nine. If he ran the table, anything was possible.

Midway through round ten, the possibilities changed. At 1:30 of the round, Forrest landed a hellacious hook to the body, and an involuntary scream escaped Mosley's lips. After the fight, Shane would acknowledge, "The left hook to the body got me. I said to myself, 'Wow; that really hurt!' But my will and my pride wouldn't let me go down. I said to myself, 'He'll have to hit me again on the jaw to put me down.'"

Forrest did just that, following with a vicious right uppercut and an overhand right that sent Mosley's mouthpiece flying. The next thirty seconds might have been the worst half-minute of Shane Mosley's life, but he wouldn't succumb. Finally, there was a break in the action, and referee Steve Smoger called time to put Mosley's mouthpiece back in. But for all practical purposes, the fight was over.

In rounds eleven and twelve, Mosley survived on courage. Great fighters don't crumble; and he didn't, but he lost. The scoring of the judges was anti-climactic: 115-110, 117-108, and 118-108. This observer had it 116-109.

One can look at the fight in one of two ways. The first is that a very good fighter had a great night, while a great fighter had a less-than-good one. The other possibility is that, when a great fighter meets a very good one, it can turn out that the very good fighter is great.

Either way, Forrest earned a lot of respect. He did things in the ring better than he'd ever done them before. He shut Mosley down, limiting him to single-digit connections in nine of twelve rounds. And he hit Mosley with more solid blows than Shane had experienced in all of his previous outings combined. Forrest hadn't been regarded as a particularly hard puncher in the pros. But against a pretty big puncher, he consistently landed the harder blows.

Afterward, Mosley said he wanted a rematch. Forrest promised he'd give him one.

"It was basic boxing," Forrest said at night's end. "I beat him before because I was a better fighter, and I beat him tonight because I'm a better fighter. Everybody was talking about his speed, but I've got speed too and power to go with it."

Mosley's take on things was a bit different. "I fought it all wrong," he posited. "I should have done more boxing instead of attacking. And Vernon fought a perfect fight; he beat me. But my heart goes deep. I always said, if I lost a fight, I'd leave it all in the ring and put myself out one hundred percent. That's what I did tonight, and that's what I'll do if we fight again. My goal is still to beat Vernon Forrest."

Meanwhile, Vernon Forrest is still the last man to have beaten Shane Mosley.

Round 2

Non-Combatants

Margaret Goodman is one of the behind-the-scenes people who make boxing work.

Dr. Margaret Goodman

When Hasim Rahman was knocked out by Lennox Lewis this past November, the first person to reach him was a woman with long red hair dressed in a black Gucci pants suit with a black leather collar. There was a time when the sight of a woman tending to a fallen heavyweight champion might have seemed incongruous. But Dr. Margaret Goodman has earned the respect of the boxing community as a pioneering ring physician.

Goodman was born in Toronto. Her father was a musician, who played the saxophone and clarinet, managed several rock groups, and ultimately became a record producer. When she was seven, the family moved to Southern California, and Margaret became a child of Beverly Hills.

"*Broadway Danny Rose* was the story of my father's life," says Goodman. "In the 1950s, he managed a group called the Diamonds that had hits with "Little Darlin'," "Walking Along," and "The Stroll." He worked with Brook Benton and Dinah Washington. He started Sonny & Cher and the Righteous Brothers. But what always happened was he'd take them to a certain point, and then somebody big with a recording studio and more clout in the industry would come along and take them away from him."

Still, music was the love of young Margaret's life. "I was a daddy's girl," she acknowledges. "I'd follow my father to nightclubs and concerts. He taught me how to read music and sing. And it was my father who got me interested in boxing. I used to watch fights on TV with him. Then I started drawing pictures of boxers in elementary school. Even at that age, I was attracted to fighters' physiques and the definition in their bodies."

Goodman was self-trained as an artist, but she was pretty good. By the time she entered college at UCLA, she was drawing a lot in her spare time, mostly black-and-white charcoal drawings.

"Several of my sketches were put on display in a local gallery," she recalls. "Someone from Collier Publishing saw them, and I was commissioned to supply artwork for lithographs that went into office buildings and hotels. Then, after college, I wasn't sure what to do. My father always wanted to be a doctor. I think that's the road he wanted me to travel, but he also wanted me to be happy. And I loved singing. That's what I really wanted to do. So I had a heart-to-heart with my father, and he told me, 'If you want to be a studio singer, you'll do fine. But if you have your heart set on becoming the next Barbra Streisand, go to medical school.'"

Ergo, Goodman enrolled at Chicago Medical School. But it was expensive, and she had to make ends meet. Thus, while some of her contemporaries were partying their way out of medicine, Goodman worked her way through school by singing on weekends at nightclubs in Chicago. Old standards—Cole Porter, Rodgers and Hart, Jerome Kern. "I always thought I'd keep that up," she says with a rueful smile. "But I haven't, and that's kind of sad."

Goodman graduated from medical school in 1984. An internship and residency at UCLA and the West Los Angeles Veterans Administration Hospital followed. Then, in 1988, she moved to Las Vegas and joined a group practice. "I was the tenth neurologist in a city of 750,000 people," she remembers. Eight years later, she went out on her own. Her practice today is roughly 50 percent headache management (migraines, head injuries, etc.) and 50 percent general neurology.

Meanwhile, boxing was working its way into Goodman's life.

"I used to watch fights on television whenever I could," she recalls. "One night, I was at home waiting to see Terry Norris against Simon Brown, when it was announced that the fight had been cancelled because Brown was experiencing dizziness. I heard Jim Lampley say, 'They're calling in Dr. Margaret Goodman, a neurologist.' And I said to myself, 'Omigod! That's me.' So I saw Simon. That was my first contact with boxing as a physician. And after that, I drove Flip Homansky crazy."

At the time, Homansky was chief ringside physician for the Nevada State Athletic Commission and chairman of the commission's medical advisory board. He and Goodman had known each other professionally through his work as an emergency room doctor and her role as a neurologist. Ultimately, they would develop a close personal relationship, and he would become her professional mentor insofar as boxing was concerned. But for a while, he viewed her as an attractive nuisance.

"For three years, I followed Flip around like a little puppy dog," Goodman acknowledges. "First, it was 'How can I get into boxing? What do I have to do to become a ring doctor?' Flip told me, 'Go to the amateurs.' So I went to the amateurs, did physicals and worked the corners. It's hard to get doctors to work the amateurs. There's no pay, no glory; you're doing forty physicals an hour under sweatshop conditions, so they were happy to have me. And at the same time, I was going to every professional fight possible. I couldn't always get passes for the big ones, but I went when I could. Finally, in 1994, a spot on the medical staff opened up and I got it. But they didn't give me fights. They sent me to cover professional wrestling."

The Nevada State Athletic Commission has ten doctors who serve on a per diem basis. Goodman is now the commission's de facto chief ringside physician and chairman of its medical advisory board. "The jobs can be distilled into two words," she says: "'safety' and 'fairness.' And you can't just show up. You have to work at it."

Goodman takes her preparation a level beyond most of her peers. She asks in advance who will be on a given fight card, learns the history of the fighters, and when possible, watches tapes of their previous bouts.

"You have to know what a fighter has done in the past," she says. "In fact, I'm more comfortable at a big fight than a small one because I know more about the fighters."

Goodman has been assigned to Felix Trinidad's corner for his bout against Fernando Vargas, Lennox Lewis's corner (against David Tua), Oscar De La Hoya's corner (versus Arturo Gatti), Naseem Hamed's (for Marco Antonio Barrera), and Hasim Rahman's (Rahman-Lewis II).

"Once a fight starts," she says, "the referee, inspectors, and doctors are a team. It's important that we read each other at the same time we're reading the fighters."

Goodman also worked two corners where high-stakes medical decisions were involved.

On December 1, 2000, she was assigned to Bernard Hopkins's corner when Antwun Echols body-slammed Hopkins to the canvas. The fear at first was that Bernard had suffered a torn rotator cuff or dislocated his shoulder. Goodman determined that the shoulder wasn't dislocated and that the pulse in Hopkins's forearm was strong, which meant there was no arterial damage. The most likely diagnosis was a strained shoulder. Thus, the question, "How dangerous would it be to let Hopkins continue?" Factoring Bernard's iron will and ring experience into the equation, Goodman allowed the fight to go on. Hopkins stopped Echols in the tenth round.

Goodman was also in Evander Holyfield's corner for his March 3, 2001, rematch against John Ruiz. In round eleven, Evander was badly hurt but, despite his staggering around the ring, Goodman let the fight continue. "I was comfortable with Evander's speech patterns and behavior between rounds," she says. "And like everyone else in boxing, I was familiar with Evander's recuperative powers. Also, I tend to let a big fight go a little longer than a small one, because at that level the fighters know how to take care of themselves and because of the stakes involved."

Marc Ratner, executive director of the Nevada State Athletic Commission, is a great admirer of Goodman. "She's more than a doctor," says Ratner. "She's as conscientious and dedicated as any ringside physician in the world."

Cutman Al Gavin, who has worked numerous big-fight corners in Las Vegas, concurs. "Margaret is a refreshing change from what we're used to in boxing," says Gavin. "She knows what she's doing, and she knows what she's talking about. I hope she's around to help us for a long time."

And Emanuel Steward is in accord, saying, "Margaret does a good job during the fights. She knows when to let them go on and when to stop them. But more important, she's pushing hard to get people to realize that boxing is a dangerous sport. A lot of people care about safety, but Margaret actually works to promote it."

That last point is important, because Goodman is more than a ring physician. She is also an outspoken advocate for fighters.

"Fighters should treat boxing as a business and take an active role in everything they do from choosing a trainer to choosing a mouthpiece," Goodman posits. "And fighters should know what boxing is doing to their brain. That's the heart of the matter, really. The fighters should be better protected physically. I'm tired of the excuses. I'm sick of it. Some of these guys are hurt; they're injured; and they're allowed to keep fighting."

In keeping with that view, Goodman and Homansky have authored and edited a collection of essays that have been published in book form under the title *Ringside and Training Principles*. The book has been distributed throughout the boxing industry and is available for free through the Nevada State Athletic Commission to every fighter who requests a copy.

The book is part of Goodman's crusade to made boxing better. Her presence in the sport also furthers that goal.

As St. Patrick's Day 2001 neared, some recognition for Gil Clancy seemed appropriate.

Gil Clancy

Boxing has a great tradition of Irish American fighters. John L. Sullivan, Jack Dempsey, Mickey Walker, Terry McGovern, Tommy Loughran, and Billy Conn all come to mind. But as St. Patrick's Day approaches, a tip of the hat to seventy-eight-year-old Gil Clancy is also in order.

Clancy's grandparents on his father's side came to the United States from Limerick, Ireland, in 1910. Gil and his wife have six children: two boys and four girls. His daughter Kathy is married to an Irish immigrant.

"I grew up in Rockaway Beach which is part of Queens, right on the Atlantic Ocean," Clancy remembers. "Back then, it was known as Irishtown. You thought you were in Ireland when you were there. A lot of policemen and fireman lived in the neighborhood, and there was one bar after another. I'm not joking; I'm talking about twenty bars in a row. There was Irish music coming out of all the bars, and the kids used to dance in the streets every night because they were too young to go inside for a drink. I still see a lot of the guys I grew up with. Some pretty famous guys came out of our gang. Al McGuire and Dick McGuire had very successful careers in basketball. Jackie Priestley won an Academy Award for cinematography. Lyn Duddy wound up doing all the music for the Jackie Gleason shows. And there were small fight clubs all over the city, including one in Rockaway Beach. It was all ethnic in the clubs; that's how they survived. They had neighborhood wars: the Irishman against the Jew, the Irishman against the Italian. But for the most part, the crowds were well-behaved."

Clancy entered the ring himself for the first time as an amateur in the Army. He'd been inducted in February 1942 and stationed in Gulf Port, Mississippi. Gulf Port and Biloxi were about fifteen miles apart, and

they had weekly fights at the Biloxi Air Force Base. By his own recol-
lection, Clancy had "about a dozen fights" and won all but one of them.

After World War II ended, Clancy was discharged from the Army and
went to college at NYU to study physical education. While he was there,
the school's job placement service got a call from the Police Athletic
League saying they needed a boxing coach, and he took the job. "It was
three hours a night, five nights a week, a thousand dollars a year," he reminisces. "Ironically, the first fighter I trained at the PAL wound up being
one of the best fighters I ever had. Ralph Jones was his name. Later on,
he fought as Ralph "Tiger" Jones, but I wasn't with him. In those days,
boxing was run by the mob, so what I had to do when Jones turned pro
was sign him over to another manager for a small percentage of his earn-
ings. Ralph never got a title shot, which is too bad because, during his
career, he beat five guys who were world champions, including Kid
Gavilan, Joey Giardello, and Sugar Ray Robinson."

Eventually, Clancy graduated from college and began working three
jobs in an effort to make ends meet. He was teaching physical education,
working for the PAL, and refereeing sports at the high-school level. Then
a kid named Emile Griffith walked into the New York City Parks
Department Gym where Gil was training youngsters and said he wanted
to box in the novice division of the Golden Gloves.

"I started with Emile at the beginning," Clancy says with a smile.
"Left foot forward, right foot back. And right away, I could see that he
was an exceptional talent. Emile won the Golden Gloves; I turned him
pro; and he's in the Hall of Fame now. Without a doubt, Emile was the
best fighter I ever had."

"As far as Irish fighters," Clancy continues, "I only trained three of
them that I remember. Ronnie Gibbons could fight like hell, but he had
a glass jaw. Pat Barry was a tough kid, but his shoulder kept going out so
I made him retire. Pat is a policeman in Las Vegas now. And there was
Jerry Quarry, who could fight but was too small for most of the heavyweights of his era. And of course, for one fight at the end of his career, I
worked with Gerry Cooney."

Meanwhile, there haven't been many world-class Irish-born fighters
in recent years. Barry McGuigan, Stevie Collins, and Wayne McCullough

come to mind. But former welterweight champion Jimmy McLarnin, one of the greatest fighters of all time, was born in Ireland. And Clancy has some interesting recollections of him.

"I was friendly with Jimmy McLarnin," Clancy acknowledges. "In fact, we went out together drinking one St. Patrick's night, and it's a wonder we didn't wind up in jail. What a night that was. People had warned me that, you know, when Jimmy gets loaded, he starts to get nasty, but I didn't realize how bad it was. Then, after a few hours of solid drinking, I could see it coming; not toward me, but toward everyone else around us. I had to deal with a couple of unpleasant situations that night."

Like McLarnin, Gil Clancy is now in the International Boxing Hall of Fame. That puts him under the same roof as the best of his Irish brethren. Yet ironically, it wasn't until 1985 that he himself went to Ireland.

"My wife is more Irish than I am," Clancy explains in closing. "She'd always wanted to go to Ireland, and I'd tell her, 'Who wants to go to Ireland and listen to a bunch of guys BS-ing in a bar all the time?' Then Juan LaPorte fought Barry McGuigan in Belfast. McGuigan was a national hero in Ireland, and CBS sent me over there to cover the fight as a TV commentator. That's when I found out you can't meet nicer people in the world than you meet in Ireland. I've gone back there twice more since then. The Irish are great people and great fight fans. I'll tell you something. If you ever get an Irish heavyweight champion of the world, there'll be singing and dancing in the streets like nothing anyone has ever seen."

Hugh McIlvanney is a patron saint for boxing writers.

Hugh McIlvanney

One can make a strong argument that the best sports writer in the world lives in London.

There are two major awards for sports journalism bestowed annually in Great Britain. The first is the British Press Award for "Sports Journalist of the Year." Hugh McIlvanney has been accorded that honor eight times. The second is "Sports Journalist of the Year" as chosen by the British Sports Council. McIlvanney won that award in each of the first three years of its existence. Then he was asked to become a judge in the selection process, which removed him from further consideration. More significantly, he is the only sports writer to ever win the British Press Award for "Journalist of the Year." And he's the first foreign-born writer designated by the Boxing Writers Association of America as recipient of the Nat Fleischer Memorial Award for excellence in boxing journalism. In sum, McIlvanney is a giant.

Hugh McIlvanney was born in Scotland on February 2, 1934. "There's no point darting around that one," he acknowledges. Four decades ago, he was working as a general news and features writer for the *Scotsman,* when the editor requested that he turn to sport. McIlvanney was reluctant, fearing that he would end up as "nothing but a football writer." To allay those fears, the editor gave him a copy of A. J. Liebling's classic work on boxing, *The Sweet Science.* "Liebling confirmed for me that writing about sport could be worthwhile," says McIlvanney. "Of course, the high standard of his writing also frightened the life out of me."

In 1962, having decided that writing about sport was in fact "a proper job," McIlvanney sent a letter of application and some clippings to the *Observer* in London. He was offered a position, and the rest is history. For three decades, McIlvanney and the *Observer* were synonymous with one another. Then in 1993, the *Observer* was taken over by the *Guardian*. "At that point," McIlvanney recounts, "The *Observer* ceased to be the paper I had worked for for so many years. The *Guardian* was behaving like an occupying army, and I had no desire to be taken prisoner, so I moved to the *Sunday Times*."

As chief sports journalist for the *Times*, McIlvanney now covers football (known in the colonies as "soccer"), boxing, horse racing, and golf. He writes occasionally for magazines. And he was the literary craftsman who pieced together the autobiography of Alex Ferguson (manager of Manchester United, the world's most fabled football franchise). To date, the Ferguson book has sold 600,000 copies in hardcover, making it the best selling sports book in the history of British publishing.

McIlvanney is also something of a pugilist himself. He is rumored to have knocked out Norman Mailer with a single punch when Mailer challenged him to a fight. And Henry Cooper, who reigned as British and Commonwealth heavyweight champion for ten years, recalls, "Once, when Hughie had a bit too much to drink, he wanted to fight me. It didn't come to anything. I said, 'Calm down, son,' and, I'm pleased to say, he did just that."

McIlvanney, for his part, doesn't remember the Cooper incident. But he doesn't deny it either and says simply, "It would have been a short fight and a long recuperation. If it happened, I'm thankful that Henry has a kind nature."

As for boxing itself, McIlvanny freely admits, "My ambivalence runs very deep. I'm aware of all the statistical evidence that boxing is less dangerous than mountaineering, and boxing is less dangerous than automobile racing. But that's not the issue. The issue is motive and a core of frightening violence. No matter how you dress it up, boxing is two men trying to batter each other senseless. And we, the public, get the charge without suffering the damage. Also, the whole circus approach to boxing that we see so much of these days appalls and depresses me. The ugly babble that comes out of Mike Tyson. Laila Ali and Jacqui Frazier shamelessly plundering their fathers' good names. Professional wrestling can say, 'We're just playing; no one is getting hurt.' But in boxing, people are getting hurt. And the more I see of that show-business rubbish, the more I feel I could turn my back on the sport."

"Now, having said that," McIlvanney continues, "I'll add that one should examine the motives of all abolitionists. I'm tired of doctors who attack the sport and say of each knockout, 'So-and-so won that fight on brain damage.' People who drink get brain damage, too. And some wonderful human activity has come out of boxing, moments of glory and fighters traveling to places inside themselves that few of us will ever reach. Still, the arguments against boxing are valid; and improved medical care, better pay for fighters; none of that will change the essence of it. Either you take boxing whole or not at all. If boxing were banned tomorrow, I couldn't raise a passionate outcry against the decision. Still, the truth is, as long as boxing exists, I suspect that I'll find it utterly irresistible."

As a writer, McIlvanney professes to be "happiest when celebrating greatness." Thus, it's no surprise that perhaps his favorite personage to write about has been Muhammad Ali. "Ali in his prime was the greatest figure in the history of sport," says McIlvanney. "He had the capacity to dream himself anew each morning and then inhabit that dream. He didn't just thrill you. He was a magical spirit of joy."

Lennox Lewis is another favorite. "Lennox," McIlvanney opines, "would have been competitive with any heavyweight in history because of his size and ability. He's a big man; he can punch; he knows how to look after himself. He's only lost one fight [McIlvanney was speaking in January 2001]. And if they'd had the same referee that night that they had when Larry Holmes fought Earnie Shavers or Renaldo Snipes, Lennox might well be undefeated as a professional. I think Ali would have beaten Lennox," McIlvanney continues. "Muhammad would have dazzled him and found a way to win. And George Foreman in his prime, before Ali broke his heart, had the size and punch to beat Lennox. But other than those two, I'd bet Lennox Lewis in a fight against any heavyweight ever. That's not a pound-for-pound assessment. I'd rate Joe Louis and a number of other heavyweights ahead of him pound-for-pound. But if you could match them up by way of a time machine, Lennox would be fifty pounds heavier than Joe Louis in his prime. Rocky Marciano fought at 186 pounds. There's no way that Rocky Marciano could give Lennox Lewis 65 pounds and beat him. Lennox lacks fire. Lennox lacks passion in the ring. He's a percentage player. But I'm prepared to accept Lennox for what he is, which is considerable, and I have no question about his heart. I just hope Lennox retires while he's still champion," McIlvanney says in closing. "He'd feel so good about it for the rest of his life."

As for his philosophy of writing, McIlvanney says simply, "It's important to maintain a sensible perspective on the relationship between sport and the world at large. For that reason, I've always been thankful for the years I spent writing about general news. And there should be a sound knowledge of the sport being covered. A good sports writer must be equipped to judge performances without waiting for experts to explain what he's been watching. That's not to say that one has to know all the answers, but a good writer knows the questions."

And then McIlvanney adds modestly, "My approach to writing is not an expectation of triumph, but a determination to avoid screwing up. When I write, I imagine people I respect scrutinizing my work. I have an almost neurotic concern to avoid making a mess of it."

One of those who McIlvanney might imagine evaluating his work is A. J. Liebling. "If you couldn't go to a fight, the best commentary you could have on it was Liebling," he says reflectively. "Of course, Liebling had a great advantage in that he was writing about boxing. It's a writer's sport. You have courage, romance, skullduggery, excitement, and moments of unspeakable horror. Liebling couldn't have written the way he wrote if he'd been writing about croquet."

A wistful look crosses McIlvanney's face. "You know, I greatly regret never having met Liebling. I wish I'd had the presence of mind near the end . . ." His voice trails off and then picks up again. "It's one of those regrets we all have."

No doubt, there will be writers who feel the same way about Hugh McIlvanney in the future. But those of us in the writing fraternity expect to have him active and with us for a long time.

To many boxing fans, Jimmy Lennon Jr. plays Avis to Michael Buffer's Hertz. But Lennon has an ardent following.

Jimmy Lennon Jr.

When Joe Calzaghe faces off against Mario Veit on Showtime this Saturday night, many viewers won't recognize the fighters. But there will be at least one familiar face. Shortly before the main event, the man who commentator Steve Albert refers to as "the classy Jimmy Lennon Jr." will take the ring microphone in hand and intone the words, "I–i–i–t–t's Showtime!"

Jimmy Lennon Jr. was born in Santa Monica, California, on August 5, 1958. His father had five children. Jimmy was the youngest of three sons, yet he was the one who inherited his father's name. All his life, people have told him that he looks and sounds like his father. That's what led him into boxing. You see, his father is *the* Jimmy Lennon, who began working as a ring announcer in Los Angeles shortly after World War II and loved the sport until his death more than four decades later.

"My father had a lot of jobs," Lennon remembers. "When I was young, he was a butcher during the day and sang at night. Then he became a salesman and emceed various events in and around Los Angeles, and that led him into ring announcing. We grew up watching Dad on television. He was big in Los Angeles. I even remember his doing a Cassius Clay fight before Clay beat Sonny Liston and changed his name to Muhammad Ali."

Lennon graduated from UCLA with a degree in psychology in 1981. That year, he announced his first fight. "It was at the Forum," he recalls. "There was a small crowd and it was an off-TV bout. I had my best suit on, and I was a little bit frightened. All I did was one preliminary bout, and my dad did the rest of the card."

Shortly thereafter, Lennon began teaching at West LA Baptist, a small private school in Los Angeles for grades seven through twelve. He is now the school principal. Meanwhile, his career as a ring announcer has flourished. All totaled, he estimates that he has served as ring announcer for 400 world title bouts and 1,500 fight cards. He is Showtime's announcer of choice and, with rare exceptions, has handled every fight for that network since Tyson-Ruddock I in 1991. That distinction will end later this year when Showtime's Saturday-afternoon series, *ShoBox,* makes its debut.

"Our budget for those shows is tight," explains Showtime boxing czar Jay Larkin. "And Jimmy is a luxury we can't afford." But Larkin goes on to sing Lennon's praises with the declaration, "Jimmy is the consummate ring announcer. It's in his genes. And he's a valuable asset to our entire boxing program. He's a true fight fan; he's well-informed. Whenever I ask him about a possible fight, I get an intelligent answer. He's fluent in Spanish, which is a tremendous plus on fight night. Jimmy has become a logo for Showtime, and we're proud to have him."

Meanwhile, Don King has hired Lennon for every major fight he has promoted since Mike Tyson was upset by James "Buster" Douglas in 1990. The King-Lennon association is ironic when one considers the fact that the fight it began with represented a huge blow to the promoter. But as King points out, "The guy on the microphone had nothing to do with the result of the fight. I'm a fair-minded man, and Jimmy announced it properly."

"Tyson-Douglas was huge for me," Lennon acknowledges, remembering that night. "It was the first megafight I ever did. My dad was struggling with his health then. And when I told him I was going to Japan for the fight, he started crying. Tears were streaming down his face. He was so supportive of me. And there are some other fights I did for Don King that stand out in my mind. One is Greg Haugen versus Julio Cesar Chavez in Mexico City in 1993. There were 135,000 people there, and the whole event was spectacular. It was great to be a part of something like that. And both Tyson-Holyfield fights are vivid for me. The first was a shock as it unfolded and the second was so bizarre."

Meanwhile, King's loyalty to Lennon has led to an interesting situation, whereby Showtime's ring announcer of choice has appeared lately on HBO in conjunction with Holyfield-Lewis, Trinidad-Vargas, and HBO's ongoing middleweight championship series. In fact, King insists that his contracts with HBO contain a clause pre-approving Lennon as the ring announcer.

"It could be awkward," Lennon acknowledges. "Jay Larkin could have told me I couldn't work on HBO and that would have been the end of it, but Jay has been incredibly kind about it all."

Before each fight card Lennon announces, he makes a point of speaking with the boxers, particularly those who will be in the undercard bouts. He asks each fighter how he pronounces his name, his nickname, his hometown, and what color trunks he'll be wearing.

"While the fight is going on," Lennon explains, "I'm a fan. I enjoy it and, like any other fan, I form an opinion as to who's winning. Naturally, there are times when I'm surprised by what the judges do. Chavez-Whitaker wasn't a great decision. And Holyfield-Lewis I stands out in my mind. When I get something like that, I read the result to myself two or three times to make sure I've got it right. Then I take my emotions and my opinion off the table and do my job. Someone has to break the news. It might as well be me."

"Sometimes it's good to build up suspense before reading a decision," Lennon continues. "And sometimes it's good to downplay it. If there's a partisan crowd and the local hero has lost, I'll make an effort to say something nice about him before I give fans the bad news. There have been a few times where I was afraid to announce a decision. In certain situations, if the crowd is hyped up and a lot of people are intoxicated, there's definitely a sense of concern for your health."

Then comes that moment when the eyes of the world are upon him.

"Boxing is unique," says Lennon, "in that it's the only major sport where, very often, people don't know who has won until someone announces the result. That means millions of people are listening to my every word. And I'll be honest, I love it. The bigger the stakes, the more the suspense, the more it means to me."

Someday, a hundred years from now, people will be looking at today's fights the same way fans now look at old fight films of Jack Dempsey, Joe Louis, and Sugar Ray Robinson. And Jimmy Lennon will be part of that. Thanks to boxing, he's part of history.

I'd planned to put this story online in conjunction with a dinner that was to be held in Eddie Futch's honor. Instead, it became his eulogy.

Mr. Futch

Every once in a while, it's nice to have a "feel-good" story about boxing. Eddie Futch, who died today at age ninety, was always a feel-good story. Whenever one talked with him—or better yet, listened—one heard words of wisdom. If the world lived by better standards, he would have been a king. As it is, it's a sign of the respect he was accorded within the boxing community, and particularly among fighters, that he was often addressed as "Mr. Futch."

Great trainers have a unique talent: the ability to recognize and develop talent in others. Futch began training fighters in 1938, and worked with twenty-two world champions including Joe Frazier, Larry Holmes, Michael Spinks, Riddick Bowe, Ken Norton, Bob Foster, and Alexis Arguello. There would have been more, but for an admirable quirk in Eddie's personality. "I never take on a fighter I don't like," he once said. "If I find myself with a fighter I dislike, I get rid of him no matter how much profit there is in it. I've seen managers who subconsciously hate one of their fighters and enjoy seeing him beat. You've got to love your fighter. Otherwise, it's dangerous. You'll send him out and get him mangled or killed."

Futch was also a disciplinarian. In the late 1930s, he was working with amateurs in Detroit. "There was a twelve-year-old who'd come to the gym," he remembered. "He wasn't there to train, just hang out with his friends and make noise. One day, he made so much noise that I chased him out of the gym and told him not to come back until he was ready to behave himself. About six months later, his family moved to New York and he began fighting as an amateur."

The story bears repeating, because the young man's name was Walker Smith Jr., later known to the world as Sugar Ray Robinson. "Ray had it all," Futch said with a trace of awe in his voice. Boxing skills, punching power, mental strength. He did things in the ring I've never seen anyone else do, before or since."

Like many of his brethren in boxing, Futch moved into the limelight as a result of Muhammad Ali. He was in Joe Frazier's corner for all three of Smokin' Joe's bouts against Ali, and saw something in Ali's style that could be exploited. "It was the way Ali pulled his head back from punches," Futch explained. "Not in the center of the ring, but when he was on the ropes. He would pull his head back from punches in a way that left his body exposed, so the body attack was the key. Most fighters, when they boxed Ali, when he went to the ropes they'd go immediately to the head. Ali would pull back so the punches passed in front of him. And once he made you miss, he'd come off the ropes and hurt you. So Joe was instructed, when Ali was on the ropes, to work the body with both hands. Let Ali pull his head back, because if he leaned back against the ropes, he'd expose his body to hard shots."

In Ali-Frazier I, it worked. "I might have cut the diamond," Yank Durham (Frazier's first trainer and manager) said afterward, "but Eddie polished it."

After Durham's death, Futch became Frazier's trainer and manager. In that capacity, he's best remembered for stopping Ali-Frazier III after fourteen brutal rounds of carnage in Manila.

"Joe kept getting hit with the right hand," Futch said later. "His left eye was completely closed; his right eye was closing. It had been a grueling fight and that's when fighters get hurt, when they get hit with good clean punches they don't see. I didn't want Joe's brains scrambled. He had a nice life and a wonderful family to live for; so I decided at the end of the fourteenth round to stop it. I just didn't think Joe should go on anymore."

Futch was also with Ken Norton for the first two Ali-Norton bouts, and devised the strategy for Ali-Norton I which led to Norton breaking Ali's jaw.

"It was the way Ali held his hands," Futch recalled. "Not that they were too low, but the placement of his right hand when he threw the jab. When a man throws a jab, his right hand should be by his chin to parry the jab that's coming back, but Ali didn't keep it there. He'd move it to the right. Norton had four inches more height than Frazier, so I told him to step toward Ali with his jab. Norton's right hand being in proper position, Ali's jab would be blocked by Norton's right. And Norton's jab would hit Ali in the middle of the face, because Ali's right hand would be out of position."

It's no wonder that, when Ali reflected back on his own career, he acknowledged, "Whenever I fought someone who was trained by Eddie Futch, I knew I was in for a hard fight."

Futch ranked Joe Louis as the greatest heavyweight of all time, with Ali and Jack Johnson in a virtual tie for second place.

"I have great memories of Joe Louis," Futch reminisced. "We came out of the same amateur club in Detroit. Joe was a light-heavyweight at the time, and I was a lightweight. But we sparred together about a dozen times, because Joe liked to work with fast fighters. He never hurt me with a punch to the head, but blocking his shots let me know how devastating his power was even then. I was too small to force him back, so I had to lead him into things. And I hit him a few times. Yes, I did; I hit Joe Louis. But he was a smart fighter, getting smarter, and his hands were so fast."

"I remember, one time we were sparring," Futch continued. "I hit Joe. He stepped back and looked at me and asked, 'How'd you do that?' I told him, 'Joe, it doesn't matter how I did it. I'm too small to hurt you.' And he said, 'I know. But if you can hit me with it, someone bigger than you can hit me with it, too."

"Maybe I'm prejudiced," Futch said in closing, "but I think Joe Louis would have beaten Ali. People remember how hard Joe punched. What they don't remember is what a good boxer he was. I always thought that Joe would have seen the flaws in Ali's style and been able to take advantage of them."

With Mr. Futch in Joe Louis's corner, it would have been quite a fight.

Meanwhile, looking back over the course of his career in boxing, Eddie Futch could say that he sparred with Joe Louis, was in the corner with two guys who beat Muhammad Ali, and kicked Sugar Ray Robinson out of the gym. That's quite a life.

Round 3

A Case Study

When Hasim Rahman knocked out Lennox Lewis in their first fight to
capture the heavyweight championship, it set in motion a series of law-
suits, betrayals, and other events that revealed the inner workings of box-
ing. But all that was in the future when Cedric Kushner appeared at the
Hammerstein Ballroom on April 28, 2001, as Rahman's "exclusive
promoter."

At the Hammerstein Ballroom

Jerry Sterner once wrote a play entitled *Other People's Money.* When
this past weekend's card at the Hammerstein Ballroom in Manhattan was
announced, it appeared as though Cedric Kushner was engaged in a varia-
tion of that theme. Call it *Other People's Work.* More specifically, Kushner,
who was feeling a financial squeeze, had agreed to do the nuts-and-bolts
promotional work for Bob Arum's *KO Nation* card for short money. Three
months earlier, he had done the same thing when Lou DiBella's Olympic
fighters made their professional debut at Madison Square Garden.

But boxing is an ever-changing puzzle, and the pieces fit together in
funny ways. How else to explain the fact that, two years ago on the night
of March 12, 1999, Lennox Lewis was resting in a Manhattan hotel room
readying to fight Evander Holyfield the following night. Meanwhile, less
than a mile away, Hasim Rahman, who had been knocked out by David
Tua in his previous outing, was entering the ring at Roseland Ballroom
to face Michael Rush. Rahman's promoter at the time was Cedric
Kushner. Now, with one explosive right hand, Rahman is the heavyweight champion of the world and Cedric Kushner is still his promoter.

Kushner was born in South Africa. A self-described "disobedient
youngster who had no interest in school," he abandoned academia after
failing the American equivalent of seventh grade and worked at a series
of jobs, including a stint as a tally clerk on the docks of Capetown. He
left South Africa as a deckhand onboard a freighter in 1970 and arrived
in the United States on his twenty-third birthday. Now, metaphorically
speaking, his ship has come in.

Ironically, the Lewis–Rahman bout almost didn't happen. The Lewis camp sent contracts for bouts against both Rahman and Kirk Johnson to Kushner. Since Kushner has exclusive promotional rights to both fighters, he was free to make the deal for whichever one he chose within the parameters of the Lewis camp's offer. Johnson wanted too much money. Initially, Rahman balked at going to South Africa. But eventually, he changed his mind; and his co-managers (Stan Hoffman and Steve Nelson) were willing to compromise on money. Thus it was that, while last night's *KO Nation* card was underway at the Hammerstein Ballroom, Kirk Johnson was stepping into the ring to fight Derrick Banks on a "Heavyweight Explosion" card in Indiana.

Meanwhile, Kushner and the Rahman team claim that the new champion is free to fight anyone he chooses (i.e. Mike Tyson) in his first title defense. That, and a possible loophole which may or may not be present in the original Lewis–Rahman fight contracts, has left the powers-that-be at HBO and Main Events as well as Lewis's business manager Adrian Ogun scratching their collective heads. When Buster Douglas upset Mike Tyson in 1990, control over the heavyweight championship moved from Don King Productions to Main Events. And HBO, which had televised twenty-one consecutive heavyweight title bouts, saw Douglas make the first (and only) defense of his reign against Evander Holyfield on Showtime. A similar shift in the balance of power between HBO and Showtime (the real heavyweights in boxing) may now occur. Showtime is believed to have offered Rahman in the neighborhood of $15,000,000 to fight Tyson. Kushner is point man for the Rahman team in the current negotiations. "Right now," he said on Saturday afternoon, "it's fifty-fifty as to whether the next opponent will be Lewis or Tyson. Maximizing the money will be our top priority. We hope to resolve things within a week." Then, on Saturday night, word spread that HBO, Main Events, and the Lewis camp had pooled their resources to offer Rahman $13,000,000 for a Lewis rematch with HBO having options on both fighters. Given the fact that the contract Rahman signed for the first Lewis fight was thought by HBO, Main Events, and the Lewis camp to bind him to a rematch for the sum of $3,500,000, someone goofed.

Regardless, Kushner and Rahman will split whatever purse Rahman gets for his next fight on terms that are expected to bring the promoter several million dollars. In other words, barring an unforeseen catastrophe, Hasim Rahman beating Lennox Lewis is the best thing that ever happened to Cedric Kushner.

Thus it was that Kushner appeared at the Hammerstein Ballroom in full glory on Saturday night. In the past, the site had been a symbol of his financial difficulties. He promoted a series of "Heavyweight Explosion" cards there and lost a lot of money. But Saturday, the Hammerstein was the site for a coming out party in honor of his success. And make no mistake; Cedric enjoyed it.

"Someone wrote that I cried for an hour after Rock won," Kushner reported. "Whoever started that rumor was talking rubbish. But there were a few tears in my eyes, I'll admit. You have to appreciate where I've come from and what I've gone through these past few years. There have been financial difficulties; people are aware of that. And some very ugly things have been said about me. The truth is, as I watched the fight, I wasn't exactly feeling sorry for myself. But I started to ask, 'What have I done wrong? Why can't I get a break? I've been a good guy. I've been fair to my fighters.' I was thinking all that in the fourth round, knowing full well what the magnitude of a win would mean to me. Then I realized that Lennox was starting to look a bit tired; Rock was doing well. And I said to myself, 'There's no reason Rock can't win this fight.' I'm not religious; but when that big right hand landed, it was an almost spiritual moment for me."

■ ■ ■

Often, at a fight, the most interesting action takes place away from the ring. And that was the case at the Hammerstein, where much of the talk revolved around Hasim Rahman's heavyweight triumph. There wasn't a whole lot of sympathy expressed for Lennox Lewis. Lennox wore his crown with dignity and grace for most of his reign. But while he might have weighed only four pounds more for Rahman than he did for David Tua, he looked like he had six pounds less muscle and ten pounds more fat. More to the point, he prepared poorly and fought a sloppy contemptuous fight.

Also, great fighters aren't supposed to be stopped by a single punch;

and that has now happened to Lewis twice. For purposes of comparison, consider Joe Louis, Muhammad Ali, Jack Dempsey, Rocky Marciano, and George Foreman. And check out the tapes of Larry Holmes versus Earnie Shavers and Renaldo Snipes. Ten days ago, Lennox wanted to fight Mike Tyson to secure his place in boxing history. Now he *needs* to fight Mike Tyson to secure his place in boxing history. Incidentally, most insiders at the Hammerstein were glad that it was Rahman, and not Tyson, who whacked out Lewis. Meanwhile, on the other side of the ocean, a lot of Brits who were fawning over Lewis earlier this month now say that he's Canadian. And the Canadians say he's Jamaican.

■　■　■

In the eyes of some, Hasim Rahman is an "interim" champion. They won't take him seriously until he beats Lewis again or successfully defends his title against Mike Tyson. In fact, when Rahman entered the Hammerstein Ballroom, he went largely unnoticed. But Rahman is already making friends and impressing people.

The man who destroyed the monarchy is bright, friendly, and unpretentious, with a good sense of humor. He seems comfortable with who he is, and the braggadocious nature often associated with world-class athletes is refreshingly absent. His wardrobe of choice consists of street fashions rather than the more glamorous elegance the world had come to expect from Lewis. But in the spotlight, he has a glow.

"Lennox was never able to impose his will on me," Rahman said on Saturday. "Everything he did, I answered back." Other choice thoughts offered by the new heavyweight champion included, "Oleg Maskaev was a wake-up call for me to get serious and not underestimate anybody. It opened my eyes. I treated him like a 'Heavyweight Explosion' opponent, and I paid for it . . . I thought it was arrogant for Lennox to dismiss what the scientists said about the altitude in South Africa. At the time, I said to myself, maybe he knows something the scientists don't know. But as it turned out, he didn't know much about altitude. The altitude was a real factor. To be honest, I don't think the month I was there was enough for me to adjust completely to it . . . I'm not interested in fighting John Ruiz.

The way they took the WBA title away from Lennox was bogus, so John Ruiz or whoever the WBA titleholder is doesn't count."

As for what it means to be heavyweight champion of the world, Rahman stated, "I'm up to the challenge, and I accept the responsibilities that come with it. People can count on me to be a law-abiding citizen; to be accessible to the media and to everyday people; to be a regular guy who lets other regular guys know that they can overcome the odds and make something good out of themselves. I hope my impact on people will be that they look at me and learn that one loss in life, no matter how bad it might be, doesn't ruin your life unless you let it, that you should never count yourself out."

This from a man who had five hundred stitches etched into his face after a devastating car accident and was considered dead in the ring after being knocked out by David Tua and Oleg Maskaev.

Meanwhile, Rahman's victory over Lennox Lewis was the greatest triumph ever for his co-manager Stan Hoffman. Unfortunately, Hoffman missed it. "I saw Lennox go down and bang his head on the canvas," Hoffman acknowledged. "Then everyone stood up in front of me. I'm a little guy, so I got on my chair and the chair fell backwards and, by the time I got off the floor, the fight was over."

■　■　■

It has often been said that politics makes for strange bedfellows, and the same holds true for boxing. When Seth Abraham was president of Time Warner Sports, he and Don King had a bitter split. After sixteen months of negotiations, the two men shook hands on a $100,000,000 contract extension that would have bound Mike Tyson to HBO for nine more fights. Then the deal fell apart over demands that Larry Merchant be fired, and King took Tyson to Showtime. Shortly thereafter, Abraham said of the promoter, "There's an old Chinese proverb that, if you sit long enough by the side of the river, eventually you'll see the bodies of all your enemies float by. I'm prepared to sit for a long time so I can be there when Don's body floats by."

Times change. Ultimately, Abraham brought King back into the

HBO fold in order to televise Felix Trinidad. Then, as executive vice president and chief operating officer of Madison Square Garden, Abraham joined forces with King to construct HBO's current middleweight championship series. April was a bad month for HBO. Two of its franchise fighters (Lewis and Naseem Hamed) were decisively defeated. Four more (Oscar De La Hoya, Roy Jones Jr., Fernando Vargas, and Floyd Mayweather Jr.) have less than inspiring matches coming up. And finding the right opponent for Shane Mosley won't be easy. Don King was absent on Saturday night, but his spirit was very much present because, ironically, his middleweight championship tournament is the most compelling drama that HBO Boxing has going for it at the moment.

■ ■ ■

Because HBO broadcast the Hammerstein fights as part of its *KO Nation* series, the audience was treated to a ring announcer named Henry "Discombobulating" Jones. Mr. Jones shouted for a long time before the TV bouts began and did his best to whip the crowd into a frenzy. The visual accompaniment to his histrionics consisted of a half dozen women wearing black high-heeled lace-up boots, pink rhinestone corsets, and black hotpants. In addition, there was extremely loud pulsating music. As for the fights themselves, Julio Diaz looked good in knocking out Justo Sencion in the ninth round, while Andrew "Six Heads" Lewis won a unanimous decision over Larry Marks.

Not long after Hasim Rahman defeated Lennox Lewis, things started to get crazy . . . and confusing.

Explaining the Heavyweights

TH: Hi, Mom. It's me. Happy Mother's Day.

Mom: Mother's Day was last weekend.

TH: I know. I'm sorry, but things have been crazy lately.

Mom: Things are always crazy in boxing.

TH: But this past month they've been certifiable. It started when Hasim Rahman knocked out Lennox Lewis. At that point, HBO, Main Events, and the Lewis camp went into something that looked suspiciously like a collective panic.

Mom: Why?

TH: HBO didn't have options on Rahman. And after Rahman beat Lewis, Showtime came into the picture, offering him a huge amount of money to fight Mike Tyson.

Mom: So both HBO and Showtime want Rahman?

TH: Actually, they don't really want Rahman. What they want is to get Rahman in the ring with their guy: Lewis at HBO and Tyson at Showtime. They figure their guy will knock him out, and they'll have a marketable heavyweight champion.

Mom: What happened next?

TH: There was a bidding war. The First Law of Holes is, when you find yourself in one, stop digging. But a lot of people ignored it. Eventually, HBO offered Rahman $14,150,000 for a Lewis rematch, $3,500,000 for two more fights if he loses the rematch, $5,500,000 to $7,000,000 for each of five title defenses if he keeps winning, and a window to fight Tyson on Showtime if he beats Lewis in the rematch.

Mom: What do you mean, a window to fight Tyson?

TH: I mean, he could beat Lewis and then go over to Showtime and get whacked out by Tyson, in which case HBO would have paid him

$14,150,000 for a fight that did maybe 300,000 pay-per-view buys and lost the heavyweight championship anyway.

Mom: I thought the alphabet-soup belts didn't matter to HBO.

TH: Under some circumstances, they do.

Mom: Wasn't there a rematch clause in the contract for Rahman's first fight with Lewis?

TH: Yes. It was in a February 13 contract between Cedric Kushner, who's Rahman's promoter, and Lion Promotions, which promotes Lewis with Main Events. That clause put significant restrictions on any fight Rahman might have before a rematch and promised him a purse of $3,150,000 for a second fight against Lennox. Also, on February 14, Rahman signed an addendum to his bout agreement with Kushner stating that, if he beat Lewis, he'd participate in a rematch upon terms and conditions negotiated by Kushner.

Mom: Why did HBO offer Rahman all that money for a rematch if there was a valid rematch clause for $3,150,000?

TH: Initially, the powers-that-be said they were increasing Rahman's rematch purse to $14,150,000 because they we're trying to do the right thing.

Mom: Did anyone in the media feel their intelligence was being insulted when HBO said that?

TH: Yes, and it's hard to insult the intelligence of the boxing media. The truth is, the rematch clause had some holes in it. Meanwhile, Showtime made an offer for Rahman to fight Tyson consisting of a $3,000,000 nonrefundable signing bonus; $13,150,000 for the fight itself; $5,000,000 to $8,000,000 for each five title defenses if he kept winning; and a window to fight Lewis on HBO if he beat Tyson.

Mom: I'll bet Rahman's face lit up when Jay Larkin looked him in the eye and made that offer to him.

TH: Actually, Kushner and Rahman's manager, Stan Hoffman, never let Larkin see Rahman face-to-face. Showtime always had to deal with Rahman through intermediaries.

Mom: Keep going.

TH: On the night of Monday, May 7, the Rahman camp in conjunction with Kushner reached an agreement in principle with HBO. They figured a Rahman-Lewis rematch was free of litigation, and

Lewis was less likely than Tyson to pull out of the fight at the last minute. But on Wednesday, May 9, Showtime made Rahman a new offer: a $5,000,000 signing bonus plus $15,000,000 more to fight Tyson. No options, no rematch clause, and a full indemnity if HBO or the Lewis camp sued.

Mom: Would HBO have retaliated against Kushner if he'd allowed the Showtime deal to happen?

TH: Maybe. That's why Showtime's offer included a significant number of dates over the next three years for Kushner on Showtime. And if Tyson beat Rahman, Cedric would have had three to five fights for a fixed fee as Tyson's exclusive promoter.

Mom: What happened next?

TH: On Thursday, May 10, Showtime had a doctor standing by to conduct an insurance physical on Rahman. Meanwhile, HBO still thought it had a deal and its contracts were ready to be signed. That's when Don King stepped into the picture. Don is amazing. He's like water on a roof. Wherever there's a crack, he seeps in. Anyway, Don met with Rahman, Stan Hoffman, and Steve Nelson, who's Hoffman's partner. And in the wee small hours of Friday morning, he gave Rahman a duffel bag filled with $200,000 in cash and a check for $4,800,000 in exchange for a promotional contract.

Mom: Wait a minute. I thought Kushner was Rahman's exclusive promoter.

TH: So did Kushner. In fact, at a press conference in New York one week to the day after he beat Lewis, Rahman said, "None of this would have happened without Cedric Kushner. I owe him everything. He's my promoter now, and he'll always be my promoter."

Mom: So how could Rahman sign with Don King?

TH: People close to Rahman leaked information to the media claiming that Kushner allowed his exclusive promotional rights to expire by not making a $75,000 payment to extend those rights in timely fashion. But Kushner has Stan Hoffman's autograph.

Mom: What good is that?

TH: It's on a document that says the $75,000 was received by Hoffman on behalf of Rahman in full satisfaction of Kushner's obligations relating to the extension of his exclusive promotional contract.

Mom: I'm confused. I understand how Rahman might have been influenced by someone handing him a duffel bag filled with cash. But why would Hoffman and Nelson let him do something so risky?

TH: I have no idea. They say they were acting in Rahman's best interests.

Mom: Is there a chance that Don King gave them a duffel bag full of cash, too?

TH: Mom, how can you suggest something like that?

Mom: I wasn't suggesting, just asking.

TH: Anyway, on the morning of Friday, May 11, Hoffman telephoned Kushner, told him that Rahman had signed with King, and said, "I hope this doesn't affect our friendship."

Mom: What did Cedric say?

TH: His response was less than encouraging on that point. The truth is, there are quite a few people who once thought that Hoffmann and Nelson were okay guys and are now very disappointed in the way they acted. In fact, there's a school of thought that it would be fitting if Carl King wound up as Hasim Rahman's manager.

Mom: So where does that leave everyone?

TH: Well, let's look at the players one at a time. HBO has taken some whacks in the media. Actually, the whacking started when Ross Greenburg was perceived, fairly or unfairly, as being responsible for keeping Lennox Lewis versus Mike Tyson from happening. And of course, HBO's hold on the heavyweight championship is tenuous now.

Mom: Would this be happening if Seth Abraham and Lou DiBella were still at HBO?

TH: Who knows? Don King said it wouldn't have happened if Seth and Lou were there. But Don has been complaining a lot about Ross and Kery Davis lately. He went off on them at the press conference at Madison Square Garden after Trinidad versus Joppy last Saturday night. And this past Monday, Don said—and I'm quoting directly—"Ross Greenburg and Kery Davis are my enemies." The truth is, when Lennox Lewis fought Frans Botha and Zelko Mavrovic, HBO didn't have options on those challengers either.

Mom: What about Lennox Lewis and Main Events?

TH: Lennox has Adrian Ogun working on his behalf, which is a great comfort to all of England, Canada, and Jamaica. Main Events is tied to Lewis, and they have Pat English as their attorney. Pat is pretty smart, although conspiracy theorists have been having a field day with him lately.

Mom: And Showtime?

TH: Showtime has an exclusive contract with Tyson, so they're joined at the hip. Tyson will become the WBC's mandatory challenger in November. But if Rahman forces that fight to a purse bid, Mike would have to settle for 25 percent of the total or pass on the fight. Also, Tyson has said he won't fight for Don King. And right now, Big Don is Rahman's promoter.

Mom: That serves Tyson right.

TH: Be fair, Mom. Tyson has the same legal rights as fighters you think are sweet. Incidentally, there's an interesting aspect to the rematch clause in the February 13 contract between Kushner and Lion Promotions. Section 10 of the Muhammad Ali Boxing Reform Act says a rematch clause is unenforceable if it's a coercive provision.

Mom: What's a coercive provision?

TH: The Ali Act describes it as a provision where a boxer is required to grant future rights in himself to a promoter as a condition precedent to his getting a fight against another boxer already under contract to the promoter. Lewis's promoters might be able to argue that requiring a Rahman-Lewis rematch was kosher because it wasn't an absolute requirement, that they paid Rahman extra for it. But things get dicey when you look at the portion of the rematch clause that allows for an interim fight. That clause says that, should an interim challenger such as Mike Tyson beat Rahman, he must fight Lewis in his first defense for $3,150,000 and that Lewis's promoters will promote it.

Mom: Where does Cedric Kushner stand in all this?

TH: Cedric's hopes hinge on the courts upholding his exclusive promotional contract with Rahman. Without that, he's dead meat. The truth is, I think HBO would offer Don King and Rahman the same deal it offered Kushner and Rahman if Cedric's contract falls by the wayside. Everybody would sell out everybody. Lewis would deal with Don King, too, if it would get him the fight. The only person who can't sell everyone out is Cedric. Cedric can't settle with Don without getting Lewis his rematch or the Lewis people will carve him into little pieces.

Mom: What are Cedric's chances of prevailing in court?

TH: That's hard to say. All of the cases have been consolidated before a federal judge named Miriam Cedarbaum. She'll hear oral argument on motions for a preliminary injunction on Friday and has set the case down for an expedited trial in June.

Mom: So if there's a big loser in this, most likely it will be Kushner.

TH: Not necessarily. Hasim Rahman could lose big.

Mom: How?

TH: There are a lot of unanswered questions about Rahman's contract with Don King. What we know is, Rahman got a $5,000,000 signing bonus and is supposed to get another $5,000,000 to fight Brian Nielsen. But the rest is speculative: $15,000,000 *if* he fights the Ruiz-Holyfield winner; $20,000,000 *if* he fights Lennox Lewis; $30,000,000 *if* he fights Mike Tyson. But what if Don doesn't deliver those fights? Is the contract just a bunch of options in Don's favor? Did Rahman have to warrant to Don King at financial risk to himself that he was free to enter into the contract? What if Rahman is stripped of the IBF title for not fighting the winner of David Tua versus Chris Byrd? You know, there's a difference between a done deal and a Don deal. With a Don deal, the real negotiations begin after the contract is signed. Plus, the original Lewis-Rahman rematch clause could conceivably be upheld by Judge Cedarbaum, in which case Rahman will have parlayed a $17,500,000 HBO offer and a $20,000,000 Showtime offer into a one-time $3,150,000 payday. It's not likely, but stranger things have happened.

Mom: And Don King will walk away unscathed by it all?

TH: Maybe; maybe not. Right now, Don is on a roll. His middleweight championship tournament is doing well, and the Rahman signing got him a huge amount of publicity for his proposed August 4 fight card in China. It's even possible that HBO and Showtime will both bid on China if the Rahman legal tangle is resolved. But everyone agrees that Ruiz-Holyfield in China ain't Ali-Foreman in Zaire. It's possible that no television network will touch it because of the potential for litigation. There are rumors that Don's Chinese financial backers might not be for real. Rahman and the winner of Holyfield-Ruiz could face mandatory challenges within a year from Mike Tyson (WBC), Kirk Johnson (WBA), and David Tua (IBF), none of whom are promoted by King. And in the best of all worlds, HBO and Showtime could get together for a tournament featuring Lennox Lewis versus Wladimir Klitschko and Mike Tyson versus David Tua, with the winners to fight for the People's Heavyweight Championship as opposed to the People's Republic of China heavyweight championship.

Mom: Is it possible that Don King outsmarted himself on this one?

TH: He's outsmarted everyone else at one time or another. Why not himself? Look, let's be honest about this. Don has an amazing ability to do things when everyone says he can't. Don't ever count him out. But I'll tell you something. Behind the bravado, Don is worried. This past week, he was complaining about AOL–Time Warner and Viacom violating the Sherman Antitrust Act. When Don King talks about going to the Justice Department for help, you know something strange is happening.

Mom: This could get ugly, couldn't it?

TH: Mom, it's already ugly. Ask Cedric.

The "Mom" format engendered an enormous amount of reader mail ask-
ing for more, so "Mom" became my vehicle for explaining the intricacies
of federal court litigation and boxing.

Don King and Tony Soprano

Mom: Thomas, it's your mother. I'm very upset.

TH: What's the matter?

Mom: *The Sopranos* is ending its season run on Sunday night, and I don't know what I'll do for a replacement.

TH: Mom, don't worry. I've got something for you that's better than *The Sopranos.*

Mom: What could be better than *The Sopranos?* I know Tony does bad things, but he's so much fun to watch. One minute, he's a big lovable teddy bear. And the next minute, WHAP!

TH: Mom, Tony Soprano is a pale imitation. The guy you want to watch is Don King. Like you said, "One minute, he's a big lovable teddy bear. And the next minute, WHAP!" Right now, Don is star-ring in the best show on television or anywhere else.

Mom: But *The Sopranos* has so many fascinating characters, like that sweet fat man Tony shot on the boat in last year's final episode.

TH: Mom, if you want sweet, chubby, fascinating, and getting whacked; how about Cedric Kushner? If you think Tony seducing Gloria was followed by chaos, check out Don King seducing Hasim Rahman. If it's scary muscle you're interested in, look at Mike Tyson. Stan Hoffman, Steve Nelson, and Bob Mittleman are just as lovable as Paulie, Ralphie, and Christopher. And the crime families in *The Sopranos* are nothing compared to the crime families in boxing. Of course, I hasten to add, Don King has paid his debt to society, whereas Tony Soprano hasn't.

Mom: I'm still not convinced.

TH: Mom, listen to me. Today's episode was riveting. There was a big argument in federal court. Lennox Lewis and his promoters want an

injunction to keep Rahman from fighting anybody except Lennox
in his next fight. Cedric wants an injunction precluding King or anybody else except Cedric Kushner Promotions from promoting
Rahman. The Lewis people said that Hoffman, Nelson, and
Mittleman would be added as defendants by the end of the day. The
judge consolidated the cases, which means they'll go to trial together.
And there were a zillion lawyers.

Mom: Was Perry Mason in court?

TH: No, Mom. Perry Mason isn't real; and besides, he only does murder cases. But Lennox and Lion Promotions were represented jointly
by Judd Burstein and Pat English. Kushner was represented by Rich
Edlin. Peter Fleming is Don King's lawyer but he had another commitment for the day, so King was represented by Joe Pizzuro and
Michael Quinn, both of whom work with Fleming. And HBO,
which isn't even a party to the lawsuits, had five lawyers there as
observers.

Mom: What about Rahman?

TH: Rahman was represented by Michael Armstrong, who's an old
friend of Fleming's. Years ago, Fleming and Armstrong worked
together in the U.S. Attorney's Office. Armstrong told the judge that
he has never met his client, didn't know anything about the case,
hadn't been retained to represent Rahman until last night, and would
be unable to talk with his client until next Tuesday because Rahman
is on Haj in Mecca.

Mom: Were any of the parties there?

TH: Only Cedric. He was quite nattily attired in a navy blue suit with
a red tie, blue-and-white striped shirt, and tassled loafers.

Mom: How is Ced holding up?

TH: Okay, I think. At times, he seems a bit taken aback by the ugliness of it all. At one point, he told me, "This might sound naive, but
it's not supposed to be like this." Cedric has been hurt by Rahman's
defection, but he's still doing business. In fact, it looks like he just
made Michael Grant versus Jameel McCline to pair with Shane
Mosley on HBO on July 21.

Mom: What did King's lawyers say in court?

TH: First they said they intend to prove that Lewis has no case because

the clause granting him a rematch was coerced from Rahman in violation of the Muhammad Ali Boxing Reform Act. There's been some
confusion over the rematch clause because, after the fight, Joe Dwyer
misspoke.

Mom: Who's Joe Dwyer?

TH: Joe is a good guy. He's chairman of the IBF Championship
        Committee. After Rahman knocked out Lewis, Joe said that the bout
        contracts filed with the IBF didn't have a rematch clause. But the
        truth is, Joe never saw the contracts. They weren't even filed with the
        IBF until after the fight, when Pat English faxed them to the IBF
        bout supervisor, Marian Muhammad. The Rahman bout agreement
        filed with the IBF contained an addendum with the more detailed
        rematch clause that everyone has been talking about.

Mom: What else did King's lawyers say?

TH: They argued that Kushner is no longer Rahman's exclusive pro-
        moter because his rights expired. You and I talked about that in our
        last conversation. The only new thing that came out was I thought I
        caught the glimmer of a suggestion from King's attorney that Kushner
        and Stan Hoffman might have colluded to defraud Rahman with
        regard to the extension of Cedric's promotional contract. If King
        winds up making that argument, it will be a real treat for Stan.

Mom: What was the judge like?

TH: Very sharp. Her name is Miriam Cedarbaum. Mom, you'd have
        liked her. At first, she seemed just like Dr. Melfi. She listened patiently
        and asked questions from time to time. Then it became clear that she
        knew exactly what was going on. At one point, she even told the
        lawyers, "I understand why it's important for a boxer who's thirty-
        six-years-old and coming to the end of his career to have an immedi-
        ate rematch."

Mom: That must have made the Lewis people happy.

TH: Absolutely. And Cedric was pleased, too. It went as well as he and
        the Lewis camp could have expected.

Mom: What happens next?

TH: King's lawyers said that extensive discovery was necessary and
        tried to push the trial back as far as possible, but the judge said, "No
        way, Jose."

Mom: Did she really say that?

TH: Not in so many words. But she did rule that expedited discovery was in order, that it would commence immediately, and told everyone to be ready for trial on June 11. There's no jury in the case, so the trial should move quickly.

Mom: What will the trial cover?

TH: The first stage will deal with whether or not to grant the injunctions sought by the Lewis camp and Kushner. Then, if necessary, there will be later testimony on the issue of monetary damages. Meanwhile, no television network is likely to touch Rahman pending the outcome of the trial. ,

Mom: Does this mean that Don King is no longer above the law?

TH: Don doesn't think he's above the law. Don thinks he's learned how to use the law to his advantage. His philosophy of life is, nothing ventured, nothing gained. Right now, he figures he can settle with Kushner if he has to. And if he wins, he figures he can use Rahman as a bargaining chip to settle his lawsuit with Mike Tyson. Meanwhile, there's a rumor going around that, on the premiere of *Sex and the City* later this month, Sarah Jessica Parker has a blind date with Cedric.

By this time, my mother was becoming a celebrity in her own right. One sports-radio station even wanted to interview her, but she declined.

The Soap Opera Continues

Mom: Thomas, this is your mother. I'm hooked on that boxing show you told me about.

TH: I told you it was entertaining.

Mom: Not entertaining, riveting. These boxing people make *The Sopranos* look like a church social. What's happening now?

TH: For starters, details are starting to leak out on the King-Rahman contract. It looks like Rahman got sucker-punched. Once you get past the five-million-dollar signing bonus and five million dollars for a title fight in Beijing, the contract is really just a series of options in Don's favor. Also, Rahman represented in the contract that he doesn't have a binding agreement with Cedric Kushner. That means, if the court upholds Cedric's contract, Rahman will be required to return the $5,000,000 signing bonus. I can imagine Don King shouting at Hasim: "You defrauded me. You told me you didn't have a contract with Kushner. Give me my money back."

Mom: What happens to Rahman if Kushner or the Lewis camp wins a judgment against him for damages?

TH: That could be big trouble for Hasim. Under the King-Rahman contract, King isn't obligated to indemnify Rahman if Kushner's contract is upheld. Plus Rahman could be held liable to King for any losses King suffers, including a court judgment in Kushner's favor against King.

Mom: Were there cash payments to Rahman that aren't mentioned in the contract?

TH: It's possible. You know, one of the problems this litigation poses is that a lot of rocks are being overturned. As I understand it, not only did King make a play for Rahman in 1998, he also made a run at him earlier this year. In fact, I'm told Don went so far as to send a draft contract to Rahman's management team four months ago. And to answer your question directly, it now looks as though Don gave Rahman $20,000 in cash when he tried to sign him in 1998 and that Don might have failed to file the federal tax form that's required when you make a cash payment to someone in excess of ten thousand dollars.

Mom: That's just a technicality, isn't it?

TH: Maybe. But you know how the government is when it comes to Don and taxes. The U.S. Attorney's Office has this totally unfair, horrible, anti-American vendetta against him.

Mom: Is Don worried about getting caught?

TH: Don doesn't worry about getting caught. Don worries about getting punished.

Mom: What about Rahman? Did he pay taxes on the twenty thousand dollars?

TH: That's a good question. Meanwhile, the Lewis camp now says that, since Rahman has breached the rematch clause, it intends to stick by the original $3,150,000 rematch figure. That might be posturing for purposes of negotiation and litigation. Showtime's lawyers were so certain the rematch clause wouldn't hold up in court that they offered Rahman a complete indemnification if he agreed to fight Mike Tyson, so I don't understand how Lewis's lawyers can be certain the rematch clause will prevail. But the $14,150,000 offer to Rahman to fight Lewis on HBO is now off the table. That means, whether or not Rahman's contract with Kushner is upheld, Hasim could be in big trouble if the judge rules in Lewis's favor. In other words, Rahman could beat Kushner in court and still wind up fighting Lewis for $3,150,000.

Mom: Do you think Rahman might be thinking now that he'd be better off if he'd never signed with Don King?

TH: I don't know about Rahman, but his attorney might be getting the idea. The truth is, the path of least risk for Hasim would be to settle with Kushner and Lewis before trial.

Mom: What else is happening?

TH: Mom; are you sitting down?

Mom: Yes.

TH: Adrian Ogun contacted Jay Larkin to explore the possibility of Lennox Lewis fighting on Showtime.

Mom: What?????

TH: You heard me.

Mom: This is better than any soap opera ever. Tell me more.

TH: Jay was in Wales for the fight between Joe Calzaghe and Mario Veit, and Ogun sent word through Frank Warren and Frank Maloney that he'd like to meet with him. Larkin, Ogun, Warren, Maloney, Judd Burstein, and at least one other person were present. Lewis's people told Showtime that there was a loophole in their contract with HBO that would allow Lennox to fight on Showtime. More specifically, they said that the HBO contract would allow Lewis to fight Mike Tyson on Showtime if Lennox lost the title to a third party who then lost it to Tyson. Larkin said he'd need documentation to support Ogun's claim that Showtime wouldn't be tortiously interfering with the HBO-Lewis contract if it made a deal with Lennox, and the Lewis people said they'd provide it. Mom, they actually worked out a deal. The Lewis people agreed to take several million dollars in step-aside money to let Rahman fight Mike Tyson on Showtime in July. Then the winner of that fight was to fight Lewis in November. If Rahman beat Tyson, Rahman-Lewis would be on HBO. If Tyson beat Rahman, Tyson-Lewis would be on Showtime. From Showtime's point of view, it was simple. Larkin wanted to get Rahman in the ring with Tyson. Don't forget, Don King wasn't in the picture yet. As far as Showtime was concerned, the only impediment to Tyson-Rahman was Lewis's rematch clause, and this was a way around it.

Mom: Was Lennox at the meeting?

TH: No.

Mom: How did the meeting end?

TH: There were handshakes all around, and the Showtime people left the room thinking they had a deal. The agreed-upon step-aside sum for Lennox was $2,150,000, and Ogun tentatively agreed to extend the time within which a Rahman-Lewis rematch had to occur from 150 to 300 days. Then, two days later, Larkin got a call saying the deal was off because Lennox wanted an immediate rematch with Rahman.

Mom: Is that the real reason the deal fell apart?

TH: I've also heard that HBO got wind of the deal and said some very unpleasant things to Lewis's people.

Mom: Like what?

TH: Things that a son shouldn't repeat to his mother.

Mom: Did Cedric Kushner and Rahman's management team know about the Lewis-Showtime meeting?

TH: Ask Cedric. I will tell you though, that, under the plan, Cedric would have promoted Rahman-Tyson and been Tyson's exclusive promoter if Iron Mike won the championship. The key to it all was that it made the rematch clause manageable. Lennox would have been paid several million dollars to sit on his butt. And then, either he would have fought Rahman in a lucrative rematch on HBO or Tyson for parity on Showtime. Only HBO would have been upset. And the truth is, Rahman still might pay step-aside money to Lewis to settle Lewis's lawsuit against him.

Mom: Are there any more juicy sub-plots?

TH: Mom, there's no bottom to this. It keeps going down and down and down. The latest rumor is that Don King has been wooing Lennox Lewis's mother in a very generous way. He wants to sign Lennox to a promotional contract.

Mom: I thought Lennox was signed with Main Events.

TH: Yeah, and Rahman was signed with Cedric Kushner.

Mom: Don is amazing, isn't he?

TH: He sure is. Other people might think of these things from time to time, but Don implements them. Just the other day, he was telling people, "I'm faster than the Roadrunner, and all them people chasing me are like poor old Wile E. Coyote." Meanwhile, I wouldn't be surprised if King makes an offer to Cedric to buy him out before trial. Then, if Cedric accepts it, I'd expect King to negotiate a Rahman-Lewis rematch.

Mom: How much money will King offer Kushner?

TH: I don't know. Cedric has a history of settling with King, first in a dispute over Gerrie Coetzee and later with Tony Tucker. Cedric said this week that he's tired of Don ruining his life and that it would take a lot of money to satisfy him. Still, there's a risk factor here for

Cedric. One of the British newspapers ran a story last week saying he's under a lot of pressure and that King's machinations could cause him to lose two million pounds.

Mom: Thomas, you're being silly. Cedric doesn't weigh that much.

TH: Mom, I'm talking about pounds sterling, not weight.

Mom: Sorry. Anyway, so what happens next?

TH: I don't know. All I can tell you is that this is another feel-good boxing story with all sorts of sub-plots and future episodes to look forward to.

After this article appeared, Don King asked—and I quote—"When are you going to stop breaking my chops?" I thought I'd been gentle with him.

The Next Episode

TH: Hi, mom. How are you?

Mom: Not so good. I watched that new HBO show, *Six Feet Under,* last Sunday night. It's awful.

TH: Not to worry. The next episode of *The Heavyweights* is ready to air, and it's fantastic.

Mom: What's happening?

TH: Depositions have been taken from Don King, Cedric Kushner, Hasim Rahman, Lennox Lewis, Adrian Ogun, Ross Greenburg, Stan Hoffman, Steve Nelson, Shelly Finkel, Jay Larkin, Milt Chwasky, and Pat English. Pre-trial document production is over, and the trial starts on Monday. Right now, Don King is digging in for the long haul. He's looking to see how strong his opponents are, testing their resolve, trying to cause panic and turn one camp against another. It's psychological warfare; and the truth is, I feel sorry for Cedric. In boxing, a clear conscience is often the sign of a bad memory. But as best I can tell, Cedric treats his fighters fairly; and unfortunately, Rahman didn't respond in kind.

Mom: How is the litigation progressing?

TH: The Kushner and Lewis camps seem happy with things so far, particularly the Rahman deposition. Hasim acknowledged under oath that he read his promotional contract with Kushner and the contracts relating to the Lewis bout before he signed them. There were some significant factual discrepancies between his testimony and King's, which made Cedric's lawyer happy. And Rahman waxed eloquent under oath about the importance of the lineal heavyweight championship, which played into Lewis's hands.

Mom: What's new in the documents that have been produced?

TH: The May 11 King–Rahman contract contains a representation and warranty by Rahman stating that he doesn't have any contracts that would keep him from fulfilling his obligations to Don King. And in the same contract, Rahman agrees to indemnify King if there's a breach of that representation and warranty and Don suffers losses as a result. There's also a letter backdated to May 9 in which King said that, based on Rahman's representation and warranty, he'd indemnify Rahman against lawsuits by Kushner and the Lewis camp. But that indemnification of Rahman by King didn't mean much because it only took effect if Hasim's contracts with Kushner and Lewis were determined to be null and void in which case Hasim wouldn't need indemnification. Then, on June 3, King sent another letter to Rahman that specifically supercedes the May 9 letter and on its face looks like a more substantial indemnification. The problem for Rahman is that King's June 3 letter doesn't revoke the representation and warranty made by Rahman in the original May 11 contract.

Mom: I'm not sure I understand all of that.

TH: Neither does Rahman. Right now, Hasim is on a high-wire without a secure safety net. He could wind up losing to Kushner and Lewis and reimbursing Don King for his losses as well.

Mom: How did Rahman get himself in that situation?

TH: In addition to being a trifle disloyal, he seems somewhat gullible. In fact, there's a school of thought that Rahman would be better off if the judge made his decisions for him.

Mom: What will the trial be like?

TH: Lennox's case will be fairly straightforward. His lawyers feel that Rahman has already admitted everything they need from him to prove their case in court. Lennox and Adrian Ogun will take the stand on Monday and say that Lennox wouldn't have signed to fight Rahman without a rematch clause. Emanuel Steward will testify about the risk that Lennox's advancing age poses in terms of being forced to wait for a chance to fight for the title again. Then Lewis's lawyers will draw upon Rahman's deposition testimony regarding the value of the lineal heavyweight championship. It shouldn't take more than a day and, after that, it will be Cedric's turn.

Mom: How long will Cedric's lawyers take to present his case?

TH: They should finish sometime Tuesday. Then, if the trial isn't done by the end of the day, the judge will recess until Monday June 18.

Mom: What are the chances of a recess?

TH: Pretty good. Don's lawyers will try to drag things out.

Mom: Why would they do that? I thought Don has to wait until the judge rules on the requests for injunctions before Don King Productions can finalize its August 4 fight card in China? The longer this goes on, the less likely it is that Rahman-Izon will be on the card.

TH: That's right. Do you think Don really wants to pay five million dollars to Rahman and one million dollars to Izon on top of what he's paying Holyfield and Ruiz?

Mom: Have there been any settlement negotiations?

TH: Just a few feelers that haven't led anywhere. My guess is that serious settlement negotiations, if there are any, won't start until the recess.

Mom: Will Cedric negotiate a settlement with King?

TH: He says he won't. Right now, Cedric feels that his credibility as a major presence in boxing is on the line, and I think he'll go into the trial with that mindset. But once the trial begins, for the right amount of money, he might be persuaded to assign his promotional rights to King?

Mom: Would he be allowed to do that?

TH: Yes. The rights are assignable under paragraph ten of Cedric's promotional contact with Rahman. Any assignment is subject to Rahman's approval, but that approval can't be unreasonably withheld. And since Rahman has already signed a contract with King, he can't very well complain if Cedric assigns his contract to King.

Mom: If that assignment takes place, what would happen next?

TH: Probably, Don would do a 180-degree turn and claim that his May 11 contract with Rahman is a null and void because the Rahman team lied to him about the validity of the Rahman-Kushner promotional contract.

Mom: Why would Don declare his May 11 contract with Rahman null and void?

TH: Because, if the May 11 contract is null and void, Rahman will have to return the $5,000,000 signing bonus that King gave him.

Also, if the May 11 contract is null and void, Rahman will have to fight Lewis as per the terms set forth in his contract with Kushner, not for the $20,000,000 that King promised him for a Lewis fight.

Mom: If Cedric makes a deal with King, what will the Lewis people do?

TH: With or without Cedric, it's possible that they'll make a deal with King. Lennox's lawyers think they have a strong case, and they might see it through to the end. But right now, there are people telling Lennox, "You'll be thirty-six years old in September. If Don King guarantees you a title shot, take it."

Mom: Who's telling Lennox that?

TH: Don King. He met with the Lewis camp to talk settlement on Thursday night.

Mom: Does Lennox want to be associated with King?

TH: No, but neither did Evander Holyfield, and look what Don did for Evander. He got him two fights against Mike Tyson. He fought for the appointment of highly qualified, fair, and impartial ring judges like Eugenia Williams for the first Holyfield-Lewis fight. And he got a federal judge to order that Lewis relinquish his WBA title, which Evander subsequently won. Don's pitch to Lennox is, "As long as you fight for the title, you shouldn't care who the promoter is." That means, conceivably, Don could wind up as Lewis's promoter even if Cedric is reinstated as Rahman's promoter.

Mom: That would be bizarre.

TH: And quintessential Don King.

Mom: What kind of deal could Don and the Lewis camp make?

TH: King might pay step-aside money to Lewis so Rahman can fight a third party with the winner to fight Lewis on HBO. Or alternatively, King could make Rahman-Lewis now. In either event, Don could assume all of the promotional rights that now belong to Lion Promotions.

Mom: Who's Lion Promotions? You told me last week, but I forgot.

TH: That's Lennox's promotional company. And I don't think Main Events would be pleased at the thought of Don King becoming Lewis's promoter. But the truth is, I get the feeling that everyone in this case could be persuaded to negotiate with everyone else to stab someone else in the back.

Mom: In other words, this is boxing; keep your hands up at all times.

TH: Mom, you're getting good at this.

Mom: I know.

TH: And there's something else to consider. Whatever happens, Don King will want to save face. Saving face is very important to Don, and that could factor into the equation.

Mom: This is exciting. I can't wait for you to tell me what happens when the trial starts on Monday.

When a federal judge stopped me in the elevator and asked if my mother was coming to court, I figured I'd created a "momster."

More Mom

TH: Hi, Mom. I called to give you an update on the trial.

Mom: Thank Goodness! I was beginning to get withdrawal symptoms. It's amazing how Don King, Cedric Kushner, Lennox Lewis, and Hasim Rahman have captured my imagination. What's happening?

TH: Cedric and the Lewis camp put the bulk of their case into evidence on June 11 and June 12. First, they called Hasim Rahman to the witness stand and got him to acknowledge that Stan Hoffman was his manager; that Stan was authorized to act on his behalf; that Stan accepted a $75,000 check from Kushner to extend CKP's promotional rights; and that the Rahman camp never returned it.

Mom: Is that all Cedric needs to confirm his promotional contract?

TH: It might be. But on top of that, Rahman admitted that he'd been medically unable to fight for a period of at least eight months during the past few years.

Mom: Why is that important?

TH: Because the $75,000 payment necessary to extend Cedric's promotional rights to Rahman was originally thought to be due on April 12, and Cedric didn't give it to Hoffman until April 24. The fact that Hoffman accepted it is important. But on top of that, paragraph 16(b) of Cedric's promotional contract with Rahman states, "Should fighter be under temporary physical disability or for any other reason be unable to engage in bouts, the term of this agreement shall be extended for a period equal to the period of such disabilities." Cedric's lawyers claim that, when you add up all the time Rahman was medically unable to fight, the renewal deadline was pushed past April 24th.

Mom: What else did Rahman say in court?

TH: He admitted that Don King gave him $160,000 to pull out of a
        fight that Cedric was promoting in 1998. In fact, Hasim acknowl-
        edged that he received $187,000 from Don in 1998 even though
        Don wasn't his promoter.

Mom: That's very interesting.

TH: It certainly is, particularly since Hasim filed tax returns declar-
        ing a total of $160,000 in income for the entire year.

Mom: Could that get him in trouble?

TH: It might. The federal government isn't real happy with Hasim at
        the moment.

Mom: Why not?

TH: Customs agents filed an affidavit in a federal court in Baltimore
        last week accusing him of laundering $37,000 in drug money for his
        cousin.

Mom: You're kidding!

TH: Unfortunately, I'm not. Rahman's cousin was sentenced to sev-
        enteen years in prison in 1998 for trafficking in cocaine and heroin.
        The government says that Rahman took drug cash from his cousin
        and gave him personal checks and cashier's checks in return, always
        in amounts less than $10,000 which would have triggered bank
        reporting requirements. The government says that the scheme was
        "designed to conceal and disguise the nature, the location, the source,
        the ownership, and the control of the drug proceeds."

Mom: Will criminal charges be filed against Rahman?

TH: Probably not in that case. To convict him, the government would
        have to prove that he knew the money came from an illegal source.
        But the Internal Revenue Service is likely to take a long look at
        Hasim's tax returns in light of his various financial dealings. In a
        worst-case scenario, he could wind up fighting Ike Ibeabuche for the
        national penitentiary heavyweight championship.

Mom: Who else testified in court last week?

TH: Cedric took the witness stand and talked about his contract with
        Rahman as well as the irreparable harm that he'd suffer if he's
        deprived of promotional rights to the heavyweight champion of the
        world.

Mom: This trial must be very hard on Cedric.

TH: It sure is. Anyone who enters the federal courthouse has to check his cell phone on the ground floor. Cedric without his cell phone is like a heroin addict without drugs. Plus Judge Cedarbaum is a stickler for rules, and she wouldn't let Cedric take his jacket off.

Mom: What do you mean?

TH: Right after Cedric was sworn in as a witness, he asked if he could take off his jacket. And the judge told him no.

Mom: Cedric is so well-mannered. I love the way he tucks his napkin in just below the top button of his shirt during meals so he won't spill on his shirt. His mother brought him up very nicely.

TH: Mom, I'm sure Cedric is very happy you feel that way about him. Anyway, after Cedric testified, Shelly Finkel took the stand and testified that, as a general rule, a manager is authorized to accept funds on behalf of his fighter. Emanuel Steward talked about the ravages of age as a reason why Lennox needs an immediate rematch. And Lennox said pretty much the same thing in addition to stating that Hasim Rahman signed a contract for a rematch and is now refusing to honor it. That was it for last week. Over the weekend, Cedric got a haircut and trimmed his mustache way back. Now, instead of calling him the "Walrus," maybe people will call him the "South African Clark Gable." And Jim DiLorenzo, who's the president of Cedric Kushner Sports Network, cut his pony-tail off. Cedric says it's their summer look.

Mom: Enough of that nonsense. Tell me some more about the trial.

TH: Testimony resumed on June 18. Bill Kozerski, who's a Michigan promoter, testified as an expert witness on Cedric's behalf regarding irreparable harm. He said it was every promoter's dream to represent the heavyweight champion of the world; that it was a unique opportunity in terms of money and collateral opportunities; and that the loss of promotional rights to Hasim Rahman would be a devastating and irreparable loss for Cedric. Irreparable harm is a key concept here because, without it, Cedric and Lennox will only be entitled to money if they win; not injunctive relief. Then the plaintiffs called Stan Hoffman as a witness. Stan acknowledged that Rahman read the bout agreement and addendum carefully before he signed them and even requested certain changes in the bout agreement.

Mom: What did Stan say about the $75,000 that Cedric claims to have offered him in South Africa to extend CKP's exclusive promotional rights to Rahman?

TH: Well, as you recall, Cedric says Stan told him that the money didn't have to be paid until Rahman returned to the United States. Stan testified that he doesn't recall such a conversation, but he didn't deny that the conversation took place. And he did remember telling Cedric that there was no need to pay Rahman his fight purse until the fighter returned to the United States. Normally, fighters like to be paid immediately after a fight, even if it's with a post-dated check. Also Stan admitted that he accepted the $75,000 check from Cedric on April 24 at the same time he signed a letter of receipt acknowledging that the payment was "in full satisfaction of CKP's obligations relating to the extension." Stan also acknowledged that his boxer-manager agreement with Rahman authorizes him to accept checks on the fighter's behalf. And he admits that he never told Cedric there was a problem with the $75,000 check or gave it back.

Mom: What else did Stan say?

TH: This is interesting. Cedric's promotional contract with Rahman provided that, should Rahman win the heavyweight championship, Cedric would get 25 percent of Rahman's championship-bout purses or such other amount as the two parties might negotiate. Hoffman testified, and Cedric later confirmed, that the two of them negotiated a contract modification calling for a new fee schedule in conjunction with HBO's multi-bout offer to Rahman. Instead of Cedric getting 25 percent of Rahman's purses, he was to get $1,000,000 out of Rahman's purse for the Lewis rematch and 10 percent of Rahman's gross purses for each bout thereafter. Documents to that effect were drafted but never executed because Rahman signed with Don King instead.

Mom: Why would Cedric agree to cut his percentage like that?

TH: He says he went along with it because the modification would have covered the full length of HBO's new offer to Rahman and thus had the potential to extend CKP's promotional rights to Rahman beyond the previous contract extension. There were other considerations as well.

Mom: Such as?

TH: Such as, Cedric might have been concerned about his $75,000
         check not being cashed.

Mom: Did Hoffman offer any other nuggets of information?

TH: Only that, as Rahman's manager, he gets 25 percent of Rahman's
         earnings and splits that 25 percent with Steve Nelson and Brendan
         Ingle (who's a stand-in for Frank Warren). Stan also testified that he
         still hasn't received any portion of the $5,000,000 signing bonus that
         Don King paid to Rahman.

Mom: Did Lewis's business manager, Adrian Ogun, testify?

TH: He was the first witness called by the defense. Peter Fleming,
         who's Don King's lawyer, wanted to prove through Ogun that the
         contract provision allowing Rahman to have an interim fight before
         a Lewis-Rahman rematch was a subterfuge inserted into the contract
         for the first Lewis-Rahman fight in order to circumvent WBC and
         IBF rules that forbid an immediate rematch. Fleming's way of prov-
         ing this was to lead Ogun through various drafts of the bout con-
         tract. But that was futile because, with regard to each draft, Ogun
         testified, "I received it but I did not read it. I only wanted to read the
         final contract." All Fleming really got from Ogun was the concession
         that the contractual framework for an interim bout was designed to
         preclude Rahman from having a major pay-per-view fight before a
         rematch with Lewis. And Ogun confirmed that, when HBO raised
         the offer to Rahman from $3,150,000 to $14,150,000 for an immedi-
         ate rematch against Lewis, $1,500,000 of that purse increase was con-
         tributed by Lewis.

Mom: Who testified after Adrian Ogun?

TH: Jay Larkin of Showtime took the stand on June 19. He confirmed
         what I told you in one of our earlier conversations about his meet-
         ing in Wales with Ogun, Frank Warren, Frank Maloney, and Judd
         Burstein.

Mom: And after Jay Larkin?

TH: The defense called Pat English, who's the attorney for Main
         Events. Fleming hoped to show through English that the contract
         provisions granting Rahman the right to an interim bout before a

Lewis rematch were designed solely to comply with the mandates of the world sanctioning bodies and the Muhammad Ali Boxing Reform Act and that Rahman's supposed right to an interim bout was "illusory" and "a sham."

Mom: How did the judge react to that?

TH: She told Fleming that lawyers are supposed to draft contracts in a way that protects their clients, and she accused him of filibustering. That brought an impassioned plea from Michael Armstrong, who's Rahman's lawyer. Armstrong leapt to his feet and declared, "Your honor, this case is about equities, clean hands, good guys, and bad guys."

Mom: And?

TH: The judge was unimpressed, but Cedric looked like he might choke on his tongue when he heard that one.

Mom: Did Don King testify?

TH: Don was the last witness. Throughout the trial, Don sat by himself at the end of the pews in the first row of the spectator section. He was conservatively dressed, very reserved and quiet. This was business, not showmanship. He seemed to be measuring the judge and opposing lawyers. Anyway, Don was only on the witness stand for five minutes. All he did was say that he wanted to clear his good name and make it clear that he didn't pay Rahman money to fake an injury and pull out of a fight that Cedric was promoting in 1998. Judd Burstein wanted to cross-examine him on that point, but the judge said it wasn't relevant to the issues at hand and told Judd, "This is a courtroom; not a circus."

Mom: Is that it as far as Don's testimony is concerned?

TH: It is indeed, although I have to say, Don is still a genius when it comes to massaging egos. He was utterly charming in dealing with the court personnel. In fact, when we went up to the cafeteria during the lunch break on Monday, one of the cashiers waved him through the line and refused to take his money.

Mom: Could that have been part of an FBI "sting" operation to indict Don for theft?

TH: You never know, but I doubt it. By the way, Don had macaroni au gratin for lunch.

Mom: Did Bob Mittleman testify at the trial?

TH: The answer is "no," but it's a longer story than that. Mittleman was named as a defendant in Lennox Lewis's lawsuit. Last week, in order to be dismissed from the case, he gave Judd Burstein an affidavit in support of Lennox and Cedric. Then, according to Burstein, Mittleman telephoned him, claimed the affidavit was a lie, and said he'd deny key parts of it if he were called as a witness.

Mom: What happened after that?

TH: Burstein sent a letter to the judge informing her that Mittleman either had committed perjury in his affidavit or would commit perjury if called to testify at trial and that the defendants might be engaging in obstruction of justice.

Mom: What happened next?

TH: Mittleman called Burstein early on the morning of June 18 and said that his affidavit was true after all with the exception of one or two points that he could "fudge" during his testimony. Then he showed up in court, but Burstein decided not to call him as a witness because he was too unreliable.

Mom: What about Burstein's suggestion that the defendants might have engaged in obstruction of justice?

TH: Burstein told the judge—and I'm quoting—"Your Honor, I'm now of the view that Mr. Mittleman did not need the assistance of anybody else to not tell the truth."

Mom: So what happens next?

TH: The lawyers will sum up before the judge this Thursday at 2:30 P.M. Then she'll rule on the Lewis and Kushner requests for injunctive relief.

Mom: Does the judge understand what's been going on in court?

TH: Absolutely. Judge Cedarbaum doesn't know much about boxing, but she's very smart. The truth is, she seemed slightly confused by Adrian Ogun's testimony. But everyone in the courtroom, including Adrian, seemed confused by Adrian's testimony. And the fact that the judge is untutored in the nuances of the sweet science is probably a plus for Cedric and Lennox. It means she's likely to base her decision strictly on the facts and the law; not on some misperceived "everybody does it" notion of boxing.

Mom: What will her ruling be?

TH: It looks good for Lennox. The judge appears to be leaning strongly in his favor. She doesn't have the power to order Rahman to fight him, but she does have the power to keep Rahman from fighting anyone else. In fact, at one point, Fleming told the judge, "Your Honor, our basic position is that Rahman was tricked into signing this [rematch clause] and did not understand its provisions." And the judge responded, "I hope you have some other positions." She even asked Lennox's lawyer to draft a proposed injunction and give it to her before summations.

Mom: What will happen if Lennox wins an injunction against Rahman?

TH: For starters, Hasim will get a lot less money than he thought he would for the rematch.

Mom: Why is that?

TH: His leverage will be gone. The only reason HBO's offer went from $3,150,000 to $14,150,000 was Rahman's threat of bolting to fight Mike Tyson on Showtime and the fact that Lewis was willing to sacrifice financially to make an immediate rematch happen. But if the judge upholds the rematch clause, the only thing Rahman will have left to bargain with is an offer of options to HBO should he win the rematch.

Mom: How soon could a rematch occur?

TH: That's uncertain. Right now, all sides are clinging to fictions. Rahman says publicly that he could be ready to fight David Izon in China on August 4, and Lewis says he could be ready for a rematch on August 18. But Adrian Ogun admitted this week that Lennox hasn't done any serious gym work since losing to Rahman, only road-work and a bit of weightlifting. And Rahman says the same thing, although he claims that, last Thursday in Baltimore, he hit the heavy bag and sparred six rounds with one of the locals. My guess is, the rematch would be held in October or November.

Mom: What about Cedric's case?

TH: The judge has given off fewer signals there, so the outcome is less certain. Cedric could lose entirely, although I don't think that will happen. He could win entirely. Or the judge could decide in his favor on the issue of liability, but rule that monetary damages will suffice.

Mom: What would happen if she did that?

TH: Cedric would continue his suit for a monetary award against Rahman for breach of contract and against King for tortious interference with contract, and the parties would present more testimony at some time in the future. But my own view is, the judge would be making a mistake if she did that. If you want to know how important it is to control the heavyweight championship, look at everything Don King has been willing to do over the years to control it, including giving Hasim Rahman a $5,000,000 signing bonus.

Mom: What's the best-case scenario for Cedric?

TH: The judge could grant an injunction AND order Don King, Hasim Rahman, or both of them to pay damages. You know, over the years, Don has shown considerable contempt for Cedric. But as Evander Holyfield once said, "In boxing, sometimes the guy you think can't possibly get you is the one who gets you." This could be Don's version of the XFL.

Mom: That bad?

TH: It's possible. But it would be premature to congratulate Lennox or Cedric yet. The judge still has to issue her ruling, and Don has won some strange decisions in boxing. Congratulating Lennox and Cedric now would be like congratulating Billy Conn after twelve rounds against Joe Louis.

Mom: How soon will the judge hand down her decision?

TH: It won't be long.

Mom: How long?

TH: Not long.

When Judge Cedarbaum handed down her first ruling on injunctive relief in the heavyweight championship litigation, I temporarily set aside the "Mom" format.

Heavyweight Trial Update

United States District Judge Miriam Cedarbaum has granted Lennox Lewis's request for an injunction against Hasim Rahman. The injunction forbids Rahman from engaging in any heavyweight fight during the next eighteen months unless he first engages in a rematch against Lewis.

The judge's decision was issued from the bench after two hours and forty minutes of oral argument by the attorneys for Lewis, Rahman, Cedric Kushner, and Don King.

The judge reserved decision on Kushner's request for an injunction regarding his claim that he is Rahman's exclusive promoter. That decision is expected early next week along with a more elaborate written explanation of the judge's decision in the Lewis–Rahman dispute.

Rahman won the heavyweight championship by defeating Lewis in South Africa on April 21. At that time, Kushner was Rahman's exclusive promoter. The Lewis camp claimed that Rahman was contractually obligated to fight a rematch against Lewis for $3,150,000 or such higher sum as the parties might negotiate. However, Rahman took the position that he was free to fight whomever he chose, and a bidding war for his services followed. HBO and the Lewis camp offered Rahman $14,150,000 and other incentives for an immediate rematch against Lewis. Showtime offered Rahman $20,000,000 and a promise of indemnification if he made his first title defense against Mike Tyson on Showtime. Then, on May 9, Rahman bolted from Kushner and signed an exclusive promotional contract with Don King.

Judge Cedarbaum ruled that Lewis had an enforceable contract with Rahman with regard to a rematch; that Rahman had breached the contract; that Lewis, because of his advanced age, would suffer irreparable harm if not given an immediate rematch; and that injunctive relief was an appropriate remedy.

Rahman's attorney had argued on summation that his client wanted a rematch against Lewis, but should be allowed to participate first in an interim bout on terms that were more reasonable than those called for by the original Rahman-Lewis bout agreements. However, the judge rejected that argument, noting that Rahman failed to take advantage of the interim bout provision in a lawful manner and instead entered into a contract with Don King Productions to fight David Izon and, after that, the winner of the proposed August 4 WBA championship bout between Evander Holyfield and John Ruiz. "To me, that's a breach of contract," the judge said. "Rahman breached the contract when on May 9 he signed an exclusive promotional contract with Don King that precluded the Lewis rematch as contracted for. We don't make promises and then walk away from them."

Kushner's case is more problematic than that of the Lewis camp. His original exclusive promotional agreement with Rahman ran through October 12, 2000. Both sides agree that a series of injuries that precluded Rahman from fighting pushed the expiration date of the contract to April 12, 2001. And both sides agree that, prior to April 12, 2001, Kushner could have extended his contractual rights for another two years by giving Rahman an additional $75,000. However, that $75,000 payment wasn't made until April 24.

Kushner's attorney advanced four arguments in support of his client's right to a contract extension:

(1) The injuries and medical suspensions that precluded Rahman from fighting were of such duration as to extend the original contract term to August 2, 2001. However, the judge has been openly skeptical of this argument in light of a March 16, 2001, letter agreement between Kushner and Rahman that, because of injuries, extended the contract expiration date to April 12, 2001. Kushner's attorney now says that the date was miscalculated.

(2) Rahman's course of conduct after winning the championship, such as allowing Kushner to negotiate on his behalf with HBO and Showtime, extended the contractual relationship between them. This is

known as a contract by estoppel. Here, again, the judge has seemed to reject Kushner's argument.

(3) When Stan Hoffman, acting on Rahman's behalf, accepted a $75,000 check from Kushner on April 24, it extended Kushner's exclusive promotional rights. Here, it's worth noting that, when Hoffman accepted that check, he signed a letter of receipt acknowledging that the payment was "in full satisfaction of CKP's obligations relating to the extension." He also acknowledged in court that his boxer-manager agreement with Rahman authorizes him to accept checks on the fighter's behalf. But—and this is a big but—Rahman's attorney argued that Kushner's exclusive promotional agreement had expired by then. And he argued further that Hoffman might have been authorized to accept checks on Rahman's behalf, but he wasn't authorized to change payment dates or modify any other contract term without first consulting Rahman. Once again, on this argument, the judge seemed to be leaning in Rahman's favor.

(4) Paragraph 1(C) of Kushner's exclusive promotional agreement with Rahman states, "In the event that fighter is declared the heavyweight world champion by any or all of the WBA, WBC, or IBF, then the term of this agreement shall be extended, if necessary, to include fighter's next four fights following his being declared heavyweight world champion." The judge has indicated that she regards this as Kushner's strongest argument. The court could rule that, even though the Kushner-Rahman contract was slated to expire on April 12, the contract automatically extended through April 21 (the date of the Lewis-Rahman bout) because that bout was negotiated pursuant to and took place under Kushner's exclusive promotional contract. If Judge Cedarbaum so rules, she could then decide that, irrespective of all other considerations, Kushner is entitled to serve as Rahman's exclusive promoter for four more fights.

All of this gives the judge four choices with regard to the dispute between Rahman and Kushner:

(1) She can uphold Kushner's claim in its entirety and rule that he properly extended the exclusive promotional agreement. This would entitle Kushner to another two years as Rahman's exclusive promoter.

(2) She can rule that Kushner is entitled to serve as Rahman's

exclusive promoter for four more fights by virtue of the fact that Rahman won the WBC and IBF heavyweight championships while under contract to Kushner.

(3) She can rule that Kushner's exclusive promotional contract has expired, but that he's entitled to negotiate on behalf of Rahman and receive 25 percent of Rahman's gross purse for the Lewis rematch.

(4) She can rule that all of Kushner's rights have expired.

The judge is most likely to chose alternative #2 or alternative #3. Alternative #2 would represent a near-total victory for Kushner. Alternative #3 would be something of a setback for him.

Kushner's promotional contract with Rahman also gives him the right to match any offer made to Rahman by a competing promoter for a period of one year after expiration of their exclusive promotional agreement. Rahman never afforded Kushner that right with regard to King's offer, and this could play into the judge's decision. If any portion of Kushner's contract with Rahman is upheld, he could then proceed against King for damages for tortious interference with contract.

Meanwhile, even after Judge Cedarbaum's next ruling, there will be many unanswered questions. Foremost among them is likely to be, "How much money will Rahman get for his rematch against Lennox Lewis?"

The answer to that question is, "A lot less than the $14,150,000 and other incentives that Rahman was once offered.

The judge noted that the rematch clause she was upholding called for Rahman to receive a minimum purse of $3,150,000 and stated, "I expect negotiations in good faith to raise that minimum." But Rahman's greatest negotiating leverage—his threat to bolt to Showtime for an immediate bout against Mike Tyson—is now gone. HBO will offer Rahman something extra for options on his future bouts. And the Lewis camp will probably throw in a million dollars or so more. But unless Rahman beats Lewis a second time, he will have suffered a deep self-inflicted financial wound.

It should also be noted that, even if Don King winds up as Rahman's exclusive promoter, King probably won't have to make good on his promise to Rahman of a $20,000,000 payday for a Lewis rematch because, in order to get that promise, Rahman represented and warranted to King that he had no contractual obligations to Lewis. That representation turned out to be false.

Shortly after Judge Cedarbaum's ruling, Rahman said defiantly, "If I don't get the purse I want, I don't fight." But if Rahman doesn't fight for eighteen months (the length of Judge Cedarbaum's injunction), he will be stripped of his WBC and IBF titles. The WBC championship would probably then be fought over by Lewis and Mike Tyson, while David Tua and Chris Byrd would do battle for the IBF crown. And eighteen months from now, the WBA champion could well be Kirk Johnson, whose promoter is none other than Cedric Kushner. Under those circumstances, Hasim Rahman would still be "the man who beat the man." But would anybody care?

By popular demand, "Mom" returned for the final installment of the heavyweight courtroom drama.

Cedarbaum Rules

Mom: Thomas, this is your mother. How dare you write last week's story, *Heavyweight Trial Update,* without me?

TH: Mom, I'm sorry. I tried to reach you after Judge Cedarbaum handed down her decision last Thursday. But you weren't home, and I was writing on deadline.

Mom: Well, I'm home now, and I hear there's a second ruling. What's the judge's latest decision?

TH: Well, as you know, last week the judge granted Lennox Lewis's request for an injunction forbidding Hasim Rahman from engaging in any heavyweight fight during the next eighteen months unless he first engages in a rematch against Lewis. Today she issued her ruling with regard to the lawsuit between Rahman, Don King, and Cedric Kushner.

Mom: And?

TH: The first part of the ruling was that Kushner did not properly extend his exclusive promotional agreement with Rahman and that the basic agreement between them has expired. Rahman was injured or medically suspended from fighting for a period of nine months during the course of the agreement, and that could have extended Cedric's rights through mid-July 2001. But on March 16, 2001, Kushner and Rahman signed a letter agreement calling for a six-month injury extension through April 12. Cedric's lawyer said that the date referenced in the letter was a miscalculation. The judge called it a settlement. Cedric also argued that his exclusive promotional agreement was extended on April 24 when Rahman's manager, Stan Hoffman, accepted a $75,000 check from Kushner and signed a letter of receipt acknowledging that the payment was "in full satisfaction of CKP's obligations relating to the extension." That payment had originally been due on April 12. The judge ruled that Hoffman was in fact authorized to extend Kushner's time to pay the $75,000, but that the letter of receipt was insufficiently drafted by the Kushner camp from a technical legal point of view. The judge ruled further that the contract provision entitling Kushner to extend his promotional rights for four more fights in the event Rahman won the heavyweight championship was immaterial, because Cedric's exclusive promotional contract had already expired by April 21 when Rahman won the crown. And she said that Hasim's repeated references to Cedric as his exclusive promoter and all the negotiating that Cedric did on his behalf after April 21 were counterbalanced by the fact that Kushner and Rahman were negotiating what she called "a new promotional agreement" between them at the same time. In other words, according to the judge, the only reason Kushner was negotiating this new promotional agreement was because, deep down inside, he knew that his old one had expired. That's a hole in Kushner's case that his side should have been able to fill during the trial. Cedric and Hasim weren't negotiating a new promotional agreement. They were negotiating a modification of the old one, which said that, for any world championship bout that Rahman engaged in, the split between Kushner and Rahman would be "negotiated in good faith."

Mom: Did Cedric win anything?

TH: The judge ruled that Cedric had a contractual right to be Rahman's promoter for the Lewis rematch. But rather than issue an injunction in Cedric's favor, she said that Don King would provide Rahman's services to the Lewis camp and Kushner would receive a percentage (probably 25 percent) of Rahman's purse.

Mom: So what happens next?

TH: Don King is now Hasim Rahman's promoter. The next step is for King to negotiate with the Lewis camp on terms for a rematch. October 6 on TVKO is being talked about as a possible date, but it could be later. After the judge's decision was handed down, Rahman told reporters, "I love it. Whenever they say, I'll be ready." So if the warring factions can reach an agreement, fine. If not, things will get messy.

Mom: What kind of deal are they likely to reach?

TH: I don't know. Technically, the way things stand at the moment, Rahman's purse for the fight will come from Lion Promotions, which is Lennox's promoter. The judge said she expected the parties to negotiate in good faith to raise the $3,150,000 contract minimum. Lion could add to the purse by paying King and Rahman for promotional options on Rahman. And HBO will sweeten the pot by offering to pay King and Rahman directly for TV options. But Rahman has no opponent other than Lewis who he can legally get into the ring with at the present time. And last week, after Judge Cedarbaum announced her decision to enjoin Rahman, HBO Sports president Ross Greenburg said the $14,150,000 rematch deal was "way off the table" and that it would be "significantly cut."

Mom: Did Greenburg say what HBO would be willing to pay as a license fee for the fight?

TH: Not specifically. He did say, and I'm quoting, "We'll figure out what the pay-per-view numbers are and pay that to the promoter. What they pay the fighters is their business."

Mom: Does the Rahman camp have any negotiating leverage?

TH: Not much, although Greenburg also said, "Obviously, Hasim Rahman is heavyweight champion of the world, and we're going to make sure we don't get caught again in the position we were in before if he beats Lennox a second time. We would offer him a deal that entertains a future for him with HBO if he wins."

Mom: So what does Rahman expect to get?

TH: Last week, Rahman said, "If they're not talking eight figures, then they're not talking to me."

Mom: What did the Lewis people say to that?

TH: Judd Burstein, Lewis's attorney, said, and I quote, "Rahman is more likely to be panhandling than he is to get $10,000,000 for this fight. Unless cows are flying, he's not getting eight figures."

Mom: What happens if the Rahman and Lewis camps can't reach an agreement?

TH: They'll go back to court on the issue of good faith. But the money behind the $14,150,000 Lewis rematch offer to Rahman came mostly from HBO because it was afraid Rahman would fight

Tyson on Showtime instead of giving Lewis a second fight. And unless Rahman can win the rematch, his threat of fighting Tyson on Showtime for the title is gone.

Mom: Can Judge Cedarbaum exert any control over HBO?

TH: No, HBO isn't a party to the court action.

Mom: What if King and Rahman refuse to negotiate in good faith or Rahman simply refuses to fight Lewis? In terms of age, he can afford to sit on the sidelines a lot longer than Lennox can.

TH: Judd Burstein said last week, "If Mr. Rahman doesn't fight, every dollar that has been paid to him by Don King will be recovered by us in damages." Also, the judge could keep the injunction against Rahman in place while Lewis has an interim fight. Plus you have to consider that, come November, Mike Tyson will be entitled to a championship bout as the WBC's mandatory challenger. That means, if Iron Mike doesn't have a title bout signed by November, the WBC could strip Rahman and order a title match between Lewis and Tyson. If Lewis and Tyson sign to fight, Lennox would get in the neighborhood of $20,000,000, so he might do it. Then I'd expect Rahman to go back to court and argue that the injunction against him should be lifted. But of course, he'd no longer have the WBC title, and Lewis would argue that the injunction shouldn't be lifted because Rahman failed to bargain in good faith. The IBF might also strip Rahman and order a title match between David Tua and Chris Byrd.

Mom: Who determines whether or not the parties are negotiating in good faith?

TH: The judge. And negotiations will be complicated by the fact that King and Rahman will try to construct the rematch contract in a way that gives them payments for future considerations and minimizes the direct payment to Rahman for the Lewis rematch.

Mom: Why would they want to do that?

TH: To cut down the amount of money received by Cedric. It's highly unlikely that Miriam Cedarbaum has heard the last of this case. And the ironic thing is, if Rahman had signed immediately to fight Tyson instead of bolting to King, the judge might have allowed Rahman-Tyson as an interim fight.

Mom: But Rahman wouldn't have been able to schedule a Tyson fight within the time limitations called for by the rematch clause.

TH: On its face, that's correct. But the judge might have stretched the rematch clause to allow Rahman to fight Tyson anyway. The thing that seemed to piss her off most about Rahman's conduct was that he signed to fight David Izon in China on August 4 and the winner of Holyfield-Ruiz III after that. He walked away from his rematch obligation entirely.

Mom: Who do you think will win a Rahman-Lewis rematch?

TH: My guess is, Lennox. Certainly, he'll be favored. But Lennox might be a head case by the time he gets in the ring again with Rahman. Remember Lewis-McCall II, when McCall wandered around the ring crying and Lennox couldn't do much with him. Part of that was because Lennox was skittish about having been knocked out by Oliver in their previous fight. I'll tell you one thing, though. If the rematch is at altitude, Lennox will get there early to acclimate.

Mom: Who do you think would win Tyson-Lewis?

TH: I don't know. But I do know that, when you've been whacked out in your last fight, it's not a particularly good idea to come back against the hardest puncher in boxing.

Mom: So who are the big winners and losers so far?

TH: Right now, the big winners are Lewis, Lion Promotions, and HBO. Lewis gets his rematch; HBO pays less for rights than it was willing to pay last month; and Lion makes more of a profit on the fight than it thought it would.

Mom: And the losers?

TH: Cedric's claim is now limited to monetary damages on one fight. He might wind up with King and Rahman owing him 25 percent of last month's $14,150,000 rematch offer, but 25 percent of whatever Rahman gets for the rematch is more likely. King will be in great shape if Rahman beats Lewis a second time. But if he doesn't, Don might be out of pocket a lot. The biggest loser though, could be Rahman. Hasim was ebullient after the judge's decision was announced. He told reporters, "I feel great. I'm free of Kushner. I can beat 'em in the courtroom, too." But the truth is, right now, Hasim is like a shakey dot-com company. After an extremely successful public offering in South Africa on April 21, Hasim has turned an asset valued at tens of millions of dollars into considerably less. If he wins the rematch, he'll be fine. But if he loses, he could have problems.

Mom: Has there been any talk of settlement between Kushner, King, and Rahman?

TH: Lou DiBella called Kushner at King's urging on Tuesday afternoon and asked if Cedric was interested in talking. Then he called again on Wednesday and said that Don had asked him to try to broker a settlement. Cedric said he'd think about it, but that was all before the judge's decision came down. Don is in Las Vegas now. He'll be back in New York on Monday. I suspect Don will sit down next week with Cedric and also with people from HBO and the Lewis camp.

Mom: What will happen to Bob Mittleman, Stan Hoffman, and Steve Nelson?

TH: That depends on the course of events. The Lewis camp still has an action pending against them for damages. If Rahman and Lewis negotiate a rematch, the issue of damages will probably become moot and Lewis's lawsuit will be dropped. If there's no Rahman-Lewis rematch, the lawsuit will continue.

Mom: Boxing is something, isn't it? It's like a chess game that goes on and on and on.

TH: You're right on that one. But I'll tell you something. I had a couple of thoughts about our judicial system during the trial. Our system of justice is quite arbitrary. Cases in the federal courts are assigned to judges by drawing their names out of a drum. It's a lottery. Lewis was lucky in that he happened to get a no-nonsense judge who believes in the sanctity of contracts and moved things along at a fast pace. That was important because Don King is more likely to get his way by attrition when the wheels of justice grind slowly. But the second thought I had is more encouraging. Anyone who wanted to could walk into the federal courthouse this month; sit in the same row of seats as Lennox Lewis, Hasim Rahman, and Don King; and watch the entire proceeding from beginning to end. There's something very nice, open, and egalitarian about that.

Round 4

The New York State Athletic Commission

By the year 2001, the New York State Athletic Commission had become a microcosm of incompetence and corruption. I'd like to think that the following articles were part of a rising tide that called attention to the situation and led to the resignation of the NYSAC's chairman and several of his top operatives.

A Scandalous Tragedy

The tragic death of Beethavean Scotland underlines the problems that permeate the New York State Athletic Commission. Many ring deaths are unavoidable. This one was not.

The basic facts surrounding Scotland's death are as follows. On the night of June 26, he fought George "Khalid" Jones in a bout that was nationally televised from the flight deck of the *U.S.S. Intrepid*. It was Scotland's first fight in 329 days, and he took a beating. On three occasions in three different rounds, there were cries from the crowd that the bout should be stopped. Finally, in round ten, he was knocked unconscious. He died six days later.

Any examination of the Scotland tragedy has to begin with the man who refereed the fight, Arthur Mercante Jr.

Arthur is a gentleman. I like him. I think he's a good person. He might be the best referee in the country but for one serious flaw. There are times when he allows fights to go on too long. It happened with Razor Ruddock against Michael Dokes in 1990. It happened with Pernell Whitaker against Diosbelys Hurtado in 1997. It happened with Michael Bennett against Andrew Hutchinson in 2001. And it happened again on the night of June 26.

Mercante's situation is analogous to that of a dedicated police officer. Picture a cop who cares about the community, is fearless in fighting crime, makes important arrests, and does his best to serve society. But once every few years, he fires his police revolver under questionable circumstances. One time, he fires at a fleeing mugger on a crowded street.

Another time, he fires when he thinks a suspect has a gun that is actually a cellular telephone. The incidents go on, but no one is hurt. Then, one day, he fires at fleeing bank robber who's running past a school playground, and a ten-year-old is accidentally killed.

Long before a cop reaches that point, the police department should sit him down and talk with him. Yet no one at the NYSAC sat down with Arthur Mercante Jr. to talk about his philosophy of refereeing and improve his otherwise sterling ring performance. Several times since the tragedy, Mercante has said, "I never thought of stopping the fight." But if Arthur didn't at least think about stopping the fight, something in his thinking was wrong. His desire to let Scottland finish the fight is understandable. Again and again, Beethavean had come back from the brink; and rather than just try to survive, he kept trying to win. Indeed, after taking a beating in round seven, Scottland won rounds eight and nine.

But the first and foremost concern of a referee during a fight must be the safety of the fighters. And here, the thoughts of Arthur Mercante Sr. are instructive. In arguing against the use of a standing eight count for fighters in trouble, the elder Mercante once opined, "I'm opposed to the standing eight count, because the point at which a referee is supposed to use it is precisely the point at which a fight should be stopped. The fighter's knees are weak; his eyes are rolling. So why prolong his agony?" And Jerry Izenberg of the *Newark Star Ledger* echoed Mercante's reservations when he observed, "A fighter can be an inch away from getting knocked out; then he's brought back; and then he can go an inch away from getting knocked out again. That's not good for the fighter." Yet that's precisely what happened to Beethavean Scottland in the fourth, fifth, and seventh rounds. Then, in round ten, Scottland's condition went beyond taking a beating. His eyes wandered. Clearly, he was no longer functioning properly. This was the point at which stopping the fight became an urgent imperative rather than a judgment call. Yet Mercante let the destruction go on.

To Mercante's credit, he hasn't gone into hiding. He has answered inquiries about the tragedy as forthrightly as possible. It has been suggested that he retire from the ring. Should he? I can't answer that. If he referees again, will he go in the opposite direction and stop fights too soon? I don't know. I'll say simply that I feel sorry for the situation that

Arthur finds himself in. Whatever course he pursues, he'll carry this tragedy with him for the rest of his life.

The men in Beethavean Scottland's corner are also to blame. Did they care about their fighter? I'm sure they did. But they saw what was happening to him and let the fight continue. However, the ultimate responsibility for Scottland's death lies with the New York State Athletic Commission, which is currently chaired by Mel Southard.

The NYSAC is a microcosm of incompetence and corruption. Yes, some dedicated public servants work there. But by and large, the most qualified employees—men like Joe Dwyer, Bob Duffy, Tony Mazzarella, and Tom Hoover—have been forced out or chose to leave the commission because of the lack of professionalism that surrounded them. Those four men cared about the fighters; they understood boxing; and they're gone.

After Beethavean Scottland underwent the second of three unsuccessful surgeries to repair the damage to his brain, Michael Katz asked Southard if any of the commissioners or other ranking NYSAC personnel had gone to the hospital with Scottland. "No," Southard told him. "Why not?" Katz queried. "Because the main event was coming up," Southard responded, "and we had to be there in case something happened." "What for?" Katz countered. "Something happened in the fight before, and you didn't do anything."

Not enough people at the NYSAC do their job. Or phrased differently, too many commission employees today view their job as one of Republican Party service rather than public service. They know next-to-nothing about professional boxing and care less. The result is that there's a shortage of qualified personnel at the NYSAC. Many of its referees, judges, and inspectors are poorly chosen and poorly trained. No one takes charge, because no one in a position of responsibility knows what has to be done.

On the night of June 26, Mel Southard should have gotten up from his seat, walked around the ring to the physician assigned Scottland's corner, and told him to examine the fighter. If he had, Scottland might be alive today. Instead, Southard's office now says it's conducting an investigation by reviewing a video tape of the tragedy. And Dr. Barry Jordan, chief neurologist for the NYSAC, explains, "We're asking, were there any opportunities to stop the fight?"

That's an idiotic question. Of course, there were opportunities to stop the fight.

Jordan observed the Jones–Scottland bout from a neutral corner outside the ring. He says that, after round seven in which Scottland took a bad beating, he told Mercante "Don't let him take too many more blows." Mercante says that Jordan's words were, "Let's keep a good eye on him." The difference is immaterial. Jordan's observation of the carnage from a distance was hardly a substitute for a closer look at Scottland by a qualified doctor.

Dr. Rufus Saddler was the ringside physician assigned to Scottland's corner. Reporters in the press section observed, and Mercante later confirmed, that Saddler examined Scottland only once during the fight. He went to the fighter's corner to check on a cut after the fourth round. No one has ever bled to death in a boxing ring. Saddler later told Dr. Jordan, that he was concerned about Scottland's condition but close enough to the corner to see and hear what was going on. I wonder if Dr. Saddler examines the patients who come to his office from across the room.

Dr. Margaret Goodman is a physician who works for the Nevada State Athletic Commission. She and Dr. Flip Homansky (a former ringside physician, who is now an NSAC Commissioner) recently edited a book entitled *Ringside and Training Principles*. The book should be mandatory reading for all fight personnel. One of the essays in it is entitled "What the Ringside Physician Is Looking for in Determining Whether or Not a Fight Should Continue." In that essay, Dr. Goodman notes that, when the physician visits a corner between rounds, "He has already seen something during the round that led him to believe there was a potential injury.... Using a penlight, the doctor looks to see how the fighter's pupils react. If they are unequal or slow to constrict, this can indicate a potentially serious brain injury." Nowhere in the book does Dr. Goodman recommend that a between-rounds examination be conducted from a seat outside the ring while the fighter is staring in another direction. Goodman also states in a section of her book dealing with acute head injuries that there does not have to be a loss of consciousness for a concussion to have occurred. "LET ME RESTATE THIS FOR EMPHASIS," she says in capital letters. "Someone can function with a concussion, but continuing to take punishment with one can lead to permanent brain damage."

Much has been made of the fact that Scottland told both his corner and Mercante that he wanted to continue. Here again, the Goodman-Homansky book is instructive. "The roles of the referee and doctor are vital," it states, "because a fighter usually doesn't know when he is hurt. He cannot think cognitively and doesn't realize his body is not functioning properly. The decision to continue should not be left up to the fighter." And to that, one can add the thoughts of Arthur Mercante Sr., who once opined, "The last thing you do is ask a fighter who's been beaten up or is dazed, a fighter who might be hurt, if he wants to continue, because if he's any kind of fighter at all, he'll say yes."

In sum, a fighter should be allowed to decide that he wants to quit. A fighter should not have the final say on whether he is allowed to continue in a fight. Dr. Jordan now says, "This is just one of those unfortunate things that happens every once in a while. Occasionally, a boxer gets hurt despite regulatory policies."

No! In this case, a fighter was killed because too many people at the NYSAC didn't do their job properly. And it all traces back to the top, although there's a school of thought that Mel Southard doesn't even run the commission. After the Scottland tragedy, several NYSAC officials spoke on condition of anonymity. "The assignments are coming from Albany," said one. "The politicians have to be satisfied that the right people are in the corner and in the ring, particularly when a fight is on television." Another commission official was more specific in his complaint, stating his belief that assignments for major fights are often dictated to Southard by Republican Party officials through State Senator Michael Balboni.

Balboni represents the Seventh State Senatorial district, which includes most of the north shore of Nassau County. Arthur Mercante Sr. is Balboni's personal trainer. Mercante describes the legislator as "a handsome, bright, intelligent guy, who's going to go a long way." Both Balboni and Southard were unavailable when interviews were sought for this article. But regardless of Balboni's role, it's clear that the New York State Athletic Commission is now an arm of the New York State Republican Party.

"We're not even a commission anymore," one NYSAC official acknowledges. "All we are is a slush fund for the party. Our primary guideline is, what will this fight or this appointment do for the party. Any guy in a local Republican club can say, 'I want to be an inspector for a night,' and it's done. Most of the inspectors have no idea what they're doing. There are a few good ones left, but the great majority just stand in the corner and have no idea what's going on. Anyone who gives enough money to the Republican Party can get a job for his son or his son's friend. It's disheartening for the few decent people who are left at the commission, and it's dangerous beyond belief for the fighters."

Tragedies happen in boxing. They're more likely to happen when a state athletic commission is run for the primary purpose of supporting a state political party. Joey Gamache was almost killed in the ring by Arturo Gatti last year in a fight that came after what is widely perceived as a phony weigh-in. But Gamache survived and the furor subsided. Maybe now those responsible at the NYSAC will be held accountable. There's a need for a full house-cleaning. A man getting beaten up on the street would have received better protection from strangers that Beethavean Scottland got from the New York State Athletic Commission on the night of June 26.

Meanwhile, earlier of this year, I wrote an article entitled "Twenty Questions For Mel Southard." I'm still waiting for answers. How about it, Mr. Southard? As a service to the boxing community, please answer the following questions:

(1)   Your predecessor, Floyd Patterson, was forced to resign in March 1998 when a deposition revealed that he didn't know his office address and was unable to remember his own wife's name. Did you ever inquire into the circumstances that enabled Patterson to remain as chairman of the New York State Athletic Commission for as long as he did?

(2)   Tom Hoover (former assistant deputy commissioner for the NYSAC) has said publicly that, before you were hired, he was offered the job you now fill on the condition that he become a Republican and campaign for George Pataki. Have you ever inquired about that? And have you done campaign work for, or contributed money to, George Pataki or Republican Party causes?

(3)   Last year, an editorial in the *New York Post* declared, "The Athletic Commission has served as a dumping ground for patronage employees with little knowledge of how boxing is meant to operate. That has resulted

in scandalous negligence in safeguarding the health and safety of boxers, routine sanctioning of outrageous mismatches, and approval of incompetent judges." Given that fact that the *Post* is thought of as a highly partisan Republican newspaper, what do you think occasioned its editorial?

(4)   There were sixteen fight cards in New York in 1999 (the last year for which the NYSAC has been willing to provide detailed financial information). The best estimate is that, during that year, the New York State Athletic Commission cost taxpayers in excess of $1,400,000. That comes to $87,500 per card. The same year, Nevada hosted forty-two fight cards, and the total budget for the Nevada State Athletic Commission was $325,000. That comes to $7,738 per card. Please explain why it cost New York eleven times as much per fight card as it cost Nevada.

(5)   Shortly after Bob Duffy resigned as director of boxing for the New York State Athletic Commission, he said, "Everybody knows what's going on at the commission. To get a job, it helps to know someone in the Republican party, contribute money to the Republican party, or work for the Republican party." Please comment on that.

(6)   How much money and how much work have current commission employees and their relatives contributed to Republican Party candidates and causes?

(7)   The most recent data made available indicates that the NYSAC has a payroll that includes ten appointees on full salary plus seventy-seven inspectors, nine advisory board members, eight "special assistants," and numerous other personnel on a per diem basis. Requests for later data have been denied. How many of these individuals are former professional fighters? Why doesn't the commission employ more former professional fighters?

(8)   Bob Duffy also said, "There are certain people at the commission on full salary who are supposed to come to work every day, and I almost never saw them." Please comment.

(9)   Last year, at least three government agencies (the FBI, the New York State Inspector General's office, and New York County District Attorney's office) began investigating the New York State Athletic Commission. It's believed that the FBI investigation was spurred by reports of "no-show" jobs and other political patronage plums being given out by the commission in return for political contributions. To what extent have you cooperated with these investigations?

(10) Jack Newfield and Wally Matthews wrote a series of articles in which they referred to Jim Polsinello as "the $70,000 a year seldom-show special assistant." Has Mr. Polsinello been given a raise since then? Also, how much time does Mr. Polsinello devote to his job at the commission and what specifically are his duties?

(11) Prior to stepping down in the aftermath of the Arturo Gatti–Joey Gamache weigh-in scandal, Tony Russo was executive director of the NYSAC. How much time did Mr. Russo devote to his job and what specifically were his duties?

(12) A NYSAC official can be seen on tape wantonly inciting the Madison Square Garden crowd during the Bowe-Golota riot. Why is this official still working for the commission?

(13) When Evander Holyfield fought Lennox Lewis at Madison Square Garden, the commission assigned twenty-five inspectors and asked for sixty-seven ringside credentials. Why? (Dear Mel, please note, the State of Nevada employs only thirteen inspectors statewide and assigns no more than five inspectors to any given fight card.)

(14) Also regarding the first Holyfield-Lewis fight, Bob Duffy has recounted the following incident: "I chose two inspectors for each corner. Bill O'Malley and George Ward were supposed to work one corner, and Mike Fayo and Harold Townes were supposed to be in the other. Then Polsinello came to me and said, 'I'm assigning the corners.' There was a lot of yelling, and he overruled me. So Chris DeFruscio and Mike Pascale worked Lewis's corner, and Marc Cornstein and Jerry Becker were assigned to Holyfield. This was Pascale's first fight in the corner. You don't start your career as an inspector in the corner at a fight for the heavyweight championship of the world. I complained to Becker, and Gerry told me, 'Hey, Duffy, you don't understand. We won the election.'" Please comment.

(15) Joe DeGuardia promoted a fight card at Yonkers Raceway on March 14 of this year. During one of the fights that night, there was loose tape on a fighter's glove. Instead of scissoring the loose end off or covering it with more tape, the referee, for some incomprehensible reason, removed all of the tape from the glove, thus completely exposing the lace, and instructed the fighters to resume boxing. Neither NYSAC corner inspector said a word in protest. The other NYSAC officials in attendance

(including yourself) seemed equally uninvolved. Finally, matchmaker Ron Scott Stevens (who wasn't even working the show) approached a commission official and explained to him that rules require tape over laces for the protection of the fighters. At that point, the fight was stopped and the glove retaped. Are you embarrassed by this incident?

(16)   Teddy Atlas has said, "The judging in New York is a joke, especially in the small local fights. It's almost as though some people at the commission are in bed with the promoters and the other money people; and the guy they're backing has to win so there can be more fights in New York. When there's a bad decision, it can be the result of incompetent judging or corrupt judging. In New York, you have both." What do you think inspired Atlas's statement? Please comment on the quality of ring judging in New York.

(17)   After Cedric Kushner acknowledged paying bribes to Bob Lee, the NYSAC announced that it would appoint a monitor to oversee Kushner's activities in New York. That monitor is New York attorney Matthew Brief, a former prosecutor who, among other clients, has represented Luchese crime family underboss Anthony Casso. Mr. Brief is slated to receive $60,000 from Cedric Kushner Promotions over a twelve-month period. What specifically has Mr. Brief done as monitor? Has Mr. Brief or his law firm contributed money to the Republican Party or Republican Party candidates in New York?

(18)   How much of the taxpayers' money does the NYSAC spend "regulating" professional wrestling in New York? Would you recommend that the NYSAC stop spending taxpayers' money to "regulate" professional wrestling?

(19)   Bob Duffy has said, "Mel Southard puts up with a lot of things that he shouldn't have to put up with. I said to Mel a hundred times, 'Let's go to the governor and tell him what's going on.' Mel said he agreed with me, but it never happened." Could you comment on these conversations with Mr. Duffy?

(20)   Have you ever discussed criticism of the New York State Athletic Commission with George Pataki? If so, what was said?

Incompetence, Corruption, and Gov. George Pataki

The New York State Athletic Commission is ideal in one respect. It provides a window on how the administration of Gov. George Pataki conducts business in New York. Enough has been written about the situation, including front-page stories and editorials in the *New York Post,* that the governor has to be aware of the fact that the NYSAC is rife with corruption and incompetence. Yet he allows business as usual to continue because the commission has become a slush fund for the New York State Republican Party.

All of this was reaffirmed at Coney Island's KeySpan Park on the night of July 7. Jesse James Leija was fighting Hector Camacho Jr. in a bout televised by HBO on *Boxing After Dark.* Unfortunately, the evening degenerated into a classic example of government out of control.

For starters, NYSAC personnel demanded forty-one ringside credentials and ten $300 tickets for the night. Then, prior to the fight, they came back and asked for more. How many of the people who received credentials actually worked the fight? NYSAC officials have refused to answer that question. What is known is that Tom Hoover, who was the on-site coordinator for the promoter, complained about the magnitude of the request. The response of Dan Goossen (president of America Presents) was, "Hey, I've got my fighter on the card. Give them what they want." After the fight, Goossen acknowledged, "What are you gonna do? They want what they want, and that's what it is. You live with it."

I like Dan Goossen. I think he's a good guy who fights for his fighters. But last week, Dan Goossen greased a corrupt system with thousands of dollars worth of seats, and it paid off for America Presents. Was he the victim of extortion? Probably. But he got his money's worth. Or as one official at the fight said, "Dan's not stupid. He knows how the game is played. Right now, these guys [at the commission] have the power to destroy careers and they're ruthless. So you give them what they want and keep your mouth shut or they'll ruin you."

As for the main event at Coney Island, NYSAC personnel acted like the Keystone Cops at KeySpan Park. The sequence of relevant events was as follows.

Early in round five, Camacho suffered a cut on his right eyelid as the result of an unintentional head butt. He took a beating for the rest of the round and returned to his corner. Between rounds, Camacho's seconds never made a serious attempt to stop the bleeding. They appeared more concerned with the fight being stopped than stopping the flow of blood. The ring physician examined Camacho and told the referee that the bout could continue. Finally, after a between-rounds break of 105 seconds instead of the usual 60, referee Steve Smoger motioned for round six to start. The fighters moved to the center of the ring. Smoger then told them to step back while Camacho's corner cleaned up some excess water that had been spilt on the ring canvas. If Smoger hadn't told Camacho's corner to wipe the canvas, the fight would have continued.

Meanwhile, Dan Goossen, who had been sitting behind the table where the judges' scores were being tabulated, stood up and began talking with Jerry Becker (one of three NYSAC commissioners). There was gesturing toward Camacho's corner. Two minutes and forty seconds after the end of round five, Camacho quit. "He claims he can't see," Smoger said. The NYSAC then declared Camacho the winner on points.

In other words, it appears as though Camacho was willing to fight until he learned that, if he quit, he'd win. He had every right to quit. He did not have the right to quit and be awarded the decision. Yes, the cut was caused by a head butt, but the alleged vision problems could just as easily have been caused by punches. The referee was correct in stopping the fight, but Leija should have been declared the winner. Emanuel Steward said as much when he opined after the fight, "I think that someone in [Camacho's] camp informed him that he was ahead on the scorecards and the best thing for him to do was to refuse to fight anymore. I saw no reason for him to not fight. What bothers me a lot is, even before he got to the corner, he was indicating in so many ways that he wanted to quit. He said, 'I want out of here; this is not the party I intended to come to.'"

In sum, what should have been a good night for boxing was tarnished. Another tourist, Jesse James Leija, came to New York and was mugged by the New York State Athletic Commission. Afterward, Goossen sought to defend his fighter's honor, but even he felt compelled to admit, "Of course, if I'm Leija's people, I'd have a different view." And Leija himself said in disgust to Camacho, "We know what happened."

The fight card at Coney Island was the first in New York since the tragic death of Beethavean Scottland. And it reinforced the view that NYSAC chairman Mel Southard and his compatriots are fast becoming New York's answer to Bozo the Clown, except the consequences of their actions are far more serious.

Meanwhile, it should be noted that the July 7 fight card at Coney Island took place five days after Beethavean Scottland died. Yet in a violation of the rules of basic decency, there was no ten-count in his honor. The people who run the New York State Athletic Commission should be ashamed of themselves. Unfortunately, they're shameless.

Fighters at Risk

The crisis at the New York State Athletic Commission has spiraled out of control. The NYSAC now threatens the well-being of every fighter who fights in New York.

Two recent incidents are instructive.

On July 26, Beethavean Scottland fought George "Khalid" Jones in New York. Scottland endured a brutal beating. On numerous occasions, there were cries from the crowd that the bout should be stopped. Finally, in round ten, Scottland was knocked unconscious. He died six days later. Arthur Mercante Jr. was the referee that night. He bears partial responsibility for the tragedy. But the New York State Athletic Commission as a whole is more at fault.

Duva Boxing, which promoted the event, reports that the NYSAC demanded forty-five credentials to "regulate" the fight card. In addition, NYSAC officials requested and were given "fifteen to twenty" free tickets. In other words, on the night of June 26, there were forty-five credentialed officials from the NYSAC onboard the U.S.S. Intrepid. A man was beaten to death in front of them. And they did nothing to save him.

During round five, Max Kellerman, who was commentating for ESPN2, cried out, "That's enough! That's it; that's it; that's it! This is how guys get seriously hurt as we saw with Jimmy Garcia, who wound up dying."

NYSAC chairman Mel Southard, NYSAC chief neurologist Dr. Barry Jordan, and Dr. Rufus Saddler (the ring doctor assigned to Scottland's corner) sat there and watched.

In round seven, Kellerman voiced his concern again: "You know what I don't like about the way he's getting hit. About four or five times a round, Jones lands two or three good sharp punches right in his face, snapping his head around, and those are the cumulative punches that lead to things you don't want to hear about after the fight. That's bothering me. I don't like it."

Mel Southard (the $101,000-a-year NYSAC Chairman) looked on. What did he think was happening in front of him?

At the end of round seven, Kellerman's voice grew more urgent: "I don't like it. I don't like it. If you're in Scotland's corner, you have to ask yourself, is it worth it, the damage he's sustaining right now? Is it worth it for the kid's life in the future, sustaining this kind of damage?"

Still, no doctor took it upon himself to visit the corner.

In round ten, Kellerman was pleading, "I don't like what I'm seeing, how much he's getting punched in this fight, how many clear shots to the head he's taking in this fight."

Yet no one from the NYSAC intervened to save Beethavean Scotland's life.

Dr. Michael Schwartz is chairman of the American Association of Professional Ringside Physicians. Schwartz says that, "During a fight, the most important thing the ring doctor can do is visit the fighter in the corner." Dr. Ferdie Pacheco, who knows a thing or two about medicine and boxing, is more direct. "The main job of the ringside doctor," says Pacheco, "is to figure out when enough is enough. If he doesn't go into the ring to examine Scotland, what's he there for?"

I don't recall Barry Jordan ever working the corner during a professional fight. Maybe he has. If so, I'd like to know how often and when? But more important, I'd like to know why Dr. Jordan didn't get out of his seat, walk over to Dr. Saddler, and tell him to check Scotland out between rounds? Dr. Jordan may have edited a book entitled *The Medical Aspects of Boxing,* but Beethavean Scotland hardly got textbook medical care.

It brings to mind a bout that occurred in 1983 between Roberto Duran and Davey Moore. The two men were battling at Madison Square Garden for the WBA junior-middleweight championship. That night, Moore absorbed one of the worst sustained ring beatings ever seen. And the referee, for some inexplicable reason, let the bout go on.

Tom Hoover was the NYSAC inspector assigned to Davey Moore's corner that night. In round eight, Hoover had seen enough. With Moore being brutalized almost beyond belief, Hoover stepped into the ring and ended the fight. Quite possibly, he saved Davey Moore's life. He took responsibility.

On the night of June 26, 2001, none of the forty-five credentialed New York State Athletic Commission employees supposedly on duty took responsibility. And the commission is still trying to evade responsibility.

Indeed, NYSAC officials have since voiced the view that the "policy and protocol" of the commission that allowed Scotland's death to occur were followed just fine. And carrying things one step further, Dr. Jordan says the commission reviewed its performance and, "We determined that every measure was taken to save the fighter's life. This is obviously a tragedy, but we feel our standards for safety are the most rigid in the country . . . There was no negligence involved."

That's idiotic! How can an internal review be conducted by the very people whose conduct is being questioned? It's standard practice in the medical profession for medical-legal reviews to be conducted by independent evaluators. For Dr. Jordan to say there was no wrongdoing is one of the most insulting things that fighters in the State of New York have ever been told.

The administrative-medical fiasco that occurred at Coney Island on July 7 offers further evidence of a commission in turmoil.

New York law requires that boxing rings used for professional fights be at least eighteen feet squared. The ring at Coney Island was sixteen-feet-three-inches. After Jesse James Leija chose the gloves he intended to wear in his fight against Hector Camacho Jr., NYSAC personnel changed the gloves without Leija's knowledge. The Leija camp objected to two of the three judges selected by the NYSAC for the fight. Those two judges were retained, and the one judge approved by Leija's people was replaced. A NYSAC inspector allowed Camacho's hands to be improperly taped in the dressing room before the bout, apparently because he had no idea what he was watching. All of this took place with forty-one credentialed officials from the NYSAC supposedly on duty.

The bout itself was worse. Early in round five, Camacho suffered a cut on his right eyelid as the result of an unintentional head butt. After the round, the ring physician examined him and ruled that he could continue. But Camacho complained of "blurry vision" and quit. That was his right. The problems arose when Mel Southard seemed to disappear, and other NYSAC personnel declared Camacho the winner.

Since that night, there has been speculation that Dan Goossen, Camacho's promoter, was improperly apprised of the judges' scoring before Camacho quit. Goossen says he wasn't. Personally, I believe him. But whether or not Goossen knew what was on the judges' scorecards, the entire Camacho camp understood that Hector had a better chance of winning by going to the scorecards than by going to the center of the ring for round six. As Ferdie Pacheco later noted, "Camacho's most pressing medical problem was that he was getting hit and wanted out. Even the dumbest, most gullible people in boxing understand what happened that night."

On July 9, the Leija camp filed a formal protest with the New York State Athletic Commission asking that the decision in Camacho's favor be overturned. Most observers expect the NYSAC to rule on the protest without holding a full hearing in order to avoid airing some very troubling issues.

If Hector Camacho Jr. really had blurred vision (or a fractured orbital bone as was later suggested), proper medical care dictated that he go to the hospital for treatment immediately after the fight. Otherwise, he risked infection, long-term eye-muscle problems, and permanent loss of vision. Dan Goossen cares deeply about his fighters. So why is it that, instead of going immediately to the hospital, Camacho went to a post-fight press conference. Also, if Camacho really had blurred vision, proper medical care dictated that his eye be covered by a patch. But at the press conference, Camacho wore a patch placed over the cut on his eyelid. The eye itself wasn't covered. Shouldn't NYSAC medical personnel have intervened to remedy this situation?

One also has to ask what medical care Camacho received at the hospital after the fight other than getting the cut on his eyelid stitched up. Was he examined by an ophthalmologist? What tests were administered? If Camacho truly had blurred vision, he should have been given a slit-lamp test to determine if there was a corneal abrasion and his pupils should have been dilated to determine if there was a retinal tear. If there was concern about a fractured orbital bone, an orbital X-ray series and maybe a CT-scan should have been ordered.

To date, America Presents, the Camacho camp, and the New York State Athletic Commission have all declined to make relevant medical records available.

Meanwhile, incompetence and corruption reign supreme at the NYSAC. That's because the New York State Athletic Commission represents politics at its worst. The week after Beethavean Scottland died, it was announced that New York governor George Pataki had raised $16,000,000 for his upcoming re-election bid. Almost $9,000,000 of that has been raised in the last six months. The New York State Athletic Commission is a slush fund for Governor Pataki and the Republican Party in the State of New York.

What's the solution? There are rumors that Mel Southard is on the way out as NYSAC chairman and will be replaced by Jerry Becker. But substituting Becker for Southard is no more of a solution than substituting Southard for Floyd Patterson was three years ago. A full house cleaning is necessary.

But more important, at some point, the fighters themselves are going to have to stand up, speak out, and take control of their own destiny.

For years, fighters have been saying that promoters are robbing them and managers don't protect them. But they've done virtually nothing to remedy the situation. Now one of their own, Beethavean Scottland, has been killed in a tragedy that could have been avoided. Another fighter, Jesse James Leija, has been victimized by inept officiating. And beyond that, every fighter who lives or fights in New York is insulted daily by a state athletic commission that treats them like garbage.

Lennox Lewis fought Evander Holyfield for the heavyweight championship of the world at Madison Square Garden, and one of the NYSAC corner inspectors who worked that fight had never worked a professional corner before in his life. That demeans fighters.

The NYSAC appoints ring officials who don't have a clue about what goes on in a boxing ring. Many of these officials have been given their jobs as a result of contributions to the Republican Party or in return for work on behalf of Republican Party candidates. Meanwhile, former fighters who seek positions with the commission can't even get their telephone calls returned.

The fighters have to do for themselves! The fighters have to stand up and say, "Our lives are at risk. Enough is enough!"

Lennox Lewis has already said privately that he won't fight Hasim Rahman at Madison Square Garden because of concerns regarding the conduct of fights in New York. Suppose Roy Jones Jr. announced that he'd fight the winner of Felix Trinidad versus Bernard Hopkins . . . but not in New York . . . ?

The NYSAC
"They Just Don't Care"

Last week, a spokeswoman for Gov. George Pataki, defended the New York State Athletic Commission. "These are accomplished qualified professionals," said Molly Fullington. "We are confident they are doing a good job."

The hard evidence suggests otherwise. At present, the NYSAC appears to be incapable of properly regulating boxing in New York. Every fight card is run on the edge of an abyss. When a bout takes place under the auspices of the NYSAC, ring announcer Michael Buffer could well begin the proceedings by intoning, "Ladies and gentlemen, let's get ready to fumble."

This website has reported at length on the death of Beethavean Scottland and the chaos surrounding the July 7 fight card at Coney Island. In an effort to sweep these incidents under the rug, the commission has investigated itself. It found no wrongdoing in conjunction with Scottland's death, despite Ferdie Pacheco's observation that, "If the doctor allowed the fight to go on without going into the ring, that's criminal." It also engaged in some of the most bizarre legal reasoning ever put on paper to declare the July 7 bout between Hector Camacho Jr. and Jesse James Leija a "no contest." Crucial to this ruling was the NYSAC's refusal to explore the issue of whether Camacho quit without cause because to do so, according to the commission, "would inject an element of uncertainty into the physician-patient relationship" between Camacho and the ring doctor assigned to his corner. The family of Beethavean Scottland will be interested in hearing more from the NYSAC about "the physician-patient relationship," which the commission declared is "a relationship that must be based on trust." And it will be particularly interested in the ugly whispering campaign emanating from the commission to the effect that Scottland was responsible for his own death.

Motrin is a common painkiller similar to Advil or Aspirin. It's sold over the counter to millions of people in the United States. Used in large doses, Motrin affects the ability of the blood to coagulate. In recent days, commission personnel have suggested that Scottland "might" have used Motrin to his detriment. This is known as grasping at straws to evade responsibility.

Meanwhile, NYSAC officials continue to perform their duties in a bizarre manner. A fighter on Joe DeGuardia's June 26 card at Roseland Ballroom was knocked down at the bell ending round two, rose immediately, and went to his corner. He was then disqualified because he and his corner hadn't waited for the referee to finish a mandatory eight count even though the bell ending the round had rung.

The next day, the NYSAC held a weigh-in for a card that was being promoted by Thomas Gallagher Promotions at Aqueduct Race Track. There's a law in New York that fighters with a weight differential of more than five pounds cannot face one another in four-round bouts in certain weight divisions. At the weigh-in, there were two instances, one of them in a junior-featherweight bout, of an unlawful seven-pound weight differential between fighters. The commission's solution to this problem was to send the "underweight" fighters out to eat two pounds of food each in order to temporarily close the weight gap between them and their heavier opponents. This is the definition of "making weight" in New York. There is no record of what the fighters weighed on the night of the fight.

Meanwhile, the NYSAC managed to regulate an April 26 fight card on Long Island with sixteen credentialed employees. That makes one wonder why Mel Southard and his brethren feel they need forty-five credentialed employees on site to do their job properly at the more prestigious televised shows.

The more one learns about the NYSAC, the worse things appear to be. On Sunday, July 29, the *New York Daily News* ran a front-page story about the commission. The *News* informed readers that, "The Commission's recent history has been marked by episodes of incompetence," and declared, "The agency remains a stronghold of Republican patronage, where who you know is more important than what you know about boxing."

Among the pieces of information contained in the *Daily News* article were revelations that (1) the father of Marc Cornstein (one of three NYSAC commissioners) has given more than $75,000 in campaign contributions to George Pataki, including $26,000 since April of this year; (2) James Polsinello, described last year by the *New York Post* as a "$70,000 a year seldom-show special assistant," has contributed $27,000 to various Pataki electoral ventures; and (3) Larry Mandelker, an attorney for the NYSAC, gave $5,000 to the New York State Republican Committee this summer and is also an attorney for the New York State Republican Party.

The latest data available from the New York State Comptroller's office shows ten employees on full salary at the NYSAC. Chairman Mel Southard gets $101,600 a year. James Polsinello's salary has been raised to $76,217.

The records also show a new employee named Ruby Marin, who was hired recently by the NYSAC as a "special assistant" at a salary of $95,000 a year. It appears that Ms. Marin was once a law clerk to Alexander W. Hunter Jr., a New York State Supreme Court judge in the Bronx. I don't know what Ms. Marin does to earn her $95,000 salary, since she and other commission officials have refused to answer inquiries from this website. It's possible that Ms. Marin is a fine public servant who combines Lou DiBella's passion for boxing with the knowledge of Teddy Atlas and the overall planning ability of Seth Abraham. But I wonder whether Ms. Marin is truly knowledgeable about boxing. Does she have any idea who people like Jimmie Glenn and Al Gavin are? Is she an independent voice? And why is she getting $95,000 a year when fighters get beaten up in four-round preliminary bouts for $250.

The comptroller's records list more than six dozen per diem employees at the NYSAC including twenty-five "monitors." I have yet to find anyone who admits to knowing what a NYSAC monitor does.

The Commission also has "slots" for seventy-seven inspectors. In other words, it is legally authorized to hire up to seventy-seven inspectors, but it's hard to know how many inspectors the NYSAC has at any given time because the numbers keep changing. This website has compiled a list of thirty-four individuals who worked for the commission as inspectors during the past year. Only two of them are black. Not one of them is a former fighter.

One former fighter who did work for the commission is Billy Backus. Backus's roots reach deep into the soil of the sweet science. He was born in Canastota, New York, home of the International Boxing Hall of Fame. His uncle is Carmen Basilio. Backus was an honest fighter with a record of 48 wins, 20 losses, and 5 draws over a career than spanned sixteen years. On December 3, 1970, he was matched against Jose Napoles, the undisputed welterweight champion of the world. It was a payday for both men and a presumed tune-up victory for Napoles, except nobody explained the latter half of that equation to Backus. Napoles suffered a horrible cut; the bout was stopped; and Billy Backus was the new welterweight champion of the world. Six months later, in his first title defense, he was knocked out by Napoles in four rounds.

In 1980, Backus began working for the NYSAC as a per diem inspector. He understood boxing and cared about the fighters. He served the commission during the tenure of three governors and five NYSAC chairmen. Last August, Backus resigned in disgust. Recently, he explained why.

"I did twenty years with the commission," says Backus. "Things weren't always the best, but at least the people there tried. Then this outfit comes in. The people at the commission now have no idea what's going on; they don't know how to treat people; and they don't care about the boxers. That upset me more than anything. They don't care about the fighters at all. I put thirty-six years of my life into boxing," Backus continues. "Sixteen as a fighter and twenty with the commission. And right now at the commission, they've got a bunch of people with big mouths and no knowledge of boxing. And when they don't know what's going on, all they do is holler at you. These guys are incompetent; they're dishonest. All they care about is the Republican Party and themselves. They got guys working there who are cousins of cousins and friends of friends, and it has nothing to do with what's good for boxing. Guys are picking up fifty thousand dollars a year for doing nothing. If you need six inspectors for a fight, they send fourteen; and eight of the fourteen guys just sit there eating and drinking, having a good time. I'd go to a show and see ten guys I'd never seen before, who didn't know anything, didn't do anything. I still get angry talking about it. Boxing is a dangerous business. If someone screws up, a fighter can get killed. But most of these guys at the commission don't care. I did my best to do my job right. I did my best to fit in. I even changed my registration to the Republican Party to try and get along with them. But in the end, I couldn't deal with the way they were treating the fighters. They're not protecting the fighters. I had to leave."

Bob Rosetta lives in the upstate town of Sherrill, New York, midway between Oneida and Utica. Like Backus, Rosetta is a boxing guy. In fact, he grew up in Canastota on the same street as Backus and Carmen Basilio and worked for the International Boxing Hall of Fame for ten years. In 1989, Rosetta became an inspector for the NYSAC. Last year, he was fired.

"It used to be," says Rosetta, "that Billy Backus and I would do a whole show with two other inspectors, one deputy commissioner, four judges, and the referees. Now they've got thirty guys showing up for the fights, falling all over each other. Billy and I did a show in Schenectady a few years ago. There were more inspectors there than spectators. They brought these guys in, put them in hotel rooms with hot tubs, gave them their money. And at the fights, these guys just sat there in the front row, eating popcorn and hotdogs. They weren't there to work. They were there to get paid and see the show. And the wrestling, I can't stand the wrestling. Why are we spending peoples' money to regulate wrestling? You have a wrestling show, and the commission appoints judges who actually get paid. All that's about is more paychecks for these guys. Three years ago, at the State Fair," Rosetta continues, "I complained to Sandy Treadwell [then New York Secretary of State and now chairman of the New York Republican State Committee]. I told him and I told Mel Southard, 'One of these days, someone is going to get killed, and it won't be because there's no way to avoid it. It will be because most guys at the commission don't know what they're doing anymore.' And it happened. That fighter who got killed in New York, there was no reason for it. When I worked the corner as an inspector, if a fighter was taking a beating, if the doctor just sat there, I'd say to the doctor, 'You better take a look at this guy because he's in trouble.' That's the way I did my job, because that was my job. But now at the commission, they're political hacks. The way the game is played: it's who's the biggest Republican? It's a shame what they've done; they've caused so much harm. This regime has completely ruined the commission. Most of these guys are in it for the money and having a good time and nothing else, and it pisses me off because you're fooling with fighters' lives. I've always been for the fighter, and these guys don't care. They just don't care."

Last year, in an article entitled *How Not to Run a State Athletic Commission,* I wrote, "There are a number of honest, knowledgeable, hard-working men and women affiliated with the New York State Athletic Commission. Their service is tarnished, and boxing is tarnished, by the corruption around them."

I still believe those words to be true. Except more and more of the good public servants at the NYSAC have been forced out of office or resigned in disgust since then. It's very sad. This isn't how government should work, but George Pataki is telling every New Yorker loud and clear what kind of government he believes in. Think about it! If this is what the Pataki administration does with a small manageable agency with a budget of between one and two million dollars, imagine what it does with the dollars that flow in sectors like public transportation and public education.

New York State assemblyman Joseph Morelle announced recently that the Assembly's Committee on Tourism, Arts, and Sports (which he chairs) will hold hearings on the New York State Athletic Commission later this year. In response to Mondelle's announcement, Eamon Moynihan (a spokesman for the NYSAC and Department of State) piously declared, "It's a shame and really kind of sad that the Assembly leadership would try to score political points by trying to exploit the tragic death of Beethavean Scottland."

No, Mr. Moynihan. Incompetence, corruption, and politics paved the road that led to the death of Beethavean Scottland.

In September 2001, Mel Southard resigned as chairman of the New York State Athletic Commission and was replaced by Ray Kelly. On November 13, 2001, the New York State Assembly Committee on Tourism, Arts, and Sports, chaired by Joseph Morelle, held a public hearing as part of its investigation into the scandals that plagued the commission. I was to have been the first witness called, but I was on assignment in Las Vegas, where Hasim Rahman and Lennox Lewis were doing battle for the heavyweight title. Thus, I submitted my testimony to the committee in writing.

Testimony

During the past month, I've been asked several times whether these hearings are necessary. After all, Mel Southard is gone; and his replacement, Raymond Kelly, is widely regarded as a man of integrity and ability. My answer is that these hearings are more important now than ever.

The past nine weeks [since September 11] have shown us all the importance of government. As New Yorkers and as Americans, we are relying on government to safeguard our lives and help us through this difficult time. Moreover, the rebuilding of downtown Manhattan will be the largest construction project in the history of New York. It will provide tens of thousands of jobs and lead to massive government expenditures. It will also provide unique opportunities for wartime profiteering and corruption.

An examination of the New York State Athletic Commission offers a window on how the present gubernatorial administration has seen fit to conduct business in New York. Enough was written about the situation, including front-page stories and editorials in the *New York Post,* that the governor had to have been aware of the fact that the NYSAC was rife with corruption and incompetence long before the tragic death of Beethavean Scottland. Yet business as usual continued because the commission was a slush fund for the New York State Republican Party.

This is not a boxing issue. It's a governmental issue. I hope that this committee will conduct its investigation accordingly.

The first step in the corruption of the New York State Athletic Commission was the appointment of Floyd Patterson as chairman. Patterson suffered from serious memory lapses and other cognitive difficulties. He was a figurehead, nothing more. Using Patterson as a cover, the powers that be filled an increasing number of commission jobs with people of questionable competence who knew next to nothing about professional boxing but were politically well-connected. Some dedicated public servants worked, and still work, at the NYSAC. But by and large, the most qualified employees—men like Joe Dwyer, Bob Duffy, Tony Mazzarella, and Tom Hoover—were forced out or chose to leave the commission because of the lack of professionalism that surrounded them. In their place, the NYSAC appointed ring officials who didn't understand what goes on in a boxing ring. Many of these officials were given their jobs as a result of contributions to the Republican Party or in return for work on behalf of Republican Party candidates. Quite a few of them had "no show" jobs.

The 1999 championship bout at Madison Square Garden between Evander Holyfield and Lennox Lewis showed a corrupt system at its peak. The NYSAC assigned twenty-five inspectors and demanded sixty-seven ringside credentials for the fight. By contrast, the State of Nevada employs only thirteen inspectors statewide and assigns no more than five inspectors to any given fight card.

There were sixteen fight cards in New York in 1999. The best estimate is that, during that year, the New York State Athletic Commission cost taxpayers in excess of $1,400,000. That comes to $87,500 per card. The same year, Nevada hosted forty-two fight cards, and the total budget for the Nevada State Athletic Commission was $325,000. That comes to $7,738 per card. In other words, it cost eleven times more to regulate a fight card in New York than in Nevada.

Meanwhile, no one has been protecting the fighters financially; no one has been protecting the fighters physically; and no one has been protecting the integrity of the fights themselves.

The demise of the NYSAC medical department is a case in point.

Bill Lathan began work with the commission as a ringside physician during the tenure of Jack Prenderville decades ago. He served as medical director from February 1996 until the summer of 2000, when he was told that the NYSAC would be "discontinuing that line in the budget." As a practical matter, the line wasn't discontinued. The duties and salary associated with it were transferred to Dr. Barry Jordan.

"The NYSAC is no longer a regulatory body," Lathan said shortly before the ouster of Mel Southard. "There's no mission or sense of purpose. And what's particularly troubling to me is, the New York State Athletic Commission had a venerable tradition when it came to its medical department, and now that tradition has been corrupted. Why would they destroy the medical department?"

In examining the medical department, it would be instructive for this State Assembly committee to look at Dr. Robin Scarlata. Dr. Scarlata is a radiologist, who received her medical degree from George Washington University. She is currently secretary of the Nassau County Medical Society and affiliated with a radiology group. These are respectable credentials. Dr. Scarlata was on staff at the NYSAC for several years, including 1999, at an annual salary of $48,205. Tom Hoover describes her as "that chick who didn't want to do anything, who never showed up and got paid. Her daddy," Hoover adds, "was someone big in the Republican Party." Of Scarlata and Lathan, Bob Duffy says, "One was political and one was there to work." Larry Mandelker, former counsel to the NYSAC, says, "Robin Scarlata is a very good doctor." Mandelker declined to discuss Scarlata's tenure with the NYSAC, although he did acknowledge that her father was "very friendly with Al D'Amato."

Dr. Rufus Saddler was the ringside physician assigned to Beethavean Scottland's corner on June 26, the night that Scottland was beaten to death. Section 8926 of the Unconsolidated Laws of the State of New York provides, "The physician shall terminate any boxing match if, in the opinion of such physician, any contestant has received severe punishment or is in danger of serious physical injury . . . Such physician may enter the ring at any time during a boxing match and may terminate the match if in his opinion the same is necessary to prevent severe punishment or serious physical injury to a contestant."

Dr. Saddler didn't terminate the bout that night. That can be forgiven. But more significantly, he never went to Scottland's corner between rounds to examine the fighter other than to check on a cut after round four.

"As a doctor, you have to be ambivalent about sitting at ringside to begin with," acknowledges Bill Lathan. Lathan is reluctant to assign blame for the Scottland tragedy. But he does say, "As a ring physician, you have to have instinct. You have to feel what's happening and know the game. Don't blame the referee if you don't do your job right. Do your job. That's what you should be concerned about, doing your job."

Tom Hoover is more direct. "I have to believe," says Hoover, "that if Bill Lathan had been in Beethavean Scottland's corner, that young man would be alive today."

Dr. Saddler was on duty again as a ringside physician at an August 4 *ShoBox* card in New York. He began the performance of his duties from a seat in the second row of the press section. Finally, before the start of round five of the first bout, Barry Jordan came over and suggested to him that he move a bit closer to the action. Fighters who fight in New York can be forgiven if they wonder whether the physicians assigned to their corner understand what they're watching as a fight unfolds.

Louis Brandeis once wrote, "Sunlight is the best disinfectant." I believe it's incumbent upon this committee to cast the strongest light possible on the workings of the New York State Athletic Commission. More specifically, regarding each person who worked for the NYSAC at any time during the past three years, this committee should demand to know (1) what were his (or her) qualifications; (2) how did he get his job; and (3) did he do his job?

Special attention should be paid to the people at the top—Mel Southard, Marc Cornstein, Jerry Becker, Jim Polsinello, Tony Russo, Lawrence Mandelker, and Ruby Marin. Moreover, this committee should track individuals within the system after they leave the NYSAC. For example, last year after the Gatti-Gamache weigh-in scandal, the *New York Post* reported that Tony Russo, then executive director of the NYSAC, was "being investigated over allegations he rarely shows up for work." Russo subsequently left the commission "on medical leave." Where is he working now?

These times present special challenges for the State of New York. We have a right to expect that our government will function at its best. With regard to the New York State Athletic Commission, there's no need to change the law, just follow it.

As this book goes to press, it remains to be seen whether or not boxing will be properly regulated in New York.

The "New" New York State Athletic Commission

On October 22, the New York State Senate confirmed the appointment of past (and now future) New York City police commissioner Raymond Kelly as chairman of the State Athletic Commission. Kelly maintained a low profile prior to his confirmation. He's becoming a lot more visible now.

Kelly took over a commission plagued by incompetence, "no-show" jobs, and other scandals linked to contributions to the New York State Republican Party. He says his top priority is the "physical and financial well-being of the fighters." Toward that end, he intends to (1) establish an "800" telephone "hot-line" for the reporting of any and all rules violations; (2) require the strict inspections of gyms where boxers train; (3) review all contracts that impact upon fighters to make certain that they're in compliance with state law; and (4) create a permanent investigative force for the commission.

"To accomplish these goals," Kelly acknowledges, "we need to establish basic business procedures at the commission; update the computer system; improve record-keeping, things like that. We also need a coordinated comprehensive training program at every level of the commission to increase professionalism. The rules and regulations are well-written. They need some changes, but it's more important to get the right people to enforce them."

That leads to the question of how political contributions and other political considerations corrupted the commission in recent years. Kelly is forthright on that matter. "I found a commission," he says, "that many years ago had a reputation for being the premier boxing commission in the country, and that has been lost. The reputation of the commission has diminished. There's a cloud over the commission, and we have to move that cloud aside."

As a first step, Kelly has asked the state police to conduct a *de novo* investigation of events surrounding the death of Beethavean Scottland this past June and the controversy surrounding last July's Hector Camacho versus Jesse James Leija fight. "Those fights are a window onto the larger picture," explains Kelly. "I want to wait for the results of these investigations to come back, because they'll tell me about the systemic problems that exist."

As for personnel changes that might take place, Kelly promises, "I'm going to take a look at all the personnel. As far as I know, I have total leeway with regard to personnel, and we'll be making some personnel changes. Most of the people here now are political appointees and don't have civil service [job protection] status. My mandate is, 'Straighten this out,' and I intend to follow that directive. I don't want to say right now what personnel changes will take place. Give us three months for that. But I want to get the best people here. And I'll choose people on the basis of merit, not political connections. That allegation is out there, and it's fair to say that's how some commission appointments came about. But from now on, it won't be a question of who knows who; I promise you that."

The point man for Kelly's effort to revive the NYSAC is Charles DeRienzo. Kelly intends to reach into the law enforcement community for many of his hires, particularly in filling inspector slots. DeRienzo is a retired New York City police inspector who spent thirty-three years as a cop. He and Kelly worked together for the first time in 1981, when Kelly was brought into the 88th Precinct in Fort Greene, Brooklyn, as a young captain and DeRienzo was one of his lieutenants. "There were some problems in the precinct," DeRienzo remembers. "There were incidents of partying and disruptive behavior that had gotten out of hand. The cops, rather than leadership, were running the command."

Thereafter, DeRienzo worked for Kelly on a number of occasions. In 1998, he left the NYPD to become director of the Insurance Fraud Bureau for the New York State Department of Insurance. He was comfortable there, but found the lure of working for Ray Kelly at the NYSAC hard to resist. He's now the commission's new executive director and, as might be expected, echoes many of his mentor's thoughts.

More specifically, DeRienzo says, "I found a place that needs to implement better management principles; that needs a comprehensive training program for its personnel; that has to make better use of technology. But if you don't have the right people, the best processes in the world won't work."

Thus, DeRienzo concludes, "I want to evaluate people to see if they're capable of doing the work that has been assigned to them. If someone is here and they're doing a good job, I don't care how they got here. You don't want to chop peoples' heads off for no good reason. You have to be careful with peoples' lives. But I want people who believe in the same things I believe in and share my philosophy. I work ten hours a day. I expect people to give me a full day's work and, if they don't, they're not going to be here. If someone isn't doing the right thing, they're going to be out the door. I don't care who they know." And then DeRienzo adds, "It's not all going to happen overnight, but I'm starting to see things I want to change, both structural and in terms of personnel. I'm starting to get a sense of the changes that have to be made. My mandate from Ray Kelly is to be concerned with the health and welfare of the boxers. We're going to provide boxers with an environment that protects them and treats them with the fairness and respect they deserve as professionals."

Well and good. Meanwhile, here are five suggestions for Ray Kelly and Charles DeRienzo to consider:

(1) The Rules of the New York State Athletic Commission are hopelessly archaic regarding the roles of promoters, matchmakers, and managers. They should be revised to reflect the present-day realities of boxing.

(2) Section 8915 of the Unconsolidated Laws of the State of New York states, "No licensed promoting corporation or matchmaker shall knowingly engage in a course of conduct in which fights are arranged where one boxer has skills or experience significantly in excess of the other boxer so that a mismatch results with the potential of physical harm to the boxer."

This provision has been long overlooked. It should be enforced.

(3) Very often, fighters are unable to pursue legitimate grievances against managers or promoters because they don't have the financial resources to pursue litigation in the courts. All promotional and boxer-manager contracts in the State of New York should contain a provision

mandating that disputes to be resolved by binding arbitration before the commission.

(4) At present, the New York State Athletic Commission wastes tax-payer dollars by "regulating" professional wrestling. Indeed, Rule 216.11 of the Rules of the New York State Athletic Commission solemnly states, "Wrestlers are forbidden from indulging in the following unfair or foul tactics: striking, scratching, gouging, butting, or unnecessarily punitive strangleholds. Any unsportsmanlike or physically dangerous conduct or tactics by any wrestler during an exhibition entitles the referee to stop the exhibition and award the decision to the other wrestler."

An athletic commission that pretends to regulate professional wrestling doesn't deserve to be taken seriously.

(5) Ray Kelly and Charles DeRienzo are men of ability. But they're not "boxing people," and they have to surround themselves with people who are. That means getting rid of some of the personnel presently at the NYSAC, and replacing them with men and women who meet a higher standard. From day one of Kelly's reign, speculation has centered on James Polsinello (executive assistant to the chairman), George Mitchell (direc-tor of boxing), Ralph Petrillo (medical supervisor), and Ruby Marin (counsel to the commission) as candidates for removal. Polsinello has now been dismissed from his job effective December 5. His departure follows that of former chairman Mel Southard, Tony Russo, and Lawrence Mandelker. Others may join in the exodus.

Meanwhile, Jerry Becker and Marc Cornstein are the two NYSAC commissioners who serve with Kelly. Their terms run until 2003. Both of them owe their appointment to politics.

Becker is a former Bronx Criminal Court and Family Court judge who has been active for years in the Conservative Party. He is currently chairman of the New York State Housing Finance Agency.

Cornstein is the son of a wealthy Republican Party contributor who has given tens of thousands of dollars in campaign contributions to George Pataki. He was brought into the commission as a deputy com-missioner in 1995 when he was three years out of college. Former chief inspector Joe Dwyer speaks fondly of Cornstein and says, "He didn't know anything about boxing when he came in, but he was more willing to learn than most of the others." Cornstein is currently president of

Pinnacle Management, an agency that represents professional athletes, including several NBA players.

Becker and Cornstein are symbols of the old regime. They should resign to give Kelly a clean slate to work with and be replaced by two new commissioners who have the confidence of the boxing community in general and the fighters in particular.

Also, one final note—

When Ray Kelly was first named chairman of the New York State Athletic Commission, he was the head of security at Bear Stearns. His intention was to keep his day job and serve without salary as chairman of the NYSAC. Now Kelly is leaving Bear Stearns to become commissioner of the New York City Police Department. His plan is to oversee the NYSAC in what is essentially his spare time.

That might not be a good idea. The job of police commissioner is one of the most demanding, unrelenting, time-consuming jobs in the world. And that will be particularly true in the years ahead when New York City is expected to face a fiscal crisis at the same time many veteran cops are retiring and police resources are diverted to the battle against terrorism.

Kelly believes he can do both jobs. Insofar as the NYSAC is concerned, he says, "I'll put in as much time as necessary to do the job right."

Time will tell.

Round 5

Issues and Answers

More than two decades after his retirement from the ring, Muhammad Ali still stirs passions.

Ghosts of Manila

Albert Einstein once remarked, "Nature, to be sure, distributes her gifts unevenly among her children. But it strikes me as unfair, and even in bad taste, to select a few of them for boundless admiration, attributing superhuman powers of mind and character to them."

But society did just that with Muhammad Ali. Few people have ever received accolades equal to those that have been showered upon him. Indeed, Wilfred Sheed, who himself was skeptical of Ali's merit as a social figure, once observed that boxing's eras would be forever known as B.C. (before Clay) and A.D. (Ali Domini).

Enter Mark Kram. Kram is a very good writer. How else can one describe a man who refers to Chuck Wepner as having a face that looks as though it has been "embroidered by a tipsy church lady," and likens Joe Frazier's visage after Ali-Frazier I to "a frieze of a lab experiment that was a disaster." Kram covered boxing for *Sports Illustrated* for eleven years. Now, a quarter-century later, he has written *Ghosts of Manila: The Fateful Blood Feud Between Muhammad Ali and Joe Frazier*. The book, in the first instance, is the story of two men whose rivalry was ugly, glorious, brutal, and enthralling. And secondarily, Kram declares, "This book is intended to be a corrective to the years of stenography that have produced the Ali legend. Cheap myth coruscates the man. The wire scheme for his sculpture is too big."

Thus, Kram seeks to raise Joe Frazier to a level virtually equal to that of Ali in the ring and perhaps above him in terms of character. And in so doing, he portrays what he believes to be the dark side of Ali.

Ghosts of Manila is divided into four parts. They cover, in order, Ali and Frazier in retirement; the emergence of both men as fighters and in the public consciousness; their three fights; and the two men, again, in retirement.

Kram concedes Ali's ring greatness. "As a fighter," Kram writes, "he was the surface of a shield, unmalleable, made for mace and chain, flaring with light." Describing Ali in the ring moments before Ali-Frazier I, he acknowledges, "Whatever you might think of him, you were forced to look at him with honest lingering eyes, for there might never be his like again. Assessed by ring demands—punch, size, speed, intelligence, command, and imagination—he was an action poet, the equal of the best painting you could find."

As for Frazier, Kram calls him "the most skillful devastating inside puncher in boxing history," and goes so far as to rank him among the top five heavyweights of all time. That seems a bit silly. Joe was a great fighter and every bit as noble a warrior as Ali. But there's a time-honored axiom in boxing that styles make fights. And the list of fighters with the style to beat Joe Frazier numbers far more than five.

Kram is on more solid ground when he catalogs Frazier's hatred for Ali. The story of how Muhammad branded Joe an "Uncle Tom" before their first fight, "ignorant" before Ali-Frazier II, and a "gorilla" before Ali-Frazier III is well-known, but *Ghosts of Manila* makes it fresh and compelling. Thus, Kram writes, "Muhammad Ali swam inside Joe Frazier like a determined bacillus. . . . Ali has sat in Frazier's gut like a broken bottle." And he quotes Frazier's one-time associate Bert Watson as saying, "You don't do to a man what Ali did to Joe. Ali robbed him of who he is. To a lot of people, Joe is still ignorant, slow-speaking, dumb, and ugly. That tag never leaves him. People have only seen one Joe: the one created by Ali. If you're a man, that's going to get to you in a big way." And Kram quotes Frazier as saying of Ali, "When a man gets in your blood like that, you can't never let go. Yesterday is today for me. He never die for me . . . If we were twins in the belly of our mama, I'd reach over and strangle him . . . I'll outlive him."

Kram writes with grace and constructs his case against Ali's supervening greatness in a largely intelligent way. But his work is flawed. First, there are factual inaccuracies. For example, Kram is simply wrong when he discusses Ali's military draft reclassification and states "Had he not become a Muslim, chances are he would have remained unfit for duty." That's not the case. In truth, Ali had been declared unfit for military duty by virtue of his scoring in the sixteenth percentile on an Army intelligence test. That left him well below the requirement of thirty. But two years after that, with the war in Vietnam expanding, the mental-aptitude percentile required by the military was lowered from thirty to fifteen. The change impacted upon hundreds of thousands of young men across the country. To suggest that Ali was somehow singled out and the standard changed because of his religion is ridiculous.

Also, there are times when Kram is overly mean-spirited. For example, Bryant Gumbel (who aroused Kram's ire with negative commentary on Joe Frazier) is referred to as "a mediocre writer and thinker" with "a shallow hard-worked ultra-sophistication and ego that not even a mother could love." Ali in his current condition is labeled "a billboard in decline," of whom Kram says uncharitably, "Physical disaster of his own making has kept his fame in tact. He would have become the bore dodged at the party. The future promised that there would be no more clothes with which to dress him up." Indeed, Kram goes so far as to call the younger Ali "a useful idiot" and "near the moronic level."

Kram's failure to distinguish fully between Nation of Islam doctrine and orthodox Islamic beliefs is also troubling. During what might have been the most important fourteen years of Ali's life, he adhered to the teachings of the Nation of Islam: a doctrine that Arthur Ashe later condemned as "a racist ideology; a sort of American apartheid." Yet reading *Ghosts of Manila,* one might come away with the impression that Nation of Islam doctrine was, and still is, Islam as practiced by more than one billion people around the world today. That's because Kram has the annoying habit of referring to Ali's early mentors as "the Muslims," which is like lumping Billy Graham and the Ku Klux Klan together and calling them "the Christians."

Then there's the matter of Kram's sources—most notably, his reliance on two women named Aaisha Ali and Khaliah Ali.

Muhammad met Aaisha Ali in 1973 when he was thirty-one years old and she was a seventeen-year-old named Wanda Bolton. To his discredit, they had sexual relations and she became pregnant. Kram makes much of the fact that Wanda was "on her way to becoming a doctor." Given the fact that she was a high-school junior at the time, that's rather speculative. Regardless, Ms. Bolton subsequently claimed that she and Ali had been "Islamically married" and changed her name to Aaisha Ali.

Muhammad acknowledged paternity and accepted financial responsibility for their daughter, Khaliah.

Kram describes Aaisha several times as "a mystery woman," which is a cheap theatrical trick. Her presence in Ali's past has been known and written about for years. More significantly, Kram uses Aaisha and Khaliah as his primary sources to trash Ali's current wife Lonnie (who Kram calls Ali's "new boss"). Indeed, after describing Ali as "a careless fighter who had his brain cells irradiated," Kram quotes Lonnie as telling Khaliah, "I am Muhammad Ali now." Then, after referring to "Lonnie and her tight circle of pushers," he quotes Khaliah as saying of her father, "It's about money. He's a substance; an item." And after that, Kram recounts a scene when Ali and Lonnie were in a Louisville hospital visiting Ali's mother, who was being kept live on a respirator. The final days of Odessa Clay's life were the saddest ever for Ali. Yet again, relying wholly on Khaliah, Kram quotes Lonnie as saying, "We can't afford this, Muhammad."

The problem is, there are a lot of people who think that Aaisha Ali and Khaliah Ali aren't particularly reliable sources. I happen to have been present at one of the incidents regarding which Kram quotes Khaliah. It involved a championship belt that was given to Ali at a dinner commemorating the twentieth anniversary of the first Ali-Frazier fight. The dinner took place on the night of April 14, 1991, although Kram mistakenly reports it as occurring on an unspecified date five years later. Khaliah left Ali's hotel room that night with the belt. I experienced the incident very differently from the way Kram recounts it.

However, my biggest concern regarding *Ghosts of Manila* is its thesis that Ali's influence lay entirely in the sporting arena. Kram acknowledges that Ali "did lead the way for black athletes out of the frustrating silence that Jackie Robinson had to endure." However, even that concession is tempered by the claim that, "Ali's influence in games today can be seen in the blaring unending marketing of self, the cheap acting out of performers, and the crassness of player interactions. His was an overwhelming presence that, if you care about such things, came at a high cost."

And then Kram goes on to say, "What was laughable, if you knew anything about Ali at all, was that the literati was certain that he was a serious voice, that he knew what he was doing. He didn't have a clue . . .

Seldom has a public figure of such superficial depth been more wrongly perceived."

"Ali," Kram says flatly, "was not a social force." And woe to those who say he was, because their utterances are dismissed as "heavy breathing" from "know-nothings" and "trendy tasters of faux revolution."

Apparently, I'm one of those heavy breathers. Kram refers to me as "a lawyer-Boswell who seems intent of making the public believe that, next to Martin Luther King, Ali is the most important black figure in the last half century." And in case anyone misses his point, Kram adds, "Current hagiographers have tied themselves in knots trying to elevate Ali into a heroic defiant catalyst of the antiwar movement, a beacon of black independence. It's a legacy that evolves from the intellectually loose sixties, from those who were in school then and now write romance history."

Actually, Kram has misquoted me. I believe he's referring to a statement in *Muhammad Ali: His Life and Times* in which I wrote, "With the exception of Martin Luther King, no black man in America had more influence than Ali during the years when Ali was in his prime." I still believe that to be true.

Was Ali as important as Nelson Mandela? No. Was Ali in the late-1960s more important than any other black person in America except for Dr. King? I believe so. Indeed, Nelson Mandela himself said recently, "Ali's refusal to go to Vietnam and the reasons he gave made him an international hero. The news could not be shut out even by prison walls. He became a real legend to us in prison."

Kram's remarkable gift for words notwithstanding, Muhammad Ali in the 1960s stood as a beacon of hope for oppressed people all over the world. Every time he looked in the mirror and uttered the phrase, "I'm so pretty," he was saying "black is beautiful" before it became fashionable. When he refused induction into the United States Army, regardless of his motives, he stood up to armies around the globe in support of the proposition that, unless you have a very good reason for killing people, war is wrong.

Dick Gregory once said, "If you wanted to do a movie to depict Ali, it would just be a small light getting bigger and bigger and bigger and bigger. That was Ali in a sea of darkness." One can imagine Kram gagging at imagery like that. But the truth is, Muhammad Ali found his way into the world's psyche.

Perhaps Reggie Jackson put it in perspective best. "Do you have any idea what Ali meant to black people?" Jackson told me once. "He was the leader of a nation, the leader of black America. As a young black, at times I was ashamed of my color; I was ashamed of my hair. And Ali made me proud. I'm just as happy being black now as somebody else is being white, and Ali was part of that growing process. Think about it! Do you understand what it did for black Americans to know that the most physically gifted, possibly the most handsome, and one of the most charismatic men in the world was black. Ali helped raise black people in this country out of mental slavery. The entire experience of being black changed for millions of people because of Ali."

In sum, Muhammad Ali might not have meant much to Mark Kram. But he meant a great deal to a lot of people. He made an enormous difference.

*Midway through 2001, one of boxing's time-honored axioms was under
siege.*

Fathers and Sons

It's often said that trainers are father figures. Still, conventional wisdom has long been that it's not a good idea for a father to train his own son. In the past, there have been boxers who were guided in the ring by their father. Wilfred Benitez, Sean O'Grady, Marvis Frazier, Billy Collins, Darrin Van Horn, Tony Ayala, and the Hilton brothers come to mind.

But there are a lot of casualties on that list. Tony Ayala and the Hiltons wound up in trouble with the law. Billy Collins became an alcoholic and died in a car crash. Wilfred Benitez suffered severe brain damage. And no less an authority than Eddie Futch declares, "I experienced some very sad situations where a father trained his son but was not qualified to take his son to the peak of his abilities and the son suffered as a result."

Thus, it's quite remarkable that the four fighters heading most pound-for-pound lists today—Shane Mosley, Roy Jones Jr., Felix Trinidad, and Floyd Mayweather Jr.—have all been trained in significant measure by their fathers. And so has Zab Judah, who's in the thick of most pound-for-pound rankings.

What's going on?

"It's a dream of many fathers to train their son," explains Emanuel Steward. "I see it in my own gym all the time these days. One success story leads others to try, and we have a lot of fathers now trying to live through their sons. I'm not saying that's the way it is with all fathers. But at best, it's a delicate situation."

The first potential problem faced by a father who serves as his son's trainer is that the father assumes dual roles that aren't always compatible.

"It's tough to be both the man of the house and the man of the gym," says Angelo Dundee. "It's two different situations and, if you try to do both at the same time, one or both roles is going to suffer."

"You can't be a father training your son," adds Lou Duva. "You have to be a trainer training your son, and that's very hard to do. There are so many conflicts. The boy meets a girl. You tell him one thing as a father and another as a trainer. He wants to quit boxing. You tell him one thing as a father and another as a trainer."

"You're put in a situation where you're teaching a young man how to live and teaching a young man how to fight," concludes Eddie Futch. "Sometimes they're the same thing, but sometimes they're not."

Also, if a father is a responsible father, he's on top of his son enough at home without adding to it in the gym. When a son is trained by his father, there's precious little room to breathe. Thus, Gil Clancy opines, "If the father is in the gym and the father is at home, the kid can never get away from boxing. Kids need a break. But if you're training your own son, it's, 'Go to school . . . Keep your left hand high . . . Clean up your room . . . Left foot forward . . . Don't eat that candy . . . Hook off the jab.' The same voice is grinding away, grinding away, telling you what to do all the time, every day from the day you were born."

Moreover, as Emanuel Steward notes, "A kid has to grow up and go out in the world on his own. But too often, when a father trains his son, he doesn't realize that the son has become a man and should be treated as an adult. Instead, the father tries to maintain control. And when the son rebels outside the ring, which sooner or later all sons do, he's likely to rebel inside the ring, too."

Eddie Futch comments further on the issue of control and recalls, "Whenever I began a relationship with a young man as his trainer, at the very start, I'd tell him, 'If you can't follow my instructions completely, I don't want to be involved.' But that's not the way the relationship between a father and his son works. There comes a time when a young man doesn't do everything his father tells him to do."

In other words, it's a combustible situation, one fraught with even more problems if a father works his son's corner during a fight, as virtually all trainers do.

"What does a father do when he sees his son getting beaten up?" asks Gil Clancy. "I know, I couldn't control my emotions, and I think that's true of most fathers."

"Let's say you're at home and your son falls and whacks his head against the edge of a table," posits Angelo Dundee. "He's cut bad over the eye or his lip is split open. You don't look at him and say, 'It's nothing; two more rounds and this will be over.' Believe me, I know. My son was in a car accident last year. Thank God, he's all right, but there was some bleeding. I saw him after the accident, and I almost fainted."

In other words, in some situations, a father is likely to think like a father and stop a fight too soon. But the converse can also be true.

"It's very difficult for a father to be objective about the course of a fight," says Teddy Atlas. "And sometimes, the father has a totally unrealistic view of his son's skills and recuperative powers."

That concern rings particularly true to Eddie Futch, who recalls, "I've seen situations where a father wanted his son to continue in a fight when the son was hopelessly outclassed and in danger of being badly hurt. In fact, I remember a fight in the mid-1940s when I was living in Detroit. A young man was actually knocked out, but the bell rang at eight and he was saved by the bell. The young man's father was there. Two of his brothers were in the young man's corner. The referee wanted to stop the fight, but the fighter's brothers dragged him back to the corner and the whole family was arguing with the referee and finally the referee agreed to let the young man continue, even though there was no way he could properly defend himself. He died in the ring that night."

There's also the issue of money. "When a fighter turns pro," observes Emanuel Steward, "there's money to be made; particularly if the fighter is good. That means, to some fathers, their son is their financial future." Lou Duva concurs, adding, "Some fathers want to capitalize on their sons. You turn around, and all of a sudden they're the trainer and the manager, living off the kid, and their thinking becomes distorted."

Still, even with all of the above caveats, there are five major success stories in boxing today, five superstars who have been trained by their fathers.

How did it happen?

For starters, the best fighters start young. Usually, when a father trains his son, they've started early and the fighter has had a long amateur career, which is an advantage. Then too, world-class boxers are superb athletes. And a father's involvement might give an adolescent the motivation to continue with boxing in a situation where he might otherwise turn his talents to another sport.

Also, a trainer has to know what makes his fighter tick in order to do his job properly. And more than the average trainer, a father is likely to know his son.

Don Turner adds to the reasons for success with the thought, "When a father trains his son, it breeds a certain kind honesty. The father doesn't go along just to get along, especially when the fighter is young." But Bobby Miles, who has worked with Turner for years, adds a cautionary note. "These relationships are more likely to work at the beginning than the end," says Miles. "Look at Roy Jones Jr. Early on, the father can use the fact that he's the father to press his point. But sooner or later, you're likely to reach that stage where the son says, 'You may be my father, but I'm a man.'"

Thus, the question: "Will the sudden explosion of father-and-son success stories continue? Do Shane Mosley, Roy Jones Jr., Felix Trinidad, Floyd Mayweather Jr., and Zab Judah represent a trend, or are they simply the product of coincidence?"

Eddie Futch opts for the latter interpretation, stating, "I'd have to see a lot more success stories before I believe that a father training his son is good. I think that what we're witnessing now is a freak occurrence." Emanuel Steward agrees with Futch and adds, "What we're seeing at the moment is an aberration. The success ratio over time won't be what it is now." And Gil Clancy concurs, noting, "I have no idea why you have all these success stories today. It's very strange. Guys like Jack Mosley and Papa Trinidad and Yoel Judah are doing a terrific job with their sons. But look at your history; go back fifty years. You've got a handful of situations that are working now against hundreds, maybe thousands, that have failed."

Also, it's worth remembering that, at the end of the day, the trainer doesn't have as much to do with the development of a fighter as the fighter himself. Lou Duva makes that point, when he declares, "These guys like Roy Jones Jr., Felix Trinidad, and Shane Mosley would have been exceptional fighters no matter who trained them. That's not taking anything away from their fathers. I'd let Jack Mosley or Felix Trinidad Sr. train my son anytime. But the fighter makes the trainer; not the other way around."

And Teddy Atlas sounds a final warning. "If you're a good trainer, you're a good trainer," says Atlas. "But I see a problem here for the future because a lot of fathers who have no idea what they're doing are going to start training their sons. That couldn't happen in another sport once you get to the professional level. Shaquille O'Neal's father can't coach the Los Angeles Lakers. Derek Jeter's father can't manage the New York Yankees. But boxing doesn't require apprenticeships or standards at any level. And you have to remember, people only hear about the fathers whose sons have relatively successful careers in boxing. We never hear about the thousands of fathers who try to turn their sons into fighters and fail."

I got a lot of negative feedback from the powers that be at HBO after this article appeared. But I still think it was fair and responsible journalism.

What's Going On at HBO?

For well over a decade, HBO has been synonymous with the best in boxing. Its first fight took place more than a quarter-century ago, on January 22, 1973, when George Foreman KO'd Joe Frazier in Kingston, Jamaica. Since then, the network has telecast 426 bouts. Roy Jones leads the pack with twenty-two appearances. Oscar De La Hoya will equal that total when he fights Arturo Gatti on March 24. Lennox Lewis and Pernell Whitaker have nineteen each. To put the growth of boxing on HBO in context, in the first ten years of its existence, the network televised an average of four fights per year. By contrast, in the year 2000, HBO telecast fifty fights on twenty-eight dates. And none of these totals include non-featured undercard bouts on pay-per-view shows. That's an impressive record. Recently, though, there have been rumblings.

Rumbling #1 stems from the fact that, over the past year, HBO's ratings for boxing have fallen significantly. In and of itself, that's not cause for alarm. Due to the internet and the ever-increasing number of cable channels, ratings have fallen for all individual networks. Indeed, since 1997, post-season ratings have dropped ten percent for the NFL, 28 percent for Major League Baseball, and 29 percent for the NBA. But while HBO's ratings have been falling, Showtime's numbers for boxing have been rising. In the case of Showtime, that's because Showtime ended its exclusive programming contract with Don King, signed some quality fighters to long-term contracts, and increased the amount it pays for fights. And it might also be that HBO is getting a bit stale. People expect more of HBO than they do of Showtime. HBO is in 25 million homes. Showtime is in 12 million. That's an enormous edge. Still, if one listens hard at HBO, footsteps are audible. Showtime broadcast twenty-two fight cards last year. And with the addition of twenty-six biweekly Saturday afternoon *ShoBox* events beginning this summer, it will have more boxing on television than HBO. Also, while Showtime is a lot smaller than HBO, Showtime is a subsidiary of Viacom, which also owns CBS, BET, and TNN. That offers some interesting possibilities for vertical integration and means HBO can be expected to lose more ground to Showtime in the near future if Showtime is aggressive about it.

Rumbling #2 revolves around the failure of *KO Nation*. The idea behind *KO Nation* was to put boxing, hip-hop, and dancing girls together and aim it at a young audience. Maybe MTV could have pulled it off. HBO didn't. *KO Nation* is the equivalent of airline food. It's virtually unwatchable.

Rumbling #3 concerns Oscar De La Hoya. After the "Golden Boy" beat Bob Arum in a California court, the first communication that HBO received from Team De La Hoya was, "We want to fight on March 24 against Arturo Gatti." HBO said fine, as long as it had assurances that the rest of its long-term contract would be fulfilled. Oscar balked, and HBO went to court. On February 15, a federal judge refused HBO's request for an injunction that would have precluded De La Hoya from fighting outside the parameters of his HBO contract. De La Hoya and HBO now have an agreement for HBO to televise Oscar's March 24 fight against Gatti, but the overall litigation goes on. De La Hoya is the bulwark of TVKO, which handles HBO's pay-per-view telecasts. If HBO ultimately loses its case on the merits, TVKO will take a hit.

Rumbling #4 involves the heavyweights. Famed matchmaker Teddy Brenner once opined, "There's boxing, and there's heavyweight boxing." The corollary to that is, "There's heavyweight boxing, and then there's the heavyweight championship of the world." On May 20, 1985, Larry Holmes defended his heavyweight title against Carl Williams in a bout that was broadcast on NBC. For the next five-and-a-half years—until October 25, 1990, when James "Buster" Douglas lost to Evander Holyfield—every single heavyweight championship fight was televised by HBO. That's twenty-one fights, an extraordinary streak by any standard. If Lewis retires, the heavyweight championship will be up for grabs. And if he loses to Mike Tyson . . . Ouch!

Rumbling #5 is "The Roy Jones Problem." The way HBO's relationship with Jones has played out has to be a huge disappointment to the network. Last year, a new leadership team replaced a very successful old leadership team at HBO Sports. Jones had been an important part of boxing at HBO in the past. Given the uncertainty surrounding Oscar De La Hoya and Floyd Mayweather Jr., the new team was under pressure to show that it was on top of things. Thus, it threw a lot of money at a great fighter. But Roy Jones has yet to prove that he's a commercial superstar. He hasn't fought an opponent who's a challenge or a major attraction for a long time. And realistically, he had no viable options other than re-signing with HBO. What was Jones going to do? Finance a pay-per-view fight against Derrick Harmon out of his own pocket like he did against Eric Harding? How much revenue would Roy Jones versus Derrick Harmon have generated without HBO? Meanwhile, it doesn't take a rocket scientist to know that HBO would have preferred not to couple Jones's re-signing with a bout against Harmon. And Derrick "Smoke" Gainer, who often comes packaged with Jones, rarely gives what boxing fans think of as an HBO-quality performance.

Meanwhile, all of the above are playing out against the backdrop of the aforementioned turnover in senior management. It starts at the top, where Ross Greenburg has replaced Seth Abraham as president of HBO Sports. Abraham was adept at corporate politics. He had a great sense of how to work the media. And he was a forceful advocate for boxing within Time Warner. Greenburg is a great producer and an HBO Sports guy to the core. He's capable and creative. Under his aegis, HBO pioneered the high-quality production of boxing in a manner that by comparison made all other boxing productions look low-rent. But Greenburg doesn't know the sport of boxing, the business of boxing, or the players in boxing the way Abraham did. Nor is he expected to be as strong an internal advocate for the sweet science. Boxing might well be just another sport to him; something to be thrown into the mix along with *Reel Sports, On the Record, Inside the NFL,* and *Sports of the 20th Century.* And the sensitivity that served Greenburg so well as a producer, particularly of documentaries, is of less value in his present job.

The second major personnel change at HBO Sports has been the departure of Lou DiBella and his replacement as senior vice president by Kery Davis. As far as the outside world was concerned, DiBella essentially ran HBO Boxing for Abraham on a day-to-day basis. He was proactive when it came to the sport. He loved the fight world. He understood, cared about, and subordinated his life to boxing. He also operated in a very personal way with everyone from the media to the fighters themselves. DiBella constantly bounced ideas off people and solicited their advice. He fought to change HBO from a network that showcased its stars in mismatches in order to groom them for pay-per-view events to a network that put fighters in tough and stood by them when they lost as long as they lost with honor. He championed the lighter-weight fighters—a commitment that's paying dividends now in the form of Naseem Hamed, Erik Morales, and Marco Antonio Barrera. And he was up front with his feelings about corruption in the sport. To a degree, his passion for cleaning up the sweet science inoculated HBO against some of boxing's broader scandals. But DiBella also ruffled feathers in-house. There were times when he upstaged some of his compatriots and neutered others. Because boxing at HBO was enormously successful under his watch, the powers-that-be gave him wide latitude. But now that DiBella is gone, there appears to be a new attitude at HBO. Some call it "a restoration of corporate order."

Kery Davis, an attorney and DiBella protege, is the new "boxing guy" at HBO. Davis comes out of the music business and appears to lack DiBella's passion for and knowledge of the sport. Whenever there was a TVKO fight in Las Vegas on a Saturday, DiBella was likely to be in attendance at the ESPN2 card the night before. Kery is more likely to be enjoying a leisurely dinner. Davis may well grow into his role. But right now, he doesn't have the personal rapport with fighters, managers, and the media that DiBella enjoyed. Part of that revolves around personalities. And part of it is the perception that Davis is less willing than DiBella was to take into account the needs of fighters. More to the point, Davis is considered far more "promoter friendly" than DiBella. By and large, DiBella scorned promoters and had no compunction about going around them to deal directly with managers and fighters. Davis is far less likely to do so.

Mark Taffet is still in place as the go-to guy with regard to pay-per-view, and his title has been upgraded to Senior Vice President, HBO Sports. Taffet spent the first half of his career at HBO in financial planning. His introduction to sports came in 1991, when Seth Abraham

needed someone with financial expertise to explore the possibility of
HBO Sports making an offer for National Football League rights. Taffet
was the guy, and Abraham was impressed with his work. Meanwhile, boxing was just beginning to evolve from closed-circuit to pay-per-view, and
Taffet's next assignment was to prepare a business model for the entity
that would ultimately become TVKO. Once TVKO was formed, its first
two employees were Taffet and DiBella (who Abraham brought in from
HBO's legal department).

Kery Davis's old position at HBO has been filled by Xavier James,
who's a capable attorney but not a boxing guy. Rick Bernstein has moved
into Ross Greenburg's old slot as executive producer of HBO Sports.
Barbara Thomas (the chief financial officer for HBO Sports) is more of
a factor now than in the past. That's because the division is currently operating under stricter financial constraints than was the case several years
ago. To a degree, Thomas has been willing to move allocated funds from
one month to another and from one boxing presentation to another—
e.g. from *HBO Championship Boxing* to *Boxing After Dark*. But HBO
Sports no longer has the checkbook to make every fight it wants happen, and there's a stricter adherence to budgets than in the past.

Still, HBO has been and is continuing to give boxing fans some very
good fights. It expects to televise thirty-four cards this year: six on pay-
per-view, twelve on *HBO Championship Boxing,* ten on *Boxing After Dark,*
and six on *KO Nation.* That includes confrontations like Mayweather-
Corrales, Hamed-Barrera, and the hoped-for middleweight championship
tournament. If Roy Jones wants to fight the tough fights, HBO will
bankroll them. And no matter what happens, the network has pockets
deep enough to buy its way out of trouble.

HBO still has the biggest checkbook in boxing, and that checkbook
is its most reliable insurance. As things stand now, for each *KO Nation*
show, the network pays a license fee of $200,000 to $300,000 plus production and marketing costs. For *Boxing After Dark,* the license fee is
$750,000 to $1,000,000. And for *HBO Championship Boxing,* it ranges
from $1,500,000 to $5,000,000. The days when HBO Sports was able to
say, "We're going to get what we want at any cost," might be over. But
there are people in the corporate hierarchy above Ross Greenburg who
weren't particularly fond of Seth Abraham or Lou DiBella. And in all like-

lihood, those people will stretch the checkbook a bit further if necessary to make certain that Greenburg's reign is a success.

All of this suggests then, not that boxing at HBO is in trouble, but that it's at a crossroads. There's an axiom in the sweet science that, if a fighter isn't getting better, he's getting worse. And the same might be said of those who televise fights. To a degree, HBO is living off the goodwill that attaches to the HBO brand. There are times when it appears to be in a maintain-the-status-quo mode. And because HBO sets the standard, if it gets sloppy it will allow everyone else's standards to drop. Thus, if boxing at HBO is at a crossroads, so is the sport.

So what happens next?

The truth is, as far as HBO is concerned, it's about branding and marketing. HBO is star driven. That's true of its concerts (from Barbra Streisand to Garth Brooks). It's true of its original movies. And it's true of boxing. In other words, boxing is basically an ongoing series on HBO, like *Sex and the City* or *The Sopranos*. And like any series, it requires familiar faces and interesting foes to build a viewer base. Viewers follow their favorite fighters and wait for the next episode. At present, HBO boxing has eight "stars": Lennox Lewis, Oscar De La Hoya, Roy Jones Jr., Felix Trinidad, Shane Mosley, Naseem Hamed, Floyd Mayweather Jr., and Fernando Vargas. These are the fighters it has signed to long-term contracts. That means the bottom two tiers in HBO's boxing programming have to feed the top two tiers in a direct and purposeful way.

Taking HBO's four boxing programs one at a time, it makes sense to start with *KO Nation*. The people at HBO like to describe *KO Nation* as "a work in progress." The role formerly played by Ed Lover has been eliminated, and HBO is currently auditioning announcers for fighter introductions. Fran Charles and Kevin Kelley are still in place. A live music act is now closing out each show. But *KO Nation,* particularly in its new late-night time slot, sends a confusing message to the public regarding the quality of HBO's telecasts. And while its new time might gain *KO Nation* some spillover fans from *Boxing After Dark,* it also might pollute *Boxing After Dark.* "BAD" made its reputation through a series of great matchups between hungry fighters. It wouldn't necessarily be bad for HBO, or for the viewing public, if *KO Nation* were to disappear and be replaced by an additional six "episodes" of *Boxing After Dark.*

HBO Championship Boxing needs fewer fights that showcase top talent against inferior opponents and more fights that put top fighters in competitive bouts. This is where long-term contracts become a problem. These contracts give HBO continuity, but they can also become a disincentive to push tough fights because (1) everyone wants to get to the end of the contract unscathed; (2) HBO has to satisfy its contractual relationship with each fighter; and (3) most fighters want the easiest fights for the most money.

As for TVKO, the simple reality is that pay-per-view fights are getting harder and harder to market. In part, that's because ubiquitous "black boxes" now reduce gross receipts by up to 50 percent. And in part, it's because there are fewer fighters with genuine crossover appeal. In the 1970s and 1980s, Muhammad Ali, George Foreman, Joe Frazier, Sugar Ray Leonard, Thomas Hearns, Roberto Duran, Marvin Hagler, Larry Holmes, and Mike Tyson all fought on network television, which enhanced their marketability to the general public. Boxing lost a valuable promotional tool when good fights on free network television became virtually non-existent. Still, certain fighters in certain fights can make the most money on pay-per-view. And TVKO is crucial to HBO in that it allows HBO to sign the best fighters in the world to long-term contracts with the promise that they will get *HBO Championship Boxing* exposure followed by megafights on TVKO.

Meanwhile, it's worth remembering that, as far as the parent corporation is concerned, this is all about money. Boxing is just one component of the HBO empire. It's a programming tool, a piece in a larger puzzle. *HBO Championship Boxing, Boxing After Dark,* and *KO Nation* sell subscriptions to viewers. TVKO brings in pay-per-view dollars directly on a show-by-show basis. That means, what's good for boxing at HBO isn't necessarily good for HBO Sports or HBO as a whole. And vice versa. Right now, there's a special bond between professional boxing and cable television in general. And as far as HBO Sports is concerned, its franchise is boxing. Virtually every survey indicates that the sweet science is a major reason why subscribers buy and retain HBO. But if circumstances change, boxing at HBO could conceivably go the way of boxing at Caesar's Palace. It's about the bottom line; that's all.

As HBO entered the post–Seth Abraham era, the original architect of its boxing strategy was making waves at Madison Square Garden.

Seth Abraham and Madison Square Garden Boxing

Last autumn, Seth Abraham left his position as president and chief executive officer of Time Warner Sports to become executive vice president and chief operating officer of Madison Square Garden. The move sent shock waves through the boxing industry. Abraham had developed and managed all sports strategies at HBO, but the sweet science had been his signature sport. Under his leadership, Time Warner Sports had become the most powerful force in boxing.

Thus, the question upon Abraham's arrival at MSG was, "Would Madison Square Garden once again become the Mecca of Boxing?"

Six months later, the answer is, "Not quite." But under Abraham's guidance, boxing is assuming a higher profile. And that's a welcome change from the last quarter of the twentieth century, when boxing at MSG fell on hard times.

Actually, the Garden's current boxing revival began in 1995. Since then, twelve fight cards have taken place in the main arena, ten in the Theater, and one at Radio City Music Hall. Now a new team is readying to take MSG boxing to the next level. It starts at the top.

There are three people above Abraham on the corporate totem pole: Charles Dolan (the chairman of Cablevision, which is MSG's parent company), James Dolan (Cablevision's chief executive officer), and Dave Checketts (president and CEO of Madison Square Garden). All three are fight fans. That's important because, as Abraham notes, "Great ideas are only pipe dreams unless someone gives you a checkbook. You can have wonderful plans, but they're only as good as the money you have to back them up."

The fifth member of the team is Kevin Wynne (vice president, MSG

Sports Properties). Abraham credits Wynne with being the architect of MSG's current middleweight championship series and adds, "What we do here is very different from what I did at HBO. There's a difference between a good TV fight and one that puts people in the arena. Here, the crucial factor isn't electronic rights. It's the value of a fight to a building and knowing the optimum ticket price in a situation where you have limited seating capacity. Kevin knows that. And overall, Kevin is very good, which is why I can get by with spending only about 5 percent of my time on boxing."

Wynne, for his part, now feels he has someone directly above him "who understands boxing, supports boxing, and lives in that world." And the team was able to hit the ground running, because Abraham had dealt extensively with Checketts and Wynne during his tenure at HBO. Meanwhile, Abraham plans on following the same type of blueprint at MSG that he followed at HBO; that is, presenting fights as part of an ongoing drama.

To put things in perspective, last year Garden properties hosted four major fights. Roy Jones Jr. fought David Telesco at Radio City Music Hall and Shane Mosley battled Antonio Diaz at the Theater. In addition, Oscar De La Hoya fought Derrell Coley and Lennox Lewis met Michael Grant, the latter two cards taking place in the main arena. These fights were significant in that MSG turned a profit on each of them. They proved the Garden could pay large site fees and still make money, which gave boxing added credibility with Cablevision. But in many respects, these fights were isolated events. By contrast, the first fight card held at the Garden this year featured six Olympians making their professional debuts, and Abraham hopes to showcase those fighters live at the Garden and on MSG network as their careers progress. The keys to his thinking are continuity and drama. The Garden's current middleweight championship series represents the next rung up on the ladder.

"We asked ourselves who was the best fighter we could have in a big fight at the Garden," says Abraham. "And the answer we came up with was Felix Trinidad. Then we went about constructing a story-line that would make Felix's next fight here more important and even more compelling than his fights had been in the past. Casinos do fights just to do fights. We wanted drama. The middleweights were once boxing's glamour division. We decided that we'd try to crown the first unified middleweight champion since Marvin Hagler."

Abraham is a student of history. He's fond of reminding people that, while there were only three middleweight championship bouts at MSG in the thirty-three years prior to the present tournament, there were twenty-seven earlier world middleweight title fights at the Garden. Harry Greb, Tony Zale, Jake LaMotta, Gene Fullmer, Dick Tiger, Emile Griffith, Carlos Monzon, and Marvin Hagler are among the great middleweights who fought in title fights at MSG. So was Sugar Ray Robinson. Indeed, on October 4, 1940, Robinson made his professional debut at the Garden. Abraham hopes that the ghost of Sugar Ray hovers over the current "middleweight world championship series."

The series began on April 14, with Bernard Hopkins versus Keith Holmes at the Theatre. In truth, it was a less-than-enthralling bout. Holmes came to win a boxing match, while Hopkins came to win a fight.

"I can't dance by myself," Hopkins had said earlier in the week. "Boxing is a two-man sport. I can't get the recognition I want when my opponent runs around and holds and cries."

Unfortunately, for most of the evening, Holmes ran around and held and cried. Hopkins was the aggressor throughout. It wasn't pretty, but he got the job done. On occasion, his punches strayed low and, from time to time, he led with his head. But over time, he wore Holmes down with a determined assault. On those few occasions when Holmes chose to trade, Hopkins traded with him and Holmes pulled out. By round eight, Holmes was fighting like a man just trying to survive. His game plan seemed to be, hold and complain and hope that the referee disqualified Hopkins for a low blow. Except for the point that Steve Smoger took away from Hopkins in round five, one could argue that it was a shutout.

But the truth is, Abraham's philosophy worked. Hopkins-Holmes was compelling drama thanks to the promise of what comes next. On May 12, Felix Trinidad will face off against William Joppy with a strong undercard in the main arena. That fight could well be a sellout. Then, barring injury, Hopkins will face the winner at Madison Square Garden on September 15.

One thing about fighting Bernard Hopkins is, you know you're in for a fight. The same is true of Felix Trinidad. Should the two men meet, Trinidad-Hopkins has "Fight of the Year" written all over it.

And after that, Abraham hopes to match the winner of his middleweight championship series against Roy Jones Jr.

"The big prize for us would Felix fighting Roy," Abraham acknowledges. "That's not meant to disrespect the other fighters involved in the championship series. It's a statement of simple economic reality."

And how confident is Abraham that Jones will be willing to fight Trinidad if Felix emerges triumphant?

"I think Roy will have a very difficult time not fighting Felix if Felix wins the tournament," Abraham answers. "If somebody else wins, the public pressure on Roy will be less. But with all due respect to Shane Mosley, the winner of a Jones-Trinidad fight would be almost universally recognized as boxing's pound-for-pound champion. If Roy were to refuse that fight, it would define his career more than any fight he ever won. He'd be remembered forever as the light-heavyweight who wouldn't fight a welterweight who was willing to go up to 168 pounds to meet him."

The middleweight championship series represents the largest financial commitment that Cablevision has ever made to boxing. If it runs its course with a Trinidad-Jones finale, best indications are that the Garden will pay Don King between $18 and $19 million in exchange for the live gate for the four bouts.

As for the future, Abraham says that the Garden is not presently planning to promote its own fights. Rather, it will continue to buy rights to the live gate from promoters or simply rent out the arena, but not on a regular basis.

"We don't plan on monthly shows," explains Abraham. "And the reality of the situation is that boxing at Madison Square Garden has to live within the confines of certain dates. At HBO, boxing was *the* sports franchise and, along with uncut movies and *The Sopranos,* one of three keys to success. At HBO, everything was movable for boxing. Schedules at HBO were torn up for boxing. But at the Garden, boxing is a smaller part of what we do. We have the Knicks, the Rangers, the circus, the annual Christmas Show; and a lot of that is immovable. I can't just pick up the phone at the Garden and say, 'We're planning a fight; could you move next month's Knicks game against Charlotte to Tuesday night?'"

"We intend to be in the boxing business, not the one-big-fight-a-year business," Abraham continues. "We're not tied to a given number of shows per year. The key is, we want quality, not quantity. We want to match A-list fighters against A-list fighters. If the middleweights go well for us, then 2001 will have been a good year. Then, maybe next year, we'll have a unification series in another weight class. Kosta Tszyu versus Zab Judah would appeal to us. So would a junior-lightweight unification series. We're interested in promoting speculation as to who will be the next great fighter to fight at Radio City Music Hall. It might be that we won't do more than three or four shows some years. But they'll be quality fights that lead to something. Less is more if you have the right less. We will be an ongoing presence in boxing."

It's to Abraham's credit that, after all the money he made and all the success he had at HBO, he's starting over again with a new challenge. Most likely, he'll succeed. Even his most ardent critics concede that, in many respects, the man is a visionary. Long ago, he saw the opportunity to take what was then a relatively small cable-TV company and make it a major force in boxing. Now he has the MSG name, three sites in Manhattan, enormous financial backing, MSG's cable network, and the attention of the media to work with. Those are pretty good ingredients for success. And Abraham himself acknowledges, "Right now, to corporate America, boxing is a rogue sport. There are only three blue-chip companies that are heavily committed to boxing: AOL-Time Warner, Viacom, and Anheuser-Busch. I think that Cablevision will be joining that group."

Meanwhile, if one is looking for an omen, it should be noted that HBO's first major commitment to boxing was a three-fight deal in 1981 with the last undisputed middleweight champion of the world, Marvelous Marvin Hagler.

Generally, I let negative things that are written about me pass without comment. On occasion, I learn from them. But there are times when enough is enough.

Enough Already!

I think Ron Borges is a good writer. I agree with a lot of what he has to say about professional boxing. But Ron is having trouble accepting the fact that Roy Jones Jr. was named "Fighter of the Decade" by the Boxing Writers Association of America a full year ago. Obviously, it sticks in Ron's craw because, a year after the fact, he keeps writing about it.

Ron's first comment on the subject appeared last March in the *Boston Globe.* He reported—and I quote: "The Boxing Writers Association of America originally named Evander Holyfield its fighter of the decade, but a second vote was demanded by Thomas Hauser, Muhammad Ali's biographer and an admirer of Roy Jones Jr.'s. Somehow, Jones nosed out Holyfield, 6-4, by a vote of the association's executive committee. I'm on that committee, but don't ask me how it happened."

Then Ron took his crusade to the HBO Boxing website, where he said essentially the same thing. That was followed by a third broadside, in which Ron declared, "Let us straighten out for all time the issue of how Roy Jones Jr. became the Boxing Writers Association's fighter of the decade. As a member of the executive board, I was polled by BWAA president Chris Thorne, who favored Evander Holyfield. I agreed and was later told Holyfield got the belt. I assumed other members had also been polled. Later, Tom Hauser—Ali's biographer and Jones's longtime supporter—apparently disagreed, and asked for a full vote. This supposedly took place, although no one called me for a second vote and Hauser says the first vote never happened, so I guess no one's formally voted yet . . . We apparently have two lobbying factions, two votes (or none) and a situation that seems a lot like the type of thing we criticize the alphabet groups for all the time."

After that, there was silence until this past week. Then Ron felt compelled to declare, "A year ago, some kind but wrong-thinking boxing writers led a revolt when the Writers Association wanted to name Evander Holyfield "fighter of the decade." At least one had a close relationship with Jones, and he led a campaign that got Jones enough votes to win that prize . . . It was a Florida election if there ever was one, just like the Bush-Gore one."

Like the rest of us, Ron has the right to complain as much as he wants. I just wish he wouldn't keep misstating the facts.

These are the facts.

In March 2000, Tom Kenville (secretary-treasurer of the BWAA) told me that Chris Thorne (president of the BWAA) had decided to give Evander Holyfield an award for being the "Fighter of the Decade." I'm a vice president of the organization. Since I hadn't been told about the award, I called Chris to ask what was going on. He said that he had "talked with a couple of the guys" who thought it was a good idea. I asked which guys. Chris then acknowledged that he had consulted with "only two or three" people and that one of them had supported Roy Jones Jr. I then suggested to Chris that he take a formal vote. He said there wasn't enough time to mail ballots to all of the writers in the BWAA because the awards banquet was fast approaching. But he agreed to poll the remaining members of the organization's executive committee. Jones outpolled Evander six to four. Ron's vote, like that of everyone else on the executive committee, was counted. There was only one vote.

There were three strong candidates in the 1990s for the honor of "Fighter of the Decade"—Evander Holyfield, Pernell Whitaker, and Roy Jones Jr.

Holyfield had a record of thirteen wins, four losses, and one draw with six knockouts in the '90s. Over the course of the decade, he captured the heavyweight championship three times, defeated Riddick Bowe in their classic second fight, won a glorious victory and an ugly disqualification over Mike Tyson, and fought (but failed to win either of) two closely-contested bouts against Lennox Lewis.

Whitaker had twenty-four fights during the same period and won all of them, except for a scandalous draw against Julio Cesar Chavez, a disputed-decision loss to Oscar De La Hoya, and lesser performances against Andrei Pestriaev and Felix Trinidad at the end of his career.

Jones had thirty-seven fights in the 1990s and won all of them, save for a ninth-round disqualification against Montell Griffin. In their rematch, Jones knocked Griffin out in the first round.

I thought that Roy Jones Jr. deserved to be named "Fighter of the Decade." Evander's supporters—Ron Borges among them—disagreed. They felt that Roy hadn't faced the inquisitors that Evander had faced. But when I looked at Holyfield's record, I wasn't in accord. Evander won the title by knocking out an undermotivated overweight James "Buster" Douglas. In the four title defenses of his first reign, he beat two men well past their prime (George Foreman and Larry Holmes), was life-and-death against Bert Cooper, and lost to Riddick Bowe. He also lost to Michael Moorer, Bowe again, and Lennox Lewis.

Then I took another look at Roy Jones Jr. Roy dominated the middleweight, super-middleweight, and light-heavyweight divisions in the 1990s in a way that few fighters ever have. He totally outclassed some very good fighters: Bernard Hopkins and James Toney foremost among them. And even more telling, at the end of the decade, you could have gone to a hundred professional fighters and asked, "Pound-for-pound, who's the best fighter in the world right now?" Virtually all of them would have answered, "Roy Jones Jr."

In other words, Evander Holyfield, like Pernell Whitaker, would have been a deserving choice for "Fighter of the Decade." But I felt that Roy Jones Jr. deserved it more.

People can disagree forever on who should have been named "Fighter of the Decade." Ron Borges is entitled to his opinion, and I'm entitled to mine. But the bottom line is that the members of the BWAA executive committee were polled one time each, and six of the ten members voted for Roy. To keep suggesting that his victory is somehow tainted is unfair to him.

And one thing more. About that comment: "It was a Florida election if there ever was one, just like the Bush-Gore one."

No, Ron. In Florida, not all the votes were counted. By contrast, your complaint seems to be that, instead of counting just three or four votes, the BWAA counted all of them.

When I started writing The Black Lights *in 1983, the first person I met in boxing was Bill Cayton.*

Bill Cayton Belongs in the Hall of Fame

One can make a strong argument that Bill Cayton belongs in the International Boxing Hall of Fame because of his accomplishments as a manager. Over the years, he guided Mike Tyson, Wilfredo Benitez, and Edwin Rosario to stardom and generated an incredible amount of money for fighters like Vinny Pazienza, Tommy Morrison, and Michael Grant. But there's no need to make that determination, because Cayton's credentials for induction are even more clear-cut with regard to another set of accomplishments. Over the course of a half-century, he amassed the greatest sports film collection ever assembled, and the heart of that collection was boxing.

Cayton began his professional career as a chemical engineer for Dupont. In 1945, he formed an advertising agency called, appropriately enough, Cayton, Inc. One of his clients was Chesebrough Manufacturing Company. In 1949, Chesebrough decided that it wanted to advertise Vaseline Brand Hair Tonic on television. Since it was a men's product, Cayton recommended sports.

In 1949, television was in its infancy. Ad agencies often produced their own programs, and most screens measured only five or seven inches diagonally. Baseball and other team sports were ill-suited for the medium, but boxing was perfect.

Thus, Cayton set out to acquire rights to memorable fights. From 1911 through 1936, it had been against federal law to transport fight films across state lines. Also, many promoters weren't just linked to organized crime; they *were* organized crime. Accordingly, many of the rights Cayton sought were controlled by the same gentlemen involved in the distillation and sale of alcoholic beverages during Prohibition. Dealing with an attorney named Godfrey Julian Jaffe, Cayton entered into a series of contracts to acquire exclusive rights, including copyrights, to the films of roughly one hundred bouts featuring boxers like Jack Johnson, Jack Dempsey, Henry Armstrong, Mickey Walker, Gene Tunney, and Joe Louis. He then created and produced a television program entitled *Greatest Fights of the Century,* sponsored by Chesebrough, that was broadcast each Friday immediately following *Gillette's Friday Night Fights.*

Those first hundred fight films were the cornerstone of Cayton's library. He built an empire from there. The economics of sports were vastly different a half-century ago from what they are today. As far as boxing was concerned, once a promoter had promoted a fight, he wasn't interested in selling eight-millimeter films and licensing fight footage. The token amounts that such transactions brought in weren't worth the administrative effort. But Cayton saw the future.

The most powerful force in boxing at that time was the International Boxing Club. The IBC was controlled by Jim Norris, who was also the principal owner of Madison Square Garden, Chicago Stadium, and Detroit Stadium. Cayton entered into an agreement with Norris to acquire film rights to all bouts promoted by the IBC. Over time, he also acquired the exclusive copyright on the films of hundreds of other contests, including virtually every Rocky Marciano and Sugar Ray Robinson bout. Young Cassius Clay was included in the dragnet. Then, when Clay won the heavyweight crown in 1964, Cayton went after Ali footage with a vengeance.

Another coup came in 1974, when Cayton and Madison Square Garden president Michael Burke negotiated a contract giving Cayton exclusive rights to the films of all fights and other sports events that had taken place at MSG from its inception through the date of the contract.

But that was just part of the worldwide hunt for fight footage that Cayton conducted. Jack Johnson versus Jess Willard and Jack Johnson versus Tommy Burns were tracked down in Australia. Cayton also acquired rights to the first boxing film ever made: a sparring session between Mike Leonard and Jack Cushing filmed by Thomas Edison in 1894. Two months after that session, James Corbett and Peter Courtney had become the first paid film actors in history when Edison hired them for a five-round sparring session that was shown in peepshows around the country. Cayton acquired rights to that film too. If there were a film of David versus Goliath, Bill Cayton would have owned it.

Over time, Cayton created hundreds of *Greatest Fights of the Century, Big Fights,* and *Knockout* segments that were televised around the world. He also produced several dozen documentaries, among them the trailblazing *a/k/a Cassius Clay* and the Academy Award–nominated *Jack Johnson.*

Finally, in the mid-1970s, fight promoters and television networks began to grasp what Cayton had understood a quarter-century earlier: that fight films had value. Bob Arum began holding onto film rights to bouts promoted by Top Rank. Don King followed suit. At that point, Cayton's virtual monopoly came to an end, but his collection remained supreme. All totaled, he had amassed film rights to roughly 1,500 significant bouts.

The films most often requested from Cayton's library over the years have been Louis-Schmeling II, Clay-Liston I, Dempsey-Willard, and Ali-Foreman. Many of the films are incomplete. That's because, for decades, Madison Square Garden would film an entire fight, edit it down to fifteen or twenty minutes for theater release, and throw away the excess footage. By way of example, out of thirty-nine minutes from Louis-Conn I, only eighteen minutes have been located as of today.

Cayton is convinced that there is existing film footage that has yet to be discovered. "Some of it still exists and is disintegrating as we speak," he says. "Any lost footage of a great fighter that we find now would be like finding a lost concerto by Mozart or a painting by one of the masters."

Three bouts constitute the Holy Grail for fight film collectors. On July 11, 1949, Sugar Ray Robinson successfully defended his welterweight title on a fifteen-round decision over Kid Gavilan. A film of that bout is rumored to exist in Cuba. Gene Tunney and Harry Greb fought five times. A copyright on a film of one of their three title fights was filed with the Library of Congress, but the film itself has never been found. And last, Greb fought Mickey Walker for the middleweight title in 1925. Walker's autobiography refers to hot lights overhead, which are presumed to have been for film cameras. But again, no film has been found.

Cayton's film collection made him a rich man. In 1999, he sold his library to ESPN and further solidified his personal fortune. But more important, Cayton's persistence and determination over a fifty-year period preserved boxing's heritage.

Most of the films that Cayton acquired were on nitrate stock, which was the only film used for motion pictures prior to 1947. Nitrate film is highly combustible and given to disintegration. Cayton transfered his early fight–film footage to acetate stock. In later years, he transferred it to tape. Without his intervention, the images on those films would have been lost forever.

Does Bill Cayton belong in the Hall of Fame?

"I'd have to do a little thinking on that," says Don King, a longtime Cayton adversary. "I'd have to separate out the merit of what the man has done from his trying to send me to the penitentiary."

But Seth Abraham, who built a boxing empire at HBO Sports and is now executive vice president and chief operating officer at Madison Square Garden, has no such reservations. "If I had a vote and Bill's name were on the ballot, I wouldn't think twice," says Abraham. "I'd vote for him wholeheartedly and enthusiastically. A Hall of Fame should take into account everyone who makes a contribution to a sport. It's not the Boxers Hall of Fame. It's the Boxing Hall of Fame, and Bill belongs in it. He has made a significant, lasting, important, unique contribution to the sport."

Ross Greenburg, who succeeded Abraham at HBO, voices a similar view. Greenburg is acutely aware of Cayton's film library, having drawn upon it many times in producing *Sports of the Twentieth Century* documentaries and other telecasts for HBO. "Bill deserves to be in the Hall of Fame," says Greenburg. "It's a no-brainer. The history of the sport would have crumbled to dust, and instead he put together and preserved the most extensive boxing film library the world has ever seen. Those films aren't just boxing history. They're American history, an incredible record of American culture in the twentieth century."

Boxing owes Bill Cayton an enormous debt. He belongs in the International Boxing Hall of Fame.

I've long said that the best way to clean up professional boxing would be for the United States Department of Justice to bring a civil antitrust action against the world sanctioning bodies and their "co-conspirators" followed by the formation of a federal boxing commission. But there are steps that can be taken in the interim.

No More Sanctioning Fees?

Last year, Congress passed the Muhammad Ali Boxing Reform Act. It was the equivalent of putting a band-aid on a gaping wound that's badly in need of sutures. The Ali Act fails to address many of boxing's ills. But a little-noted provision in the statute could bring an end to the world sanctioning organizations as boxing knows them.

Section 11(d)(1) of the Ali Act reads as follows: "A sanctioning organization shall not be entitled to receive any compensation directly or indirectly in connection with a boxing match unless, not later than January 31 of each year, it submits to the Federal Trade Commission and to the Association of Boxing Commissions . . . a complete description of the organization's ratings criteria."

Each of the major sanctioning organizations purports to have filed this information with the Association of Boxing Commissions. The problem is, some of the filings appear to be fraudulent.

The much-publicized case of Darrin Morris is instructive in this matter. Last month, Steve Bunce of the *Independent* in London summarized the salient facts of Morris's career. In July 1999, Morris defeated a fighter named Dave McClusky on a third-round TKO. The victory raised Morris's record to 28-2-1. A full year later, without having had another fight, Morris appeared in the number-ten slot in the World Boxing Organization's super-middleweight ratings. Then, without fighting again, he continued to climb upward, reaching the number-seven slot in October 2000. That was when Morris died of HIV-related meningitis, but his career continued to flourish. By the time Bunce broke the story, Morris had climbed to number five. In sum, the WBO had a corpse ranked in the top ten of its super-middleweight division for four months. And—no religious overtones intended—that corpse continued to rise.

The Morris fiasco gave rise to some whimsical observations:

> • George Kimball: "In most sports, death is considered hazardous to one's health. But in the case of Morris, it appears to have been a good career move."

> • Ron Borges: "Morris did this the hard way. That's no joke, although the ratings and the organizations that put them out are. If Morris had died a little sooner, he might be champion by now."

> • Tim Graham: "Maybe it was a posthumous tribute."

But the Morris fiasco also revealed the hypocrisy inherent in the WBO's ratings procedures and the fraudulent nature of the WBO's filings. That much is clear from an examination of the document entitled "Ratings Criteria" that the WBO filed pursuant to federal law.

The first ratings criteria listed by the WBO is "a positive record with special emphasis on recent activities." Darrin Morris fought only once in the forty months prior to his being rated number five by the WBO.

The second ratings criteria listed by the WBO is "a positive amateur record with special emphasis on medals obtained in international and Olympic tournaments." However, I don't recall seeing Morris standing on the winner's podium while the star-spangled banner waved.

The third ratings criteria listed is "a titleholder in our regional division." Morris wasn't.

The fourth rating criteria is "quality of competition." In Morris's final four fights, his opponents had a combined record of 38 wins, 185 losses, and 7 draws. That's not a typographical error; 185 losses is correct.

The fifth ratings criteria is "frequency of competition." To repeat, in the forty months prior to his being rated number five by the WBO, Morris fought once.

The sixth ratings criteria is "positive TV exposure." Morris hadn't been on television in years.

Ratings criteria seven and eight are "good relations with the community" and "no drug or crime-related problems." No problem here. Morris was dead.

WBO president Francisco "Paco"Valcarcel tried to explain away the Morris fiasco when he told Steve Bunce, "It is sometimes hard to get all the information on boxers and we obviously missed the fact that Darrin was dead. It is regrettable." Later,Valcarcel added,"It could happen to any ruling body.You have seen retired boxers rise in other sanctioning body rankings."

Then GordonVolkman (the WBO's fourth vice president and one of three men who rate boxers for the WBO) poured more fuel on the fire. Volkman was contacted byTim Graham a week after Bunce's story broke, and he still hadn't heard that Morris was dead. "With the many different divisions that we have,"Volkman acknowledged,"it's impossible to keep up with everyone intelligently."Volkman also told Graham that, although he sends in a monthly ballot, the WBO uses it only as a "recommendation" before finalizing the ratings in Puerto Rico.

The Morris case appears to be about incompetence, not a ranking in exchange for dollars. And in fairness to the WBO, I should note that its criteria don't specifically state that a fighter must be alive in order to be ranked. But at this juncture, it's also worth mentioning that nowhere in the WBO's "Ratings Criteria" does one see the names "Klaus-Peter Kohl" and "Frank Warren" mentioned.

Klaus-Peter Kohl is the most powerful promoter and manager in Germany. Frank Warren is the most powerful promoter in England. At present, the WBO has sixteen champions. Kohl and Warren control fourteen of them. They also appear to control the number-one or number-two contenders in eight of the WBO's top twelve weight divisions.

The WBO, of course, is not alone in this matter. The WBC, WBA, and IBF have track records that are just as bad, and that makes for an interesting situation. At least one and possibly all four major world sanctioning organizations have filed phony ratings criteria with the Association of Boxing Commissions in flagrant violation of federal statutory requirements. That gives rise to the question: "What is the penalty for a false filing?

Here's where things get particularly interesting.

Section 6 of the Ali Act provides that violation of the disclosure requirements is a criminal offense punishable by up to one year in prison and a fine of up to $100,000. The criminal division of the Justice

Department is responsible for prosecuting any criminal action. John Ashcroft, are you listening?

Section 6 also provides that the chief law-enforcement officer of any state may bring a civil action to enjoin the holding within the state of any professional boxing match related to the false filing and to obtain such other relief as a court may deem appropriate. Marc Ratner and other state athletic commission personnel, please contact the chief law enforcement officer in your state.

And perhaps most significant, under the Ali Act, any world sanctioning organization that files incomplete or false information "SHALL NOT BE ENTITLED TO RECEIVE ANY COMPENSATION DIRECTLY OR INDIRECTLY IN CONNECTION WITH A BOXING MATCH." That means, if a world sanctioning body is found to have filed incomplete or false ratings criteria, a boxer who fights for one of that organization's titles in the United States should be free of any obligation to pay a sanctioning fee to the organization.

Fighters and honest managers, take note.

As a general rule, I get a dozen e-mails in response to an article. This one—written after Lennox Lewis and Hasim Rahman engaged in their now-infamous studio brawl—engendered more than three hundred.

The Bigot

Five years ago, Muhammad Ali and I co-authored a book entitled *Healing: A Journal of Tolerance and Understanding.* In explaining our purpose, we wrote, "We want to make a statement about bigotry and prejudice. We believe that most people are tired of the hating. We believe that most people are saying, 'If there's a way to solve this problem, let's solve it.'"

Last week, Hasim Rahman became part of the problem. Referring to the fact that Lennox Lewis sued to force him to live up to a rematch clause in their contracts, Rahman declared, "It was gay to take it to the court."

There are a lot of things wrong with Rahman's comment. First, it was a nonsensical non-sequitur. In the ugly world of bigoted stereotyping, Jews are typecast as "money-grubbing" and African Americans are typecast as "shiftless and lazy." But prior to Rahman doing his imitation of an intellectually challenged Ku Klux Klan member, I'd never heard anyone suggest that gay people are particularly litigious.

Moreover, Rahman didn't even have the moral courage to acknowledge the nature of his remark. In the next breath, he feigned innocence with the words, "I don't know why [Lennox] was so offended."

Hasim might be stupid, but he's not that stupid. He has to know that his statement was an ugly, overtly bigoted taunt.

Stan Hoffman (Rahman's manager) took advantage of a contract loophole and betrayed his friend Cedric Kushner for monetary gain. Was that a "Jewish thing" to do? Mike Tyson was convicted of rape. Was that a "black thing" to do? Roberto Duran said *"no mas."* Was that a "Panamanian thing" to do? Hasim Rahman says he's a devout Muslim. Was seeking to break his contract with Lewis a "Muslim thing" to do?

Maybe Rahman is fixated on the movie *Philadelphia*. Or maybe he's embarrassed by the fact that he's the one who sought to avoid a rematch with Lewis, and Lennox had to sue to force him into the ring again. Either way, Hasim's words and subsequent protestations of innocence last week remind me of a scene I saw many years ago when a white man in a mob threw a rock at a ten-year-old black girl being escorted by federal marshals into a previously all-white public school in the Deep South. After throwing the rock, the man hid his hand behind his back.

What makes this all particularly sad, of course, is that Rahman is currently heavyweight champion of the world. By virtue of his position, he's a role model. Prejudice is learned. It's not a self-winding watch. Some of the things that lead to prejudice might be human nature, but prejudice itself is not. Babies don't know prejudice; they have to be taught. And the lesson Hasim Rahman taught last week was that gay-bashing is all right.

There's a quotation in silver letters on a gray wall in the United States Holocaust Memorial Museum in Washington, DC. It reads as follows:

> First they came for the socialists.
> And I did not speak out because I was not a socialist.
> Then they came for the trade unionists.
> And I did not speak out because I was not a trade unionist.
> Then they came for the Jews.
> And I did not speak out because I was not a Jew.
> Then they came for me.
> And there was no one left to speak for me.

With that in mind, it's incumbent upon every decent person to speak out against overt expressions of bigotry. Let's see if the people who have condemned Bernard Hopkins for throwing a Puerto Rican flag to the ground are as vehement in their criticism of Rahman. Initially, it's easy to hate. For some people, being prejudiced might even be fun at first. But after a while, hating becomes a full-time job and the hours suck.

The jury is still out as to how good a fighter Hasim Rahman is, but he's starting to look like a shabby human being. People can speculate all they want regarding whether or not Lennox Lewis is gay. What we know for a fact is that, last week, Rahman acted like an ignorant bigot.

There's one honorable road for Rahman to travel. He can sincerely and genuinely apologize. If he does, he'll redeem himself and raise his stature. Meanwhile, the slur he uttered last week tells us far more about himself than it does about Lennox Lewis.

The volume of, and thoughts expressed in, my reader mail led to the following column.

More on Hasim Rahman's "Gay" Comment

Two days ago, I posted a column on this website entitled "The Bigot." In it, I criticized Hasim Rahman for his comment that it was "gay" for Lennox Lewis to sue him. Since then, I've received hundreds of e-mails in response. Many were supportive of my thoughts. Others voiced disagreement. As expected, some of the e-mails were ugly and blatantly homophobic. Others expressed disagreement in a way that was intelligent and carefully thought out. I'd like to continue the dialogue with this latter group of readers.

Most readers who disagreed with me voiced one or more of the following objections to my thoughts.

(1) Rahman's use of the term "gay" wasn't intended as homophobic. Rather, it was street slang commonly used by people who are younger than I am.

It might be street slang. But given the rumors about Lennox's sexuality, the remark wasn't innocent. I thought it was intended as a taunt; and obviously, Lennox thought so, too. Also, just because something is street slang, doesn't mean it's acceptable. Various readers have advised me that, in street slang, "gay" means "weak . . . wimpy . . . poor effort . . . etc." That, to me, is no better that saying, "He tried to jew me out of ten dollars," or "There's a nigger in the woodpile." Oftentimes, prejudice is spread through the careless use of language.

(2) Lennox's reaction was inappropriate.

I agree. Saying that he was "one hundred percent man" and suggesting that Rahman bring his sister for a demonstration was not a good way to handle the situation.

(3) It was wrong for me to compare Rahman's remark to the Holocaust.

Thomas Jefferson once wrote, "All bigotries hang to one another." I believe that to be true. The message inherent in the words that I quoted from the Holocaust Museum is that all acts of prejudice should be rebutted.

(4) Muhammad Ali once called white people "devils" and was merciless in deriding Joe Frazier as ignorant, an Uncle Tom, and a gorilla. That's worse than anything Rahman said.

Ali stepped far over the line when he was young, and I've commented on that at length. So has Muhammad. Twelve years ago, when I was researching *Muhammad Ali: His Life and Times,* Ali told me, "I'm sorry Joe Frazier is mad at me. I'm sorry I hurt him. Joe Frazier is a good man. I couldn't have done what I did without him, and he couldn't have done what he did without me." Also, in the book on bigotry and prejudice that Ali and I co-authored, Muhammad wrote, "When I was young, I followed a teaching that disrespected other people and said that white people were devils. I was wrong. Color doesn't make a man a devil. It's the heart and soul and mind that count."

(5) Homosexuality is a choice.

I'm not an expert on the subject, but I don't think being gay is a choice. One might choose to act or not act on sexual desires, but people are what they are. I'm heterosexual. That's not a "choice" I made. It's what I am. Given the "choice" of a sexual liaison with a round-card girl or a male fighter, I'll take the round-card girl every time. People don't choose their sexual preference the way they choose a political party or their religious beliefs.

(6) I shouldn't have said that Rahman is "stupid."

Actually, I didn't say that Rahman is stupid. I said he "might be stupid." Regardless, it was a poor choice of words, and I retract them. I should have written, "Hasim isn't stupid. He has to know that his statement was an ugly, overtly-bigoted taunt."

I could go on at length but, at this point, I've pretty much had my say. What I'd like to do, however, is quote from one of the many letters I received in response to my first column on this subject. It's from a reader in South Africa, who wrote as follows:

Dear Mr. Hauser:

Thank you for addressing the core issue surrounding the fracas that ensued on television between Rahman and Lewis. It seemed that nobody in boxing had cottoned on to the simple fact that Rahman had essentially committed an act of prejudice. Just because you're black does not mean that you are naturally exempt from committing prejudice against other people. I'm a black South African, and we suffer very much from the same mentality in our society. Everybody is prejudiced. While the roots of the prejudice may lie in slavery, subjugation, and colonial rule, it does not mean that the victims of prejudice are innocent of the very same crime. Rahman, as a black Muslim in America should at least carry himself with enough grace not to engage in bigoted stone throwing in an attempt to ruffle his opponent. If he himself is not enough to inspire fear or doubt in Lennox, then he has no business dragging in and abusing some already marginalised sector of society. Gay people are easy to pick on. They're characterised as weak effeminate men and have traditionally made easy targets for abuse. Rahman has chosen them as his target. Maybe some part of him thought that nobody would really mind if he picked on gay people, and sadly, he's probably right.

Those words speak volumes. And there's one last thought I'd like to add to them. After Hasim Rahman defeated Lennox Lewis in South Africa, both men were invited to meet with Nelson Mandela. Lewis was bitterly disappointed by the loss of his title, but he stayed in South Africa to meet with Mandela. Rahman, by contrast, said he was "tired" and returned to the United States.

Nelson Mandela is one of history's great men. His peers are true heroes like Martin Luther King Jr. and Mahatma Gandhi. Rahman should have met with Mr. Mandela. He might have learned something.

After the September 11 terrorist attack, Michael Katz, Tom Gerbasi, and I co-authored the following editorial regarding the upcoming middleweight championship fight between Felix Trinidad and Bernard Hopkins.

Reschedule the Fight

Thirty-eight years ago, an assassin tore at the fabric of the United States when John F. Kennedy was assassinated in Dallas. Two days later, the National Football League played its regularly scheduled contests. Pete Rozelle, the NFL commissioner at the time, later acknowledged that it was the biggest mistake he ever made.

That bit of history is relevant now in the wake of today's horrifying terrorist attack. The most important, most exciting fight of the year, Felix Trinidad versus Bernard Hopkins, is scheduled for this Saturday night at Madison Square Garden.

It should be postponed.

Reasonable arguments can be made in support of holding the fight as planned. Disrupting the rhythm of everyday life is a form of collateral damage that, in a way, plays into the hands of terrorists. Economic losses will result from a postponement. And a postponement will weigh particularly heavily on the fighters' shoulders.

But even if all the logistical problems caused by today's events are overcome, there are compelling reasons why the fight should not take place on Saturday night. Prior to today, there were safety concerns regarding the fight. These concerns pale following today's events. Madison Square Garden sits on top of Penn Station, which has been evacuated as a prime terrorist target. And more important, there can be no joy in a fight that is contested this Saturday night. The loss of life that occurred today is simply too great. Two men punching each other in the head is an inappropriate memorial to the thousands of men and women who died this morning.

American enterprises from Major League Baseball to Disneyland have shut down today. This is not a time to play. Fights are often rescheduled because of injury to one of the participants. Felix Trinidad versus Bernard Hopkins should be rescheduled because the nation has suffered a grievous wound.

After Trinidad-Hopkins was postponed, I visited an empty Madison Square Garden on the night that would have been.

Madison Square Garden
September 15, 2001

This was to have been "ground zero" tonight. Bernard Hopkins versus Felix Trinidad for the undisputed middleweight championship of the world. Screaming partisans had been expected to turn Madison Square Garden into a sea of red, white, and blue flags. Puerto Rican flags. The cops would have been here in full force because of security concerns stemming from incidents in which Hopkins was perceived as having disrespected that flag. It was feared the night would turn ugly. But another four-letter word—EVIL—intervened.

Tonight was a perfect mid-September evening. Clear skies, temperature in the low sixties, a hint of autumn in the air. No events were listed on the Garden marquee, just the digital image of an American flag at half-mast. A giant multi-colored banner advertising the fight stretched from the first floor to the top of the building. Inside the Garden, three box office windows for advance ticket sales were open. The main arena itself was dimly lit, its floor still covered with ice put in place for New York Rangers practices earlier this week.

A half-dozen uniformed New York City cops stood outside the employees entrance at the corner of Eighth Avenue and 33rd Street. "Normal security," they said. Other cops were sprinkled in and around Penn Station, which lies beneath the Garden.

Eventually, things will return to normal in America, although the definition of "normal" will change. There will be added security. But no matter what measures are taken, seeing the World Trade Center towers sliced in two by a handful of madmen leaves all of us feeling vulnerable.

We are.

Maybe we'll find a way to make our own airlines secure. But what about foreign airlines? What about personnel who work for Pakistan

International Airlines, Saudi Arabia Airlines, Royal Jordanian Airlines, and Egypt Air? What about car bombs, biological warfare, poisoned reservoirs, and other acts of terrorism? Are there pilots on domestic carriers who admire Timothy McVeigh?

The acts of terror that occurred on September 11 make us realize how insignificant our games are. All of us who live in New York know someone who perished in the World Trade Center. We just don't know yet who they were.

When Bernard Hopkins and Felix Trinidad ultimately meet, American flags will be waved along side their Puerto Rican counterparts. Fans will be shouting "USA! USA!" Let's hope the flags are waved in unity. This fight was never about Bernard Hopkins versus Puerto Rico or Puerto Rico versus the United States. It was always a fist fight between two men, nothing more.

Meanwhile, there's a horrible feeling in waking up each day and knowing right away that something is wrong. The mourning over this week's events has barely begun. The implications are far from fully understood. It feels like a death in the family.

When Bernard Hopkins and Felix Trinidad finally fought each other, reminders of September 11 were everywhere.

Madison Square Garden
September 29, 2001

Autumn is the nicest time of year in New York. Summer is too hot, winter too cold, and spring too short. Autumn is glorious. From the middle of September until the days just before Thanksgiving, the skies are often cloudless. Autumn leaves fire the imagination, and the temperature is just right.

The weather was glorious on September 11, the day the World Trade Center was attacked. On September 29, the skies alternated between sunlit and overcast. The mood at Madison Square Garden was festive one moment and somber the next. Normally, big fights are the boxing community's version of a family holiday. Hopkins-Trinidad was both holiday and wake.

Meanwhile, two blocks away from the Garden, the Empire State Building was bathed in red, white, and blue.

For those of us who grew up in an earlier era, the Empire State Building was the most visible symbol of New York. King Kong met his destiny there with Fay Wray at his side. The Kong who perished at the World Trade Center decades later after a liaison with Jessica Lange was a pale imitation.

In 1945, a B-25 bomber lost in blinding fog crashed into the seventy-ninth floor of what was then the world's tallest building. Thirteen people were killed. The Empire State Building survived. Now it gives every appearance of standing guard over New York.

On November 23, 2001, Lou DiBella held a boxing fundraiser for victims of the World Trade Center attack. The following article was written for that night's program.

September 11, 2001

I'm very down on the overall state of boxing. From top to bottom, the sport is a mess. The business is endemically rotten. People lie and misrepresent and cheat as much on twenty-thousand-dollar club-fight cards as they do on the multi-million-dollar pay-per-view shows. There's endless scheming and plotting to hurt other people. The negative energy is overwhelming. One of the few good things about it for me so far has been dealing with the fighters. A lot of people told me that being on the side of the business that I am now would teach me that the fighters are as bad as everyone else. But that hasn't been the case. So far, I've found most of the fighters to be very special decent individuals. There have been disappointments, but I love working with fighters. I enjoy the mentoring aspect of my relationship with the Olympians. There are times when I'm proud to be a member of the boxing community, and November 23rd will be one of them.

— Lou DiBella

Roseland, where tonight's fights are being held, stands a block from Broadway. For a long time, in New York's theater industry when someone died young, the question asked was is, "Did he die of AIDS?" Now, for a horrible ten weeks, when we hear of someone dying young, the question asked is, "Did he die at the World Trade Center?"

The human mind is capable of conjuring up evil that, for some of us, is literally unimaginable. Any individual can end another person's life and wreak havoc on the lives of the victim's loved ones. A small group of plotters, indeed a lone assassin, can cause incalculable harm.

Once something has happened, we can't change it. We can't undo what has been done.

Yet one day can change the world. It happened in 1914, when Archduke Ferdinand was assassinated in Sarajevo, lighting the conflagration that became World War I. It happened at Pearl Harbor. And it happened again ten weeks ago.

On September 11, we all died a little. America was the target, but the entry point for the wound was New York.

We are aware of the twin towers more now in their absence than ever before. We're also uncomfortably aware of the fact that evil lurks just beneath the surface of our lives. There are places in the world where the type of violence we've just experienced is part of everyday life. But Americans have been largely immune to such cares. Most of us have had the luxury of going through life confident that the sudden ending, the tragic accident, the unspeakable horror, won't happen to us. To a friend, perhaps. To someone we know, probably, as a matter of statistical likelihood. But not to me.

Now the certainty we seek in our lives has been undermined, and in its place we have fear. The fear that someone wants to kill us; the fear that, just as terrorists were trained as pilots here in the United States, their brethren might be learning the nuances of lethal biology at universities and laboratories in America; the fear that this is the start of a long hard difficult time.

Many of us have been traumatized by the visual image of United Airlines Flight 175 hitting the south tower of the World Trade Center more than we understand. "People keep saying 'like a movie, like a book,'" Stephen King wrote recently. "And I keep thinking, 'No, not at all like a movie or a book. This is what it really looks like when an actual plane filled with actual human beings and loaded with jet fuel hits a skyscraper. This is the truth.'"

That scene will stay with us forever. It is the signature image of horror in our times.

Now comes the response. Makeshift shrines to honor lives lost have sprung up outside fire stations across New York. People seem friendlier, warmer, and more polite. They smile and nod in acknowledgment to one another more now than before. They look at cops and firefighters with new appreciation and respect.

One of the ironies of our democratic society is that, in recent decades, only one segment of society has been called upon to do the hard dangerous dirty work. In World War II, people of all classes fought in the military. But since then, America's armed forces have been comprised largely of men and women who come from poverty and see the military as a form of upward mobility.

The World Trade Center attack struck at Americans of all classes. With terrorism, we are all soldiers. And on September 11, we were reminded of who our real heroes are. Now, we say to the perpetrators of this horror as Winston Churchill once spoke to Adolph Hitler, "We will have no truce or parlay with you or the grisly gang who do your wicked will. You do your worst, and we will do our best."

That brings us to tonight's fights. Everyone talks about how superstar athletes are heroes and role models. But most professional athletes, like the rest of us, do first and foremost for themselves.

The fighters on tonight's card are making a true sacrifice. Like cops and firefighters, boxers know what reality is. In our video-game culture, every time they enter the ring they put themselves on the line. They know that a single moment of violence can change everything. Yet many of the fighters here tonight are entering the ring for free, and their opponents are appearing for greatly reduced purses. That's part of the good in boxing.

I've often said that, if I went to war, I'd want professional fighters beside me. Professional fighters and trainers like Teddy Atlas and a young Eddie Futch. I still believe that to be true. Meanwhile, conventional wisdom dictates that a fighter isn't considered truly great until he has gotten up off the canvas to win. New York will rise from the canvas and win.

I'm a big Ali fan. But there are limits to his talents.

Ali As Diplomat
"No! No! No! Don't"

In 1980, in response to the Soviet Union's invasion of Afghanistan, the Carter administration sought to organize a boycott of the Moscow Olympics. As part of that effort, it sent Muhammad Ali to five African nations to gather support for American's position.

Ali's trip was a disaster. *Time* magazine later called it, "The most bizarre diplomatic mission in recent U.S. history." Some African officials viewed Ali's presence as a racial insult. "Would the United States send Chris Evert to negotiate with London?" one Tanzanian diplomat demanded. Ali himself seemed confused regarding the facts underlying his role and was unable to explain why African nations should boycott the Moscow Olympics when, four years earlier, the United States had refused to join twenty-nine African countries in boycotting the Montreal Olympics over South Africa's place in the sporting world.

"Maybe I'm being used to do something that ain't right," Ali conceded at one point. In Kenya, he announced that Jimmy Carter had put him "on the spot" and sent him "around the world to take the whupping over American policies," and said that, if he'd known the "whole history of America and South Africa," he "probably wouldn't have made the trip."

That bit of history is relevant now because Jack Valenti (president of the Motion Picture Association of America) has unveiled tentative plans for a one-minute public service announcement featuring Ali that will be broadcast throughout the Muslim world. The thrust of the message is that America's war on terrorism is not a war against Islam. The public service spot would be prepared by Hollywood 9/11—a group that was formed after movie industry executives met on November 11 with Karl Rove (a senior political advisor to George Bush). In Valenti's words, Ali would be held out as "the spokesman for Muslims in America."

The proposed public service announcement might be good publicity for the movie industry, but it's dangerous politics.

Ali is universally respected and loved, but he isn't a diplomat. He doesn't understand the complexities of geopolitics. His heart is pure, but his judgments and actions are at times unwise. An example of this occurred on December 19 at a fundraising event for the proposed Muhammad Ali Center. The center is intended to be an educational facility designed to promote tolerance and understanding among all people. At the fundraiser, Ali rose to tell several jokes.

"No! No! No! Don't," his wife Lonnie cried.

Despite her plea, Ali proceeded. "What's the difference between a Jew and a canoe?" he asked. Then he supplied the answer: "A canoe tips." That was followed by, "A black, a Puerto Rican, and a Mexican are in a car. Who's driving?" The answer? "The police."

Afterward, Sue Carls (a spokesperson for the Ali Center) sought to minimize the damage, explaining, "These are not new jokes. Muhammad tells them all the time because he likes to make people laugh, and he shocks people to make a point." Two days later, Lonnie Ali added, "Even the Greatest can tell bad jokes."

The problem is, this is a situation where misjudgments and bad jokes can cost lives.

Ali is not a bigot. He tells far more "nigger" jokes than jokes about Hispanics and Jews. But Ali sometimes speaks and acts without considering the implications of his words and conduct. And he can be swayed by rhetoric, particularly when the speaker is a Muslim cleric with a following in some portion of the world.

What happens if, six months from now, Ali makes an intemperate statement about Israel? What happens if Ali calls for a halt to all American military action against terrorism in the heartfelt belief that a halt will save innocent lives? Will he then still be "the spokesman for Muslims in America."

Muhammad Ali leads best when he leads by example and by broad statements in support of tolerance and understanding among all people. To ask more of him in the current incendiary situation is looking for trouble.

In December 2001, Bernard Hopkins turned against Lou DiBella. As someone who had liked and respected both men, I was disappointed.

The Handshake

It's a time-honored axiom in boxing: "Never fall in love with a fighter, because if you do, sooner or later, he'll break your heart."

Lou DiBella fell in love with Bernard Hopkins. Now Hopkins has broken his heart.

DiBella and Hopkins joined forces after the fighter defended his IBF middleweight title against Antwun Echols in December 1999 for $100,000. With DiBella's guidance, Hopkins made $500,000 for a May 2000 defense against Syd Vanderpool and $600,000 for a rematch against Echols later that year. Then, in 2001, DiBella engineered Hopkins's entry into the middleweight championship series. For that bit of business, Hopkins received $1,000,000 for fighting Keith Holmes, $2,750,000 for fighting Felix Trinidad, $50,000 in expenses for each fight, and a $200,000 signing bonus. In sum, before DiBella, Hopkins was an extremely talented fighter with limited name recognition who rarely made big money. With DiBella in his camp, he became a star.

Hopkins was aware of DiBella's contributions to his cause. In the ring immediately after knocking out Trinidad, he praised Lou on national television. Two days later, he summoned DiBella to his room at the St. Regis Hotel in Manhattan and gave him the gloves he'd worn in the signature bout of his career.

But Hopkins and DiBella never had a written contract. Rather they had what both sides called "a handshake agreement."

Not long after defeating Trinidad, Hopkins felt he no longer needed DiBella. There were rumors, unreturned telephone calls, negotiations that took place without DiBella's knowledge. But never anything between them man-to-man or face-to-face. Finally, Bernard let Lou know through intermediaries that his services were no longer desired.

Then came the *coup de grace*. Hopkins accused DiBella of arranging to receive a $50,000 kickback from him while DiBella was still at HBO.

There's no gray area here. Either DiBella took a bribe or he didn't. I don't think he did.

Seth Abraham, DiBella's former boss and now chief operating officer of Madison Square Garden, concurs. "I can tell you this," Abraham said recently. "I worked at HBO for twenty-four years. In the thirteen or fourteen years Lou worked with me, no fighter, no promoter, and no manager ever came to me and said Lou did anything improper. Even his enemies on the outside, and there were more than a few, never made such an accusation."

Meanwhile, the damage to DiBella's fledgling company goes far beyond the loss of income from Hopkins. The major promoters are already gunning for him because he represents a threat to the status quo. Lou's relationships with HBO, MSG, and other centers of power are prickly at best. DiBella's success, if it is to be, will be founded on the good will of fighters who understand that he knows boxing, will battle on their behalf, and will never betray them. Bernard Hopkins was to have been the cornerstone of that trust.

Why did Hopkins turn on DiBella?

The guess here is that it began with money. Once Bernard made it to the top, he wanted to share the wealth as little as possible. It's also not unreasonable to suggest that Bernard might have been helped toward his conclusion by Don King. King understands the darkness in people as well as anyone ever. Whether it's greed, the willingness to cheat on one's wife, ethnic animosity, whatever, Don can find the darkness and, when he chooses, play on it.

Why didn't Hopkins, who's supposed to be a stand-up guy, tell DiBella to his face that he wanted to end their relationship?

Maybe he was embarrassed. Maybe he sensed that what he was doing was wrong.

Why the accusation of bribery? Larry Merchant thinks he knows the answer.

"After Trinidad-Hopkins," says Merchant, "we all celebrated Bernard as an anti-boxing-establishment force who had prevailed against the odds.

And that fit perfectly with Bernard's self-image, since he likes to think of himself as a rebel and as the good guy when it comes to confrontations. But then, as soon as he beat Trinidad, Bernard did the same thing to Lou DiBella that he used to accuse everyone else of doing to him. And it sounds to me now as though he's striking out in a rage because he's angry at having been branded an ingrate and a betrayer."

The irony of it all is that casting DiBella aside might not turn out to be very smart. The list of fighters who thought they could deal successfully with Don King on their own is painfully long.

Also, it should be noted that, despite his penchant for confrontation, Hopkins is quite facile and diplomatic when he wants to be. Bernard tells people off. But Bernard is also quite adept at telling people what they want to hear. He has stroked more than one writer with the words, "You're the only one who understands me." And he won a lot of praise after defeating Trinidad when he pledged in the ring to go to Puerto Rico and apologize to Trinidad's fans for his actions vis-a-vis the Puerto Rican flag. The people of Puerto Rico are still waiting.

Bernard Hopkins is a captivating individual. He's also a great fighter. And I understand full well that, when he goes in the ring, no one is in there with him taking the punches. Still, like a lot of people, I'm disappointed by his recent conduct.

Hopkins himself once said, "You can't stay champion forever. If I only get respect for being champion and I don't carry myself properly, what happens when I'm not champion anymore?"

That's a good question. Bernard thrived in adversity. It remains to be seen whether or not he can handle success. Meanwhile, Hopkins used to be one of the few people in boxing I thought you could do business with on a handshake. No more.

The infamous Lewis-Tyson press conference took place on a stage at the Hudson Theatre in New York. That gave it a bizarre aura as the media sat in theater seats watching a man self-destruct.

Lewis-Tyson
Cancel the Fight

First, the facts.

A press conference was scheduled to take place at the Millennium Hotel in Manhattan on Tuesday January 22 to announce a heavyweight championship fight between Lennox Lewis and Mike Tyson. The promotion is a joint venture between HBO and Showtime, whose parent companies—AOL/TimeWarner and Viacom—are two of the biggest media conglomerates in the world.

Tyson was introduced first. Dressed in black, he strode onto the stage and took his place, as planned, on a small platform. Lewis was introduced next. At that point, Tyson left his platform and walked in menacing fashion toward Lewis. Lewis's bodyguard stepped between them. Tyson threw a left hook at the bodyguard; Lewis retaliated with an overhand right; and all hell broke loose. Tyson was the instigator, plain and simple.

During the scuffle, Tyson bit through Lewis's pants and into his thigh, causing significant bleeding.

Once semi-order was restored, Tyson moved to the front of the stage, grabbed his crotch, thrust his hips back and forth, and began screaming obscenities at the media. Someone in the crowd hollered, "Get him a straight jacket." At that point, Tyson shouted back, "Fuck you, you white faggot. I'll fuck you up the ass, white boy. I'll fuck you till you love me," and other obscenities.

The press conference was terminated. An hour later, Lennox Lewis issued a statement that read, "As a result of today's events, I will re-evaluate my options after the relevant boxing commission has ruled."

Later in the day, Tyson's camp issued a statement that quoted Tyson as saying, "My motivation for approaching Lennox was to stage a face off which I was told both camps had agreed to. It was Lennox's bodyguard who panicked and shoved me. Lennox then threw a right. I was here to promote a fight, not be intimidated. I will never be intimidated by anyone, and Lennox will pay in April."

The Tyson statement was dishonest spin-doctoring. Lennox's bodyguard was simply doing his job.

After the chaos subsided, Jay Larkin (Tyson's primary patron at Showtime) acknowledged, "That was an astounding display of rage. I've been doing this for eighteen years and I've rarely been speechless, but I'm speechless now. Tyson is the anti-Midas. He touches gold and it turns to shit."

Lennox Lewis versus Mike Tyson was to have been an unprecedented economic venture. Now, for the fight to proceed, three conditions must be met: (1) The Nevada State Athletic Commission must grant Tyson a license to box; (2) Lewis must to agree to go ahead with the fight; and (3) Tyson has to control himself between now and April 6.

Condition number one should render conditions two and three moot. A license to box is a privilege, not a right. The Nevada State Athletic Commission should deny Tyson's request for a license.

Last Thursday, Shelly Finkel (Tyson's advisor) sent a letter to the NSAC asking that it begin the process of granting Tyson a license to fight. The commission is expected to consider the matter at a meeting on January 29. Its members are Luther Mack (chairman), Flip Homansky (vice-chairman), Amy Ayoub, Tony Alamo Jr., and John Bailey. They will be called upon to consider a long list of Tyson misdeeds, both in and out of the ring.

In Tyson's three most recent fights in Las Vegas, he (1) bit Evander Holyfield; (2) tried to break Frans Botha's arm off at the elbow; and (3) hit Orlin Norris on the break twice; the second time, after the bell. Out-of-state, Tyson refused to take a drug test prior to fighting Andrew Golota in Michigan and tested positive for an illegal substance after the fight. In Scotland versus Lou Savarese, he punched referee John Coyle so he could punch Savarese some more after Coyle had stopped the bout.

Outside the ring, Tyson has been imprisoned for rape and sent back to prison for assaulting two motorists after a traffic accident. The Clark County District Attorney's office, which has jurisdiction over Las Vegas, recently received a recommendation from the Las Vegas Police Department that Tyson be indicted for sexual assault. Tyson is also under investigation by the United States Attorney's Office for a recent trip to Cuba, and several lower-profile incidents have been reported.

But Las Vegas needs this fight. Business is slow, and each member of the NSAC will be subjected to a variety of political and economic pressures.

If Tyson were a four-round preliminary fighter, there's little chance that his request for a license would be granted. It shouldn't be granted here either. This isn't just an economic issue. Legal and moral issues are involved. A society needs standards and accountability in order to survive. How will the NSAC commissioners explain their vote to the children in their lives if Mike Tyson is rewarded with a license after his most recent antisocial outburst?

What happened at the Lewis-Tyson press conference wasn't a black eye for boxing. It was a black eye for Mike Tyson. Boxing will only be punched in the eye if the Nevada State Athletic Commission grants Mike Tyson a license to fight.

The Nevada State Athletic Commission hearing at which Mike Tyson
was denied a license to box was as dramatic in its own way as the press
conference that preceded it.

Nevada Says "No" to Mike Tyson

The Nevada State Athletic Commission has denied Mike Tyson's
request for a license. The decision came after a two-and-a-half hour hearing with Tyson present and was by a four to one vote. The sole dissenter
was commission chairman Luther Mack.

The decision came after days of intense lobbying. During the past
week, pro-Tyson forces repeatedly made the argument that the Las Vegas
economy needs the proposed championship bout between Tyson and
Lennox Lewis. Sources close to the NSAC report that Jesse Jackson was
even called upon to do some last-minute lobbying on the questionable
grounds that Tyson's civil rights would be violated if he were denied a
license. But Tyson's history of antisocial behavior, past and present, was
too much to overcome.

The rallying point for those opposed to licensing Tyson was a
January 22 press conference in New York intended to announce the fight.
According to the Lewis camp, Tyson and Lewis were to stand on plat-
forms on opposite sides of the stage at the Hudson Theatre and glare at
one another. Because of the uniform black-curtain background, split-
screen television technology would make it look as though they were
engaged in a staredown in close proximity to each other.

Tyson was introduced first. Dressed in black, he strode onto the stage
and took his place, as planned, on a small platform. Lewis was introduced
next. At that point, Tyson left his platform and walked in menacing fashion toward Lewis.

"He definitely was coming to sucker-punch me," Lewis said later. "I
could see it in the way he was moving and in his eyes."

Lewis's bodyguard stepped between the two men. Tyson threw a left
hook at the bodyguard, and Lewis retaliated with an overhand right.

During the scuffle, Tyson bit through Lewis's pants and into his thigh, causing significant bleeding. At the instruction of Lewis's attorney, the wound was later photographed and Lewis was given a tetanus shot.

After the combatants were separated, Tyson moved to the front of the stage, grabbed his crotch, thrust his hips back and forth, and began screaming obscenities. Someone in the crowd hollered, "Get him a straight jacket." Tyson shouted back, "Fuck you, you white faggot. I'll fuck you up the ass, white boy. I'll fuck you till you love me," and other obscenities.

The press conference was terminated. An hour later, Lewis issued a statement that read, "As a result of today's events, I will re-evaluate my options after the relevant boxing commission has ruled."

The commission referred to, of course, was Nevada. Tyson's license had been revoked by the NSAC after he bit Evander Holyfield twice during their 1997 rematch. Fifteen months later, it was reinstated. Thereafter, Tyson fought in Las Vegas against Frans Botha and Orlin Norris. In the Botha fight, he tried to break Botha's arm off at the elbow. Against Norris, Tyson hit his opponent on the break twice, the second time, clearly after the bell. Norris fell to the canvas and injured his right knee. The bout was ruled a no-contest. The NSAC then held a hearing on the matter and decided that Tyson should be allowed to receive his purse. At that hearing, then-commissioner Lorenzo Fertitta told Tyson's promoter to, "pack Mr. Tyson's bags up and take this act on the road. I'm not so sure we need him here in the state of Nevada."

Last weekend, Larry Merchant of HBO framed the core issue. Noting that the Nevada State Athletic Commission had told Tyson to clean up his act before reapplying for a license, Merchant cited a long list of subsequent transgressions and queried, "Is this a serious discussion of whether Mike Tyson abided by the terms of their mandate to clean up his act? Because, clearly, he didn't. So either they condone his behavior or they punish him for it. There's perfect clarity to the issue."

There are five commissioners on the NSAC. Luther Mack (who owns several McDonald's franchises), Flip Homansky (a physician), Amy Ayoub, (a political consultant), Tony Alamo Jr. (also a physician), and John Bailey (an attorney). Since Tyson's meltdown, two of them—Homansky and Ayoub—were believed to be leaning "no." Mack was considered a "yes" vote. Fairly or unfairly, the public perception was that Alamo would vote whichever way his father told him to. Tony Alamo Sr. is a vice president at Mandalay Bay. And even though Lewis-Tyson was to take place at the MGM Grand, all of the Las Vegas casinos stood to benefit from the bout. That left John Bailey as the likely swing vote.

Surprisingly, a number of major Nevada media players opposed Tyson's license request. An editorial in the *Las Vegas Review-Journal* declared, "Even if the MGM or some other Nevada venue is desperate enough to risk its reputation in hopes of cashing in on a Tyson fight, now is the time for the Nevada Athletic Commission to do its job. Mike Tyson is not mentally fit to step in the ring. He should never again be licensed to fight in this state."

A strongly worded column by Royce Feour, the most influential boxing writer in Nevada, followed. "Why shouldn't Tyson be licensed?" Feour asked. And then he answered, "The health and safety of his opponent and the referee, for starters. And the safety of the spectators, should he start a riot. How much more evidence does the commission need? There is only one proper thing to do: deny Tyson's application. If that means the Lewis-Tyson fight goes to another state or country, so be it. That would be the new site's problem."

Other sports columnists such as Kevin Iole, Dean Juipe, and Joe Hawk followed suit. And behind the scenes, HBO also reportedly weighed in.

HBO, of course, is tied to Lewis, while Showtime is tied to Tyson. The two cable giants had agreed to finance, publicize, and televise the fight as a joint venture. But after Tyson's press conference behavior, HBO decided it wanted out. How to get out legally and gracefully was the issue. HBO didn't want to do anything that would render it liable for breach of contract. But a clause in one of the many bout contracts relieves HBO of certain obligations if Tyson can't get a license to fight in one of several specified states. Accordingly, HBO discreetly let it be known to the powers that be in Las Vegas that it wouldn't be displeased if Tyson's request for a license were denied. That would make Tyson exclusively Showtime's problem.

The hearing on Tyson's license application began at 1:35 P.M. Pacific Coast time. Tyson was represented by Las Vegas attorney Bob Faiss. Also present on his behalf were attorney Elizabeth Brennan, business manager Matthew Johnson, physical conditioner Keith Kleven, and adviser Shelly Finkel.

Faiss coordinated Tyson's presentation, which consisted largely of videotapes and expository argument. The attorney began by telling the commissioners that Lewis-Tyson would take place whether it took place in Nevada or somewhere else. He also criticized the "unceasing media pressure" on his client, and said he would forbid questions regarding allegations of rape and other criminal conduct currently pending against Tyson in order to "preserve Mr. Tyson's constitutional rights." He then likened Iron Mike's obscenity-laced press conference tirade to John L. Sullivan's boast, "I can lick any son-of-a-bitch in the house." And he drew an analogy between Jack Dempsey's ring savagery and Tyson biting off part of Evander Holyfield's ear.

Faiss's explanation regarding the press conference debacle was as follows. At the last minute, Tyson was advised by a member of his team that the Lewis camp had agreed to a face-to-face staredown. Indeed, Faiss claimed that "Mr. Tyson's intent was to play an assigned role in another production of boxing theater." Thus, Tyson crossed the stage and was surprised when he was shoved by Lennox's bodyguard. Thinking that they were "play-acting," Iron Mike threw a left hook in response, deliberately missing his target. Then Lewis "suckerpunched" Tyson. In other words, Tyson was "a powerless non-participant." He was "shaken, beaten, and bloodied," and believed he had been "doublecrossed." Furthermore, Feiss said in closing, "Mr. Tyson states he did not bite anyone."

Returning to the obscenities, Faiss likened Tyson's use of what he referred to as "the 'F' word" to *The Sopranos* and added that it was constitutionally protected speech. He also claimed that none of the offensive language would have been uttered but for the fact that Tyson had been provoked by a reporter. This overlooked the reality that the reporter's insult was occasioned by the fact that Tyson was standing on the stage, already screaming obscenities and simulating masturbation.

Faiss's presentation ended at 2:40 P.M. PST. Then the statements and questioning by commissioners began.

Tyson had an answer for every allegation. To hear him talk, none of the chaos that has marked his life has been his fault. Referee John Coyle got punched in the Savarese fight because "he didn't stop the fight in an appropriate way." Tyson tried to break Frans Botha's arm in a clinch because Botha was "fighting dirty." The Lewis-Tyson press conference fisticuffs were the result of Lennox's camp not following the agreed-upon script. The obscene diatribe that followed occurred because, "After the mayhem, a gentleman said something humiliating and embarrassing to me, and I tried to inflict similar pain on him. He violated me as an individual, and I violated him. He was at liberty to say what he wanted to say to me, and I was at liberty to say what I wanted to say to him."

Tyson also stated that he was not on medication, hadn't been for six months, and that his psychiatric therapy ended last spring. "I'm no longer in need of treatment," he said in response to a question. That seemed to trouble the commissioners. "How are you controlling your tendency toward violence without medication?" Amy Ayoub wondered. "Whatever the [psychiatric] plan was," John Bailey offered, "it didn't work."

There was also one moment of pathos, when Tyson was asked if he had any friends (as opposed to business associates) who he could sit down and talk things out with.

"I don't have one friend in my entire life," Tyson answered. "I was never successful with friends."

The questioning ended at 3:25 P.M. Then, after a seven-minute break, each commissioner made a statement and the pattern of votes became clear:

Amy Ayoub: "We respect the presumption of innocence until proven guilty, but there's also guilty when proven guilty. Why have laws if we're not going to enforce them?"

Flip Homansky: "From the bottom of my heart, I wish things had gone better. We're all losers here."

John Bailey: "When everything is at stake, you're unpredictable and capable of the very worst conduct. When you have uncontrolled rage, you put peoples' lives in jeopardy. And ultimately, you're the one who is responsible."

Bailey was articulate and thoughtful. His statement was a moment of high drama, and it sealed Tyson's fate.

At 3:55 P.M., Faiss asked for a ten-minute recess. When the hearing resumed, Tyson, Shelly Finkel, and Matthew Johnson were no longer present. Faiss sought to withdraw the license application, but his request was denied. At 4:05 P.M., the vote was taken and Mike Tyson went down to defeat.

So what comes next?

For starters, Madison Square Garden is out as a possible site. Previously, MSG pushed hard for the fight, and Garden officials had discussions with New York State Athletic Commission personnel that left them confident Tyson would be licensed to fight in New York. But a New York license is far less likely now. And in any event, MSG chief operating officer Seth Abraham says, "Madison Square Garden will no longer take the fight. We closed the book on Lewis-Tyson as of Monday, January 21st, [when Abraham learned that the fight was slated for the MGM Grand]." Also, Abraham acknowledged, "When the Garden was putting together its bid, we contacted our biggest sponsors and had difficulty getting sponsor support. Our sponsors were concerned about participating in a Tyson fight, and that was before January 22."

Also, it's unclear that Lewis still wants the fight. Last Saturday at Madison Square Garden for Shane Mosley versus Vernon Forrest, Lennox was non-committal when asked on-camera. Off-camera, he was slightly more revealing.

"Do you still want to fight Tyson?" someone queried.

"We already fought," Lewis answered. "Although I only hit him a glancing shot. He didn't feel my full power."

But then Lennox grew more serious.

"There are rules of conduct that all people are supposed to follow," he said. "I follow those rules. I follow them outside the ring, and I follow them as a boxer. I try to beat a man down fairly with my hands. Not bite him, not headbutt him, not try to break his elbow."

"Lennox genuinely has not made up his mind yet as to whether or not he will fight Tyson," Adrian Ogun (Lewis's business manager) said that night.

The ambiguity remains; although shortly after the NSAC vote, Lewis issued the following statement: "Prior to today, I've made no public statements concerning the events of January 22nd. I remained silent at the direct instruction and insistence of my attorneys, who advised me that revealing the truth about what occurred would have undoubtedly led to a lawsuit by Mike Tyson claiming that I interfered with the licensing process. In addition, I believed that the Nevada State Athletic Commission, for whom I have the greatest respect and whose integrity is beyond dispute, should make its decision in the best interests of boxing without regard to what I may or may not have wanted. However, now that the licensing proceedings are over and a license has been denied, I am no longer bound to remain silent. The fact is that Mike Tyson bit through my trousers and took a significant piece of flesh out of my thigh. I was particularly disturbed by the fact that he went before the commission today and did not tell the truth by denying what he knows occurred. I have made no decision yet about the possibility of fighting Mike Tyson in another jurisdiction that may license him because I want to consider carefully the reasons expressed by the commission in denying the license. In addition, I am still consulting with my attorneys as to the legal consequences should I declare that I will not go forward with the bout. I know that all of my fans were looking forward to the Lewis-Tyson fight, as was I. I am sorry that the situation has not yet been resolved."

None of this means that the chaos is over. Unless Mike Tyson is indicted for sexual assault, he'll be licensed somewhere. Maybe he'll even get a title shot. Jose Sulaiman will most likely rule that Iron Mike is still the WBC's mandatory challenger. Or Tyson could wind up in the ring with WBA "champ" John Ruiz.

But no one fight or athletic contest makes or breaks a sport. And more importantly, the Nevada State Athletic Commission sent a crucial message today. The way to dispose of Mike Tyson isn't to beat him up in a boxing ring. It's to resolve his fate as a matter of law.

Round 6

Curiosities

This was an article I particularly looked forward to writing.

Hello, Joe
A Letter to Joe Louis

Hello, Joe. October 26 is coming up. That's the fiftieth anniversary of the last fight of your career; the one against Rocky Marciano. I remember what you said after you fought Jersey Joe Walcott in 1947: "I saw openings I couldn't use. A man gets old, he don't take advantage of those things as fast as he used to." This from a man whose fists were once weapons that seemed to fire automatically.

When you fought Marciano, you were older. There's a photograph of you, knocked through the ropes, lying on the ring apron with your bald spot showing. KO by 8. From then on, things weren't good for you. Americans have a gift for creating heroes, but we tend to discard them once they're used up. Anyway, I thought I'd drop you a line and bring you up to date on what's happening here.

I was too young to see you fight. I've only watched films and read about you. I know that you were born in 1914 in a sharecropper's shack in Alabama. Your family moved north to Detroit, and you had your first pro fight in Chicago against Jack Kracken on July 4, 1934. KO 1. Three years later, you were the first black man since Jack Johnson to challenge for the heavyweight championship. KO 8 over James Braddock. Afterward, Braddock said your jab felt like someone jammed an electric light bulb in his face and busted it. He was courageous. After the umpteenth knockdown, when one of his cornermen said he was going to stop it, Braddock told him, "If you do, I'll never speak to you again." So they let you finish the job, and Braddock said of those final punches, "I couldn't have got up if they'd offered me a million dollars."

That night launched your twelve-year reign as heavyweight champion of the world. I'm told that fighting you when you were in your prime was like staying in the casino too long. Eventually, anyone foolish enough to try was going to lose. Johnny Paycheck said it best: "God, how the man can punch!" And along the way, you became the first black man to be viewed as a hero by Americans of all colors. Your fight against Max Schmeling in 1938 was deemed the clearest confrontation between good and evil in the history of sports. It was the first time that many people heard a black man referred to simply as "the American." On that night, you were the greatest fighter who ever lived. KO 1.

When World War II broke out, Franklin Roosevelt felt your biceps and proclaimed, "We need muscles like yours to beat Germany." You had your own say at a 1942 armed forces benefit at Madison Square Garden. "We'll win," you told the overflow crowd, "because we're on God's side." Later, Jimmy Cannon wrote, "Joe Louis is a credit to his race; the human race."

Anyway, here we are in 2001 and a lot of things about boxing have changed. The top fighters today are virtually all black and Hispanic. And you can't duck them. I mention that only because, in your first fifty-four bouts, the only black men you fought were Wille Davies and John Henry Lewis. Then, at the end, there were Jersey Joe Walcott, Ezzard Charles, and Jimmy Bivens.

When you fought, there was one heavyweight champion of the world. Now, at any given time, there can be up to four claimants. In fact, five years ago, boxing suffered the indignity of dividing its greatest prize among Frank Bruno, Bruce Seldon, and Frans Botha. The world sanctioning bodies that control the sport today are as bad as the mob ever was.

Overall, the heavyweights aren't as good as they used to be. That's because a lot of guys who would have been heavyweights in your day are going to college now on football and basketball scholarships. And heavyweight champions today seldom get off the canvas to win. When guys like Mike Tyson and Lennox Lewis go down, they lose.

Championship fights are twelve rounds now instead of fifteen, which could have meant trouble for you the first time around against Billy Conn.

The fighters are bigger now than they used to be. These days, 210 pounds is a "small" heavyweight. Fighters in the other weight classes are larger, too. For example, welterweights in championship bouts usually enter the ring somewhere between 154 and 160 pounds because they're allowed to weigh-in thirty hours before they fight.

You defended your title seven times at Yankee Stadium and twice at the Polo Grounds. The Polo Grounds was torn down in the 1960s, and the last fight at Yankee Stadium was a quarter-century ago. Live ticket sales are now a secondary consideration for promoters. Their big money comes from site fees and cable television.

The print media is of secondary importance as far as publicizing fights is concerned. TV exposure is considered far more valuable, and a new communications outlet called the Internet is gaining ground.

Superstar fighters make more money today than you would have dreamed possible. A featherweight named Naseem Hamed was paid more for one fight earlier this year than you earned in your entire career.

Incidentally, speaking of Hamed, his ring entrances are bizarre. "Ring entrance" is a term you might not be familar with. In your day, fighters simply walked to the ring before a fight. Suffice it to say, I was watching television not long ago and one of the fighters delayed his entrance because the CD player that was supposed to play his ring-walk music malfunctioned. Some other time, I'll explain CD players to you.

These days, ring canvases are blue, and fighters generally wear red gloves. But sometimes the gloves are green, black, white, or yellow. This past July, a pugilist named Hector Camacho Jr. opted for pink.

At the big fights, you see almost as many women as men in the expensive seats. And this will throw you for a loop, Joe. Nowadays, they've got women fighters. Most of them aren't very good, but a few are for real.

Some things, though, haven't changed. There's still the thrill of a great fight. And the glory. We have a fighter in 2001 named "Sugar" Shane, who looks a lot like the original Sugar Ray. Fights like him, too.

You had a bum of the month club. There's another extraordinarily talented fighter named Roy Jones Jr., who fights a bum every six months.

There's a fighter named Mike Tyson, who never fulfilled his promise as a boxer but he's still awfully good. All fighters, in a manner of speaking, come to hurt their opponents. But some are more fervent about it than others, and Mike seems to derive more pleasure from that aspect of the game than his brethren.

Fighters still lose their money. A lot of them end up in debt to the government for back taxes.

And the great ones still never quit when they're on top. Virtually all of them fight too long. A fellow named George Foreman came back at an advanced age and made it work to his advantage. But not many champions get out in time on their own terms.

Quite a few fighters have drug problems. Like you, some have been hospitalized for psychiatric difficulties.

And then there's Muhammad Ali.

Ali has slowed down some. I remember how you spent your last four years wheelchair-bound after a heart attack and stroke. You had trouble speaking at the end. Ali now has difficulty with words, too. The young Ali threw punches faster than most people could think them. But the hands that once flicked out jabs in four-hundredths of a second tremble a lot these days. I know there were harsh words between you and Ali way back when. But Muhammad now has more appreciation for what you went through than he did when he was young. We all get wiser as we get older.

For you, the reader.

Reader Mail

One of the nicest things about writing for a living is the realization that, on occasion, someone actually reads what I write. That's important for you, the reader, to remember as you read this article. Writing is about sharing ideas, and the new technology allows for instantaneous communication. Part of that dialogue is e-mail. I seriously consider every letter I get if—and this is an important "if"—if it reads like it has been written by a rational person. I add that caveat because, whether we agree or disagree, most of you out there are very nice. But a small percentage of you are letter-writing versions of John Rocker.

As with Rocker, the irrational and ugly correspondence tends to focus on national origin, religion, and race. That's nothing new. Jerry Izenberg was one of the first writers of national stature to defend Muhammad Ali in the 1960s. "I got thousands of letters," Izenberg recalls. "And the level of discourse was quite low. Essentially, people wrote that I was a nigger-loving-commie-sympathizer-Jew-bastard, although they had trouble spelling some of the words because, in addition to being bigots, a lot of them weren't very bright. As a general rule, I didn't answer the ugly letters. Although sometimes, I'd write back saying, 'I want to thank you for your support. I've told Muhammad about your letter, and it makes him feel better to know that you're on his side in this difficult time.' That would drive them crazy, so they'd send me a second letter even uglier than the first and I'd write back again, saying, 'Muhammad and I are heartened to know that you continue to be on our side.'"

Izenberg's most memorable moment with a literary critic occurred in a hotel lobby. "This man and woman were looking at me," he remembers. "They were pointing and whispering. Finally, they came over, and the man said, 'You're Jerry Izenberg, aren't you?' I told him I was, and his next words were, 'I thought so. You're a horse's ass.' Anyway, it was one of those days when I wasn't in the mood. So I looked at him and said, 'Why don't you take your fat wife and fuck off,' at which point woman interjected, 'See, Herbie, I told you he wouldn't be nice.'"

My fellow writer Michael Katz estimates that he gets forty e-mails a week, many of them, to use his words, "written in crayon . . . About half of them are positive," Katz continues. "Positive that I don't know anything about boxing. The others are worse."

Still, there's a bright side to reader mail. Editor Doug Fischer opines, "One of the nicest things about the Internet is that it encourages a dialogue between readers and writers. If you write a letter to a boxing magazine, it's weeks or months before there's a response and often there's no response at all. But online, the interaction is immediate. If someone writes and tells me that I'm an asshole, I don't respond. And I get letters like that; we all do. But beyond that, the contact is incredible. I did a story last month on Eddie "Bossman" Jones, and people sent me scanned photographs and magazine articles from thirty years ago. As a writer, positive feedback is the most gratifying thing in the world. There are times when letters from readers make my day."

Tom Gerbasi echoes Fischer's thoughts and adds, "A lot of the e-mail I get comes from rabid local fans. I can write something about a major fight and get nothing. Then I do a piece on Paul Spadafora and the letters pour in. I even got an e-mail from Spadafora's aunt. She seemed very nice. Some of the mail is ugly. 'You suck . . . You don't know blankety-blank . . .' Stuff like that. But a lot of the people who write are intelligent boxing fans. Even when we disagree, very often their letters help me see the other side of an issue more clearly."

Steve Kim builds on Gerbasi's thoughts and observes, "A lot of the mail I get is incredibly detailed and well-thought-out. Some of the letters read like articles. And it's interesting. You can break a major news story, and very few people will respond to it. But give an opinion and everyone wants to be heard."

Certain issues engender more reader mail than others. Pound-for-pound is one hot button. Many readers don't just have an opinion; they have a passion for the issue. The day after I posted a column entitled *Pound-for-Pound 2001,* I received sixty e-mails in response. Most of them were well-reasoned and articulate. Where there was disagreement, it was intelligently expressed. But then there were the nut letters . . ."Fuck you, asshole . . . You don't like Hispanics cuz you dissed Tito and put Mosley first . . . Naseem Hamed is best unless you hate Muslims . . . Your a big-git . . ." Et cetera, et cetera, and so forth.

It's easy to be ugly when you're anonymous. And it's interesting to note how much of the ugliness reflects the prejudice of the letter writer. Jerry Izenberg puts it in perspective when he says, "These are people who view everything through a prism of race and religion, so they accuse any-one who disagrees with them of doing the same thing."

Thus, when I broke a story last year that Roy Jones Jr. had decided to leave promoter Murad Muhammad, one angry letter writer accused me of being a racist and said that I was "out to get" Mr. Muhammad sim-ply because, in her words, "You don't like successful black people." The fact that Jones did, in fact, change promoters was irrelevant to her. If some-day I break a story that Roy Jones has signed with Don King, I doubt very much that the same woman will write, "Gee, Mr. Hauser, I was all wrong. You're a true humanitarian, and obviously, you love successful black people."

Mike Tyson is another magnet for ugly e-mail correspondence. Criticize Iron Mike, and the letters come pouring in. Some of those let-ters make valid points. Others simply confirm the view that there's a lot of free-floating rage in our society and that rage has to attach to some-thing. My guess is, the people who write the ugliest letters are the ones who are angriest in general. And I suspect they're also the ones who are rude to waitresses and most given to road rage.

Still, like Doug Fischer, I have to say, as a writer, feedback is impor-tant to me and positive feedback is particularly gratifying. So to those of you who disagree with me, I respectfully say, you're entitled to your opin-ion. But remember, so am I. Let's keep the dialogue on a high level.

There's a humorous and ironic side to happenings outside the ring in professional boxing.

Insights and Nuggets

Andrew "Six Heads" Lewis will make the first defense of his WBA welterweight title against Larry Marks at the Hammerstein Ballroom in Manhattan on Saturday April 28. The fight will be promoted by Top Rank in association with Cedric Kushner Promotions and telecast by HBO as part of its *KO Nation* series.

According to Arum, HBO was insistent that the show emanate from the Hammerstein. Unfortunately, the ballroom had already been booked for a bar mitzvah on the same night. "No problem," said HBO, which agreed to pay $30,000 to the young man and his family on the condition that they relocate their ceremony to another venue. This is believed to be the first instance of "step aside money" being paid to a thirteen-year-old in conjunction with a world championship fight.

■ ■ ■

Bob Arum waxed eloquent today about Oscar De La Hoya, who is engaged in ongoing litigation with the promoter. "I have to make a conscious effort to put him out of my mind and stay busy with other promotions," said Arum. "Otherwise, it will eat me up. I expect to win on appeal in the California litigation [which De La Hoya won at trial] and in a separate federal court action in New York. Meanwhile, I'm happy not stopping Oscar from fighting. The more he fights, the more money I'll get when this is over."

Arum was then asked about rumors that De La Hoya has said he wants Arum to return the Olympic gold medal he gave to the promoter. According to at least one report, the Golden Boy claims Arum promised to return the medal if there ever came a time when he was no longer Oscar's promoter.

"Not true," said Arum. "The little motherfucker gave it to me at my sixty-fifth birthday party. It's all on tape. Now he wants it back, and I'll tell you what: if Oscar wants to return gifts, he can give me back the Ferrari I gave him and I'll give him back his medal."

■ ■ ■

Is Lennox Lewis looking past his April 21 title defense against Hasim Rahman? That's the opinion of some observers, who say that Lewis hasn't trained seriously enough for his opponent and arrived in South Africa too late to adjust to the high altitude. Now comes a report that Lennox might indeed be thinking ahead.

Last week, Lewis finished training in Las Vegas and spent several days on the set of *Ocean's Eleven*. The Rat Pack–era Hollywood film is being remade with Julia Roberts, George Clooney, Matt Damon, and Andy Garcia in starring roles. Steven Soderbergh is directing.

The plot revolves around a plan to rob several Las Vegas casinos coincidental with a city-wide power blackout at the start of a heavyweight championship fight. Initially, the producers wanted to cast Lewis against Mike Tyson. But there were fears that Iron Mike might not show, or worse, that he would show and the make-believe fight would become real. Thus, Lewis was put in the ring with WBO heavyweight champion Wladimir Klitschko.

All of this led to an unscripted scene last Thursday afternoon, when Lennox was in the make-up trailer, chatting animatedly with Matt Damon and Julia Roberts. Klitschko walked into the trailer. Dead silence followed. No one said a word. Wladimir stood by awkwardly, with Lewis following his every move in the mirror.

Finally, Roberts spoke. "Have you two guys fought each other?" she queried.

"Not yet," Klitschko answered.

"Actually," Lewis told her, "the fight just began."

■ ■ ■

Don King's handling of the middleweight championship series at

Madison Square Garden proves that the Great One hasn't lost his promotional touch. Nor has he lost his entertainment value.

Several hours before Bernard Hopkins and Keith Holmes stepped into the ring to face one another, King waxed eloquent on a number of subjects. First, he advised his listeners, "A lady came up and grabbed me on the street the other night and shouted, 'Praise the Lord! Hallelujah! It's finally happened!'"

Since it was Easter weekend, one might have assumed that the lady was referring to the Resurrection.

But no. As King explained, "Then she said it again. 'Praise the Lord! Hallelujah! It's finally happened! Christy Martin and Cathy Collins have signed to fight one another on the undercard of Felix Trinidad versus William Joppy at Madison Square Garden on the night of May 12th.'"

While the middleweight championship series was the focal point of King's remarks, he did digress long enough to tell reporters, "You all don't know this, but the great horror writer Stephen King is my cousin."

■ ■ ■

The recent flurry of fights at Madison Square Garden brought to mind a moment that occurred in 1995, when Oscar De La Hoya made his first appearance at the Garden in a bout against Jesse James Leija.

At one point, I was standing near a man and his daughter, who looked to be about ten years old. He was doing his best to keep her interested, but the goings-on in the ring bored her so he turned his attention to the crowd.

"Look, sweetie, there's Danny Aiello. And over there, that's Tony Lo Bianco."

Finally, the girl got into the spirit of things. "Daddy, look, over there. That's Jay Leno."

"No, sweetie," her father told her. "That's Gerry Cooney."

■ ■ ■

Dr. Ferdie Pacheco has suffered a stroke. Pacheco rose to prominence as Muhammad Ali's ring physician, and later carved out careers as an author, painter, and television commentator. The stroke occurred in early September. Pacheco said today that he's progressing nicely and expects a full recovery within six months.

Pacheco also spoke of the hours immediately after his stroke. "I was in the emergency room, hovering between life and death," he said. "And out of nowhere, a vision of Eddie Futch came to me. I actually saw Eddie's face above me. Eddie said, 'Take an eight count and get up.' I told myself, 'Goddammit! If Eddie Futch can live to be ninety, so can I.'"

"After I got home from the hospital," Pacheco continued, "I wrote Eddie a letter thanking him for saving my life." Then Eddie wrote back to me, thanking me for my letter. I got Eddie's letter the day after he died."

Marilyn Cole Lownes and I collaborated again on a look at Don King's jewelry.

The King of Diamonds

Long before Michael Jordan wore a diamond stud in his ear, long before it was fashionable for professional athletes to resemble a walking version of the Crown Jewels, there was Don King.

King is a large bulky man; six-feet-two-inches tall, weighing 270 pounds. Charismatic, flamboyant, spellbinding, ostentatious, he has dominated professional boxing since the mid-1970s.

"Like me or dislike me, my longevity is unquestioned," King says in a voice as rich as his bank account. "I've been on top for twenty-five years, number one against insurmountable odds. Others try to emulate and imitate me, but I'm the trailblazer and the pioneer. I've set the tone for the whole business of boxing, and there ain't no stopping me now."

"The jewelry started when I became a promoter," King explains, speaking in rushes. "I determined that it would be to my advantage to dress the part of success. People like shiny things, so I put on shiny things to attract attention. I couldn't afford what I can afford now. But sparkling gems, real or not, were my entree. Now," King continues, "I wear them for show business. If you've got it, flaunt it. The baubles get attention. You see, the system puts diamonds at the top. If I wear diamonds, I get the ear of those within the system who are less fortunate than I am and who want to get to the top like I did. It's like the bait going on the hook for the fish. Young pugilists see the glitter and sparkle, and it draws them to me like a moth to a flame. Then, once I do my job properly, the job supercedes the baubles."

King's collection includes his famous diamond-studded crown-logo necklace, a larger crown-logo necklace, and assorted diamond-studded crucifixes, bracelets, watches, and rings.

"I have an array of jewels," the promoter says. "But without question, my favorites are the crown necklaces, which were designed by my wonderful wife Henrietta. I love them because they're beautiful and because they're the symbol of kings and the symbol of my achievement and success."

Is the jewelry real?

"Some of the baubles are more valuable than others," King acknowledges. "It's in the perception. Some say they're real; some say they're not. Sometimes people give me imitation and, if the gift comes from the heart, I accept it as though it's real because what comes from the heart is priceless. But I will tell you, I do like quality."

The jewelry is insured. Not long ago, King was robbed at gunpoint in Mexico City. Reimbursement for a $125,000 watch followed.

Most of the jewelry that King buys today comes from a jeweler in Las Vegas. Before that, he bought in New York.

"Jewelers come to me in droves," King reports. "They're always bringing me sacks filled with baubles and doo-dads, showing me their wares. But I'm reluctant to treat dollars with reckless abandon, particularly when they're mine. You see, the Queen of England inherited her jewels, but I worked for mine. I wasn't born with a silver spoon in my mouth. So when faced with temptation, my number-one rule is, 'Keep common sense.' You know, the value of jewels doesn't go down if you buy wisely. You've heard the saying, 'Diamonds are a girl's best friend.' It's the same for a man."

And then King adds one final thought: "The jewels are grand. But the jewels don't make me. I make the jewels."

Bob Duffy is one of the many good guys who are part of the mortar of professional boxing.

The Small Promoter

Bob Duffy was born and raised in New York. His resume includes two years in the army, a stint as a deputy U.S. marshal, and twenty years as a New York City cop.

From 1988 through 1995, Duffy served as a per diem inspector for the New York State Athletic Commission. In 1996, he was named director of boxing. Four years later, he resigned in protest against the incompetence and corruption that had become endemic at the NYSAC.

Last year, Duffy founded a small promotional company called Ring Promotions. He's president. Tony Mazzarella (who owns the Waterfront Crab House and is one of the financial angels behind Ring 8) is Duffy's partner and vice president. The matchmaker is Pete Brodsky. In 2001, the company promoted three shows on Long Island and one in Miami Beach. This year, it hopes to promote six to eight fight cards at the Park Central Hotel in Manhattan. January 24 marked Duffy's New York City debut.

The Park Central is a great venue for fights. The room is small. The sight lines are good. And there's the oddity of a mirrored ceiling, which means that a fighter who's knocked on his back can look up and see himself on the canvas. A balcony overlooks the ring, so fans are literally on top of the action.

Still, the economics of boxing are stressful for small promoters. The Park Central seats seven hundred for fisticuffs. If Ring Promotions sells out, it might gross $30,000. But there are expenses: fighters' purses, $12,000; rent, $5,000; NYSAC fees, $2,500; insurance, $1,500; an ambulance, $700; security guards, $700; publicity, $1,000; tickets, programs, and posters, $600; an announcer and time-keeper, $300; the ring, $500. That leaves a pretty small profit margin, assuming a full house and no unforeseen expenses.

But wait! The NYSAC requires that promoters supply it with a Fight

Fax record for every fighter on a card. Fight Fax records cost nine dollars each. And more hurtful, on the evening of the twenty-fourth, fifty fans barged in through an unmanned emergency exit without paying. At night's end, Duffy and Mazzarella were lucky to break even.

Why do small promoters put themselves through the wringer like this?

"I love boxing," Duffy answers. "I want to be involved. I'm hoping to build certain fighters. Each show, I learn a little more. My feeling is, if I break even and persevere, I'll be rewarded at the end. I don't want to steal anything from anyone. All I want is to be part of the process and maybe, someday, I'll get lucky."

The club fight promoter is like a preliminary fighter. He dreams.

Mike Tyson and the media are a formula for satire.

The New Mike Tyson

Boxing fans, take note. A major anniversary is approaching.

On March 1, 2001, Mike Tyson invited twenty members of the national media to his palatial Las Vegas home. During their hour-long get-together, Iron Mike was reported as being comfortable and friendly. At one point, he slipped a bit, acknowledging, "I can't believe I have all you bastards in my house." Nonetheless, the public was besieged with reports of a "new" Mike Tyson:

Tom Spousta of the *New York Times:* "Meet the new Mike Tyson; a more humble and mature version."

Bernard Fernandez of the *Philadelphia Daily News:* "Tyson was remarkably relaxed and charming."

Dan Raphael of *USA Today:* "He was a model host . . . smiling, laughing, and looking happy."

W. H. Stickney of the *Houston Chronicle:* "The Mike Tyson that sits and chats amicably with members of the media these days is calm, serene, even friendly. Just a plain average likable guy. It's a change long in coming, but welcomed by all."

George Kimball of the *Boston Globe:* "We were greeted by a warm fuzzy Tyson."

Tim Smith of the *New York Daily News:* "It was a kinder gentler Mike Tyson."

Michael Katz of Houseofboxing.com: "Tyson was on his most charming behavior; as mellow as a fine Chateauneuf de Pape white."

The new Mike Tyson was only accused of rape twice in 2001: once in Big Bear and once in Las Vegas. There was also the matter of an alleged scuffle with boxer Mitchell Rose in a New York nightclub. And on New Year's Day, Tyson was involved in a confrontation with journalists in the lobby of a Havana hotel. According to Reuters, Iron Mike shouted at the journalists; threw three crystal balls, each one the size of a grapefruit; and "lightly hit a camera operator twice on the back of the head with his fist." I'm not sure what it's like to be "lightly hit" in the head by Mike Tyson. I am sure that I don't want to find out through firsthand experience. Staff members at the hotel said that Tyson appeared "irritated."

Then, on January 22, Mr. Impulse Control let it all hang out in a televised crime spree when he assaulted Lennox Lewis and spewed obscenities at the kick-off press conference for what could have been the largest-grossing fight in the history of boxing. Thereafter, the Nevada State Athletic Commission denied Tyson's request for a license to box, marking the end of the "new" Mike Tyson.

What's next for Iron Mike? That's hard to say. Lewis versus Tyson is still a possibility. Or maybe we'll see the Mike Tyson Channel. Mike Tyson all the time, the ultimate in reality television. Just follow him around with a TV camera crew twenty-four hours a day.

Meanwhile, now that the "new" Mike Tyson is down the drain, it's worth speculating as to what boxing fans might expect from other reincarnations in the future.

Muhammad Ali: "For twenty-two years, I was Cassius Clay. For thirty-eight years, I was Muhammad Ali. Now I'm shaking up the world again. I just changed my name to Irving Goldberg."

Lou Duva: "I ate a salad the other day. It was really good. Carrots, bean sprouts, yum-yum-yum. No more heavy Italian food for me."

Michael Buffer: "I always wanted to shave my head. Doesn't it look great!"

Max Kellerman: "That's an area where I'm uninformed, so I'm not going to comment on it."

Norm Stone: "I just realized that all John Ruiz has is a bogus WBA title. Lennox Lewis is the real heavyweight champion."

Oscar De La Hoya: "It's all my fault."

Bernard Hopkins: "I'm through talking."

Laila Ali and Jacqui Frazier: "No more boxing for us. We felt guilty about ripping off the public."

George Kimball: "I quit smoking last month. You know, cigarettes can kill you."

Roy Jones: "From now on, I'm getting places on time. Until recently, I never thought about how much I was inconveniencing people."

Harold Lederman: "No more Mr. Nice Guy. In the future, when people disagree with me, I'm punching them in the nose."

Stan Hoffman: "Hasim Rahman, Steve Nelson, and I feel guilty about the way we treated Cedric Kushner, so we're giving him 25 percent of the total purses from Rock's next five fights."

Ross Greenburg: "Don King wants to make Roy Jones versus Bernard Hopkins on Showtime? No problem."

Bob Arum: "Yesterday I was telling the truth. Today I'm lying."

Boxing, like many sports, is founded on tradition.

Everlast
The Choice Of Champions

Everlast is the oldest major brand name in boxing. The company was founded in 1910 by a seventeen-year-old Bronx resident named Jacob Golomb. Golomb, the son of a tailor, wanted to manufacture swimsuits that lasted a full summer. Thus, the name "Everlast." Several years later, he opened a small retail store to sell his swimwear and began manufacturing other sports equipment.

In 1917, Golomb was approached by a young fighter named Jack Dempsey, who wanted to know if Golomb could provide him with protective headgear that would stand up to the rigors of training. Golomb agreed; and Dempsey, in effect, became Everlast's first boxing consultant. In 1919, when Dempsey knocked out Jess Willard to capture the heavyweight championship, he wore gloves made for him by Golomb. Six years later, Golomb expanded his line by designing elastic-waist boxing trunks to replace the leather-belted trunks worn by most boxers.

By the 1930s, Everlast was America's premier manufacturer of boxing equipment and the standard against which all others were judged. At one point, the New York State Athletic Commission went so far as to require that Everlast gloves be worn in bouts contested in New York. And to the public, Everlast became known as "The Choice of Champions," with its equipment worn by the likes of Joe Louis, Rocky Marciano, and Sugar Robinson.

Jacob Golomb died in the 1950s, and the company was taken over by his son, Dan. In 1958, the Golomb family sold a 50 percent interest in Everlast to a businessman named Ben Nadorf. Then, in 1995, Dan Golomb died and Nadorf purchased the remaining 50 percent. But a problem was brewing. Over the years, the quality of Everlast equipment had deteriorated, and an increasing number of marquee fighters were opting for other manufacturers.

Enter George Horowitz.

Horowitz was born into a lower-middle-class family in Brooklyn in 1950. "It was very important to my parents that my brother, three sisters, and I graduate from college," he says. "And we all did."

In George's case, that meant graduating from Long Island University. He planned on going to law school, but the war in Vietnam was raging. And rather than go into the military, Horowitz taught social studies in the New York City public school system, which exempted him from the draft. Then, in 1976, he was laid off during the city's budget crisis. That left him with a pregnant wife, no money, and no job. He sold insurance for a year, and was good at it but hated it. So when a family friend started a small apparel business, Horowitz joined him.

In 1990, Horowitz went out on his own and formed a company, later known as Active Apparel Group, to design, manufacture, and market women's sportswear. In 1992, he licensed the Everlast name and logo for use on what he called women's "activewear." Essentially, Horowitz was putting a men's label on sportswear and fitness clothing for women. "It was about empowerment," he says. Six years later, Active Apparel acquired an Everlast license for men's sportswear as well. Then, in October 2000, it acquired Everlast itself for stock and cash valued at $60,000,000 and changed its name to Everlast Worldwide, Inc. "It was a case of the guppy swallowing the whale," says Horowitz.

And Horowitz was like a kid in a candy store. "I'd loved boxing since I was five years old," he remembers. "My father took me to the Golden Gloves when I was a kid. We went to club fights and closed-circuit telecasts. I even saw Ali fight at Madison Square Garden. I was a fan of many sports, but boxing always had a special charm for me."

Everlast now has executive offices and a showroom at 1350 Broadway in Manhattan. Horowitz is its president and chief executive officer. The company has roughly 275 full-time employees. At the retail level, it generates sales of $300,000,000 annually.

Everlast's income flows from three sources.

First, it manufactures eighty separate sportswear products featuring the Everlast logo. This apparel is manufactured by independent contractors (65 percent in the United States and 35 percent in Asia) and sold by mail order, over the Internet, and in 20,000 retail locations. "Probably

about 10 percent of our apparel is worn to work out in for fitness reasons," Horowitz posits. "The rest is worn for comfort and casual
sportswear." Within the United States, this generates annual wholesale
sales of $36,000,000.

Second, Everlast licenses its logo for use by other manufacturers on
everything from clothing and watches to weight-training equipment. This
generates roughly $6,000,000 in licensing fees for the company on
$100,000,000 in wholesale sales worldwide.

And last, Everlast remains committed to the manufacture of sporting
goods related to boxing. Gloves, trunks, robes, mouthpieces, protective
cups, heavy bags, speed bags, boxing rings, and other equipment gener-
ate $22,000,000 in wholesale sales annually.

Everlast's boxing equipment is manufactured in two facilities: one in
the Bronx and one in Missouri. It is both standard and custom-made,
although less than $1,000,000 flows from sales to boxing professionals.
That's partly because the market is small. And its partly because Everlast
lost a significant portion of its professional market share in the 1990s.

"The product was awful by the late 1990s," Horowitz acknowledges.
"The shoes were terrible. All they did was throw an Everlast logo on a
stock shoe made in Pakistan. The basic Everlast glove design hadn't
changed for years. It was an embarrassment to the company. You have to
understand, Everlast was boxing. Fighters of every ethnic background had
worn Everlast equipment for decades. And it was all falling apart. There
was no way I could continue the company like that when I took over."

In one of his first moves after acquiring Everlast, Horowitz hired
Teddy Atlas as a consultant regarding the redesign of the company's boxing equipment.

"I'm very cynical about people," says Atlas. "But I think George
Horowitz is a good guy. He tries to do things in a way that's good for
business but is also the right thing to do. And he's doing right by the boxing equipment. I'm not a fashion expert," Atlas continues. "I know that
Everlast has to balance its traditional look for robes, trunks, and shoes
against what fighters today want in the way of style, but that's not my job.
My job is to be concerned with the effectiveness, safety, and comfort of
the equipment. For example, the old Everlast shoes weren't comfortable.
Putting them on was like putting boxes on your feet. They're much

better now. With the gloves, Reyes gloves are known as puncher's gloves, and there's some truth to that. With Reyes, there's less cushion around the punching area and the leather is pulled tighter. For that reason, Reyes gloves are also known as cutting gloves. And what we did at Everlast with our gloves was, we kept the stitching and outside of the glove the way we had it, but we redesigned the inside to conform more to the boxer's hand and give the glove a puncher's grip."

Horowitz elaborates on the redesign of Everlast gloves, which is symbolic of the company's commitment to the future. "We went to the experts," he says. "People like Dr. Charles Melone, who told us there are new ideas medically about hands today. We took advantage of modern materials for moisture management. We converted to new forms of padding that are more protective and more comfortable and don't break down during a fight. The first step toward getting marquee fighters to use your equipment is making the best equipment, and I think we're doing that now."

Horowitz has tried to keep Everlast in the public eye through a series of boxing seminars, other promotional events, and endorsement deals with fighters like Shane Mosley. He'd like as many big-name fighters as possible to return to Everlast trunks, shoes, and gloves. "That's a given," he says. "It helps at every level of sales to have champions wearing your equipment; and in addition, it would be an honor for us."

Certainly, in that regard, Everlast has a leg up on the competition. "We have an advantage," Horowitz says in closing. "With a name like Everlast, we can get the fighters to give us a fair hearing and listen to what we have to say. You can't buy authenticity. Either it's there or it isn't; and Everlast has it."

And to prove his point, Horowitz refers to Clarence Vinson, who represented the United States in the 119-pound division at the 2000 Olympics. A reporter once asked Vinson what Everlast meant to him. Vinson responded, "Everlast, when I hear that name, it touches me deep."

Often, at boxing press conferences, the real action takes place away from the microphone.

Overheard at Gallagher's

On Monday at Gallagher's Steakhouse in Manhattan, Bernard Hopkins was presented with the newly-minted Sugar Ray Robinson Trophy, emblematic of supremacy in boxing's middleweight division. Everyone expected the winner of Saturday night's fight to be presented with the trophy immediately after the bout. So why didn't it happen that way?

"I know what the deal was," says Hopkins. "After the fight, they told everyone that the trophy was locked in an office and no one had the keys to get it out. But the real reason is, they were so sure Trinidad was going to win that they already had his name engraved on the plate."

Hopkins got his trophy on Monday and reports, "You can tell by the scratches on it that they changed the plate."

But not so fast—

Eric Gelfand of Madison Square Garden reports, "It *was* locked in the Garden's Box Office and the alarms had been set. The post-fight press conference went off so late we couldn't get it out." Then Gelfand adds, "The truth is, the plaque originally was mistakenly engraved by the sculptor to Don King and was then switched to be generic with no name on it."

Meanwhile, as is often the case, the most interesting thoughts were expressed away from the podium:

Bernard Hopkins: I knew what I had to do to beat Trinidad. Joe Frazier can't box like Ali, and Ali can't box like Joe Frazier, so I was confident that Trinidad wouldn't change his style. I had top sparring partners with me in training camp. They weren't punching bags. They were trying to nail me. And I got used to staying out of a trading-punches mentality.

Don King: I've never seen Bernard Hopkins fight like he did on Saturday night.

Bernard Hopkins: I've got one of the best chins in boxing. I don't want to prove that to you, but it's true.

Don King: I'm getting calls from Oscar De La Hoya's people. But they want Trinidad, not Hopkins.

Bernard Hopkins: I'm old at thirty-six, and my birthday is January 15. By the time I fight again, I'll be thirty-seven. I'll have a cane and be walking with a limp.

Ross Greenburg: HBO is fine with Bernard winning the fight. We've been doing this for twenty-five years, so we know that anything can happen in boxing. Bernard is a great fighter. And he can go up in weight, down in weight, or stay the same. There are a lot of attractive matchups for him.

Bernard Hopkins: Roy Jones is always in the picture. Money talks, and the undisputed middleweight champion of the world fighting the undisputed light-heavyweight champion of the world is big. And I respect Roy, even if Roy hasn't given proper respect to me. But I don't know about Roy. Roy plays basketball; Roy feeds his chickens. That's a sign of being punchy, when you follow animals around like a big flood is coming.

Ross Greenburg: There's Oscar De La Hoya, Roy Jones, Fernando Vargas, Shane Mosley . . .

Bernard Hopkins: I won't fight Shane Mosley. It's personal. Fights sometimes get nasty, and I like Shane. I have too much respect for him to let it get that way. Of course, if the money is right and Shane gets nasty first—

For many of us, September 11 will never be completely out of mind.

A Prayer from Naseem

In January 2001, I interviewed Naseem Hamed in his home town of Sheffield, England. It was a good visit and, for much of our time together, we talked about Islam. Hamed is deeply religious. At one point, he told me, "The most important thing in my life is to worship Allah. I believe that everything is created by Allah, and everything is created by Allah for a reason."

When we said good-bye, Naseem told me, "I'll pray for your safe flight home."

Three months later, I was on National Airlines Flight 14, traveling from New York to Las Vegas for the championship bout between Hamed and Marco Antonio Barrera. As the plane began its descent into McCarren Airport, it was hit by lightning. There was a loud crack that sounded like an explosion. One of the two engines stopped running. For the rest of the descent, the plane wobbled slightly, as though it were flying through turbulent skies. The pilot brought it down to the runway. And then something scary happened, scarier than what had happened before.

The plane touched down on the runway, and passengers had the feeling of being in a car that was skidding out of control. There were a few cries . . . most of us held our breath . . . and the plane lifted up off the runway into the air.

Twenty minutes passed. There was no explanation from the pilot or any of the flight crew as to what was happening. None was needed. Everyone understood that the plane was burning off its remaining fuel before the pilot attempted to land again. Most people in the cabin were silent. Everyone was well-behaved.

I'm not a religious person. I have certain beliefs regarding God, but I don't believe that God hears and directly answers individual prayers. Yet there I was, in a dangerous situation. I asked myself if it would be hypocritical for me to pray. Then I remembered Naseem's parting words when

I left Sheffield: "I'll pray for your safe flight home." Coming as they did from a true believer with a generous spirit, those words gave me comfort.

Much has happened in the seven months since then. None of us will get on an airplane with a feeling of total security ever again. September 11 will always be somewhere in our mind. It has made us acutely aware of our own mortality.

On November 13, 2001, I boarded National Flight 14, traveling from New York to Las Vegas for the championship bout between Hasim Rahman and Lennox Lewis. As the plane took off, I hoped that Naseem Hamed's prayer was still with me.

To bring down the curtain on another year . . .

George Foreman on Christmas

Traditions evolve in a particularly nice way. Two years ago, I authored a poem entitled *A Christmas Eve Visit from George Foreman*. Last December, as the holidays approached, I wrote an article entitled *Two Conversations with George Foreman* and closed with the thought, "He's a good messenger for this holiday season and every other day of the year." Now, as we await another Christmas, it seems appropriate to turn again to one of the most popular men in boxing. Here are some of George Foreman's thoughts on Christmas:

I'm low key about the holidays. In fact, I put all the holidays into one basket. Everyone has been so prosperous in recent years that the buying and gift-giving never stops. People are overly generous. The machinery of giving expensive things has gotten so well-established that nothing stops it. It starts with birthdays and goes on through Christmas and every other day of the year. It's "let's see how much we can buy," and a lot of people have forgotten about giving of themselves instead of giving things.

I got a giant music box from Motown last Christmas. Very expensive. You could see it was something they sent to the elite. But not a letter asking, "How are you? What's happening?"

I get Christmas cards in the mail from people I hardly know, and I know it's "let's send him a card and him a card." My parents are dead and gone, and they still get Christmas cards from people who haven't checked for years to see how they're doing. I send out hellos and how-you-doings all the time. There's never one day a year that people have to wait for to hear from me.

You know, when I was growing up, Christmas was the most dangerous time of the year for me. We didn't have a tree or anything like that. We were poor. In the summer, we had a choice between electricity and gas, and we chose electricity. In the winter, we chose heat.

Christmas trees cost money and, once you had a tree, you had to put something on it; so no tree at Christmas. But when I was young, I'd hear people saying, "I'm giving my mother this; I'm giving my girl-friend that." So I'd go out and prowl the streets—fourteen, fifteen years old, a mugger, to outdo people and get money for presents.

Even now, I don't have a tree at Christmas. Why not? Just because. And I don't get into gift-giving at Christmas. The only gift that really matters is the gift of love.

So if a young child asked me what Christmas is about, I wouldn't say anything; I'd just hug him. Words can mess up anything, but a hug is always good. I'd hug him and spend the day with him. And the wonderful thing about a hug is, you don't have to wait for Christmas to give it. You can give hugs every day of the year.